OECD Development Pathways

Multi-dimensional Review of Kazakhstan

VOLUME 2. IN-DEPTH ANALYSIS AND RECOMMENDATIONS

OECD

dev
DEVELOPMENT CENTRE

This work is published under the responsibility of the Secretary-General of the OECD. The opinions expressed and arguments employed herein do not necessarily reflect the official views of the member countries of the OECD or its Development Centre.

This document, as well as any data and map included herein are without prejudice to the status of or sovereignty over any territory, to the delimitation of international frontiers and boundaries and to the name of any territory, city or area.

Please cite this publication as:
OECD (2017), *Multi-dimensional Review of Kazakhstan: Volume 2. In-depth Analysis and Recommendations*, OECD Development Pathways, OECD Publishing, Paris.
http://dx.doi.org/10.1787/9789264269200-en

ISBN 978-92-64-26919-4 (print)
ISBN 978-92-64-26920-0 (PDF)
ISBN 978-92-64-26921-7 (ePub)

Series: OECD Development Pathways

ISSN 2308-734X (print)
ISSN 2308-7358 (online)

The statistical data for Israel are supplied by and under the responsibility of the relevant Israeli authorities. The use of such data by the OECD is without prejudice to the status of the Golan Heights, East Jerusalem and Israeli settlements in the West Bank under the terms of international law.

Photo credits: Cover © design by the OECD Development Centre.

Corrigenda to OECD publications may be found on line at: *www.oecd.org/about/publishing/corrigenda.htm*.

Foreword

Kazakhstan embarked on an OECD Multi-dimensional Country Review (MDCR) in December 2014. The review is implemented as part of the 2015-16 Country Programme signed between Kazakhstan and the OECD. This review aims primarily at supporting public action by the national authorities of Kazakhstan in sustaining inclusive growth and progress in the well-being of its citizens.

MDCRs are an OECD tool aimed at helping countries achieve their development goals and were launched as part of the OECD Strategy on Development, adopted in 2012. MDCRs identify and analyse major constraints to a country's development and make practical policy recommendations. They reviews take a cross-sector rather than sectoral approach so as to consider the multi-dimensional nature of economic policies and challenges. The MDCRs are implemented in three distinct phases, giving rise to as many volumes. Volume 1 of a country review describes the economy and highlights the main obstacles to development. Volume 2 conducts in-depth analysis of a number of key constraints and makes policy recommendations. Volume 3 proposes concrete application of these recommendations.

This report is the second volume of the MDCR of Kazakhstan. This report focuses on four key issues: i) diversification; ii) financing development; iii) privatisation and the role of the state; and iv) environmental regulation. The focus issues respond to four of the key constraints identified in the diagnostic phase of the review. Volume I identified seven key constraints to development: i) natural-resource dependency; ii) the concentration of economic clout in the hands of the state and a small number of private actors; iii) the fragility and underdevelopment of the financial sector; iv) the insufficient effectiveness of environmental regulation; v) corruption; vi) limited implementation capacity for certain government functions; and vii) a skills system insufficient to equip the labour force adequately for a number of sectors. A number of concurrent OECD Reviews, co-ordinated through the Kazakhstan Country Programme provide further insights on other key policy areas, including public governance, competition law and practice, investment policy, innovation policy, and education policy.

This MDCR is designed to assist Kazakhstan in formulating development strategy and to support the policy reforms needed to achieve further sustainable and inclusive development. This report comes at a time where Kazakhstan faces stronger headwinds in external conditions for development than it has for over a decade. In response, Kazakhstan is accelerating structural reform processes to transit towards a more sustainable and resilient development model. While the recommendations are intended to support policy action by Kazakhstan's national authorities, the findings are also relevant for academics, the private sector and civil society.

Acknowledgements

Multi-dimensional Country Reviews are the result of a collaborative effort of the OECD and the country under review. Work on the second phase of the MDCR of Kazakhstan was carried out jointly by the OECD Development Centre in collaboration with the OECD Environment Directorate, with support from the Ministry of National Economy of Kazakhstan.

The review was produced under the guidance of Mario Pezzini, Director of the OECD Development Centre, and the leadership of Jan Rieländer, head of the MDCR Unit at the Development Centre. The review was co-ordinated by Juan Ramón de Laiglesia (OECD Development Centre) and drafted by Tim Bulman (OECD Development Centre), Juan Ramón de Laiglesia (OECD Development Centre), Krzysztof Michalak (OECD Environment Directorate) and Arto Honkaniemi (independent consultant), with significant inputs from Deirdre Culley (OECD Development Centre), Balász Egert (OECD Economics Department), Guy Halpern, Sam Mealy, and Joanne Tang (OECD Development Centre). Deirdre Culley (OECD Development Centre) managed the workshop "Scenarios for the future of Kazakhstan", jointly organised by the OECD Development Centre and the Graduate School of Public Policy of Nazarbayev University in Astana on 3 November 2015. The MDCR team is grateful to Fatima Zhakypova, Executive Director of the GSPP and to Saltanat Janenova (GSPP, Nazarbayev University) for their contribution to this review. The review also benefited from the contributions made by Toma Savitki, who provided excellent research assistance, as well as from administrative support provided by Myriam Andrieux, Georgina Regnier and Ly Na Dollon, and logistics support provided by Saltanat Janenova (Nazarbayev University). Jean-François Lengellé (OECD Global Relations Secretariat) and his team provided essential co-ordination across OECD activities in Kazakhstan.

The team is grateful for insightful comments on draft versions of the report provided by Federico Bonaglia, Elisabeth Lambrecht, Lorenzo Pavone, and Alexander Pick from the Development Centre, as well as Tihana Bule, Hans Christiansen, Thomas Dannequin, Iota Nassr, Lynn Robertson, Frédéric Wehrle (OECD Directorate for Financial and Enterprise Affairs), Osamu Yoshida (OECD Centre for Tax Policy and Administration), Philippe Larrue (OECD Directorate for Science, Technology and Innovation), Paulo Magina (OECD Directorate for Public Governance and Territorial Development), Shigeo Katsu (Nazarbayev University), Aktoty Aitzhanova (National Analytical Centre), and participants in the workshop organised on 11 April 2016 by the Ministry of National Economy to discuss preliminary findings and recommendations of the second phase of the review.

The Multi-dimensional Country Review of Kazakhstan is made possible by the financial contribution of the Ministry of National Economy of Kazakhstan. The review benefitted from the support of Erbolat Dossayev, who was Minister of National Economy of the Republic of Kazakhstan during the fact finding phases of the review, and his staff. Zhandos Shaimardanov (Director of the Department of Strategic Planning and Analysis) and his team have been a valuable counterpart throughout the process. The contributions of Olzhas Zhumagulov and

Dauren Zakumbayev have been particularly valuable to gathering the necessary data and improving the pertinence of the report, and ensuring continuous and seamless interaction between the OECD and the administration of the Republic of Kazakhstan. Other ministerial departments and agencies also provided useful contributions, namely, the Ministry of Energy and the Committee on Environmental Regulation and Control, the Ministry of Investment and Development, the Ministry of Finance, and the National Bank of Kazakhstan. The team is also grateful for inputs received from Baiterek, the Confederation of Employers of the Republic of Kazakhstan, the Economic Research Institute, the Entrepreneurship Development Fund DAMU, Kazagro, the Kazakhstan Development Bank, the Kazakhstan Industry Development Institute (KIDI), the Kazakhstan Stock Exchange (KASE), Kazakhstan Temir Zholy, Kaznexinvest, KEGOC, the National Analytical Centre, the National Chamber of Entrepreneurs Atameken, the National Wealth Fund Samruk-Kazyna, the NGO "Consumers' Advocate", the NGO "Coordination Center for Climate Change", the American Chamber of Commerce in Kazakhstan, the EBRD and the World Bank.

The team is grateful for Stephen Jessel for editing the manuscript and for the OECD Development Centre's Communications and Publications Unit, especially Aida Buendía, Delphine Grandrieux, Vanda Lintott and Elizabeth Nash for their support in editing, laying out and producing the report.

Table of contents

Tables

Figures

Boxes

Follow OECD Publications on:

http://twitter.com/OECD_Pubs

http://www.facebook.com/OECDPublications

http://www.linkedin.com/groups/OECD-Publications-4645871

http://www.youtube.com/oecdilibrary

http://www.oecd.org/oecddirect/

This book has...

StatLinks

A service that delivers Excel® files from the printed page!

Look for the *StatLinks* at the bottom of the tables or graphs in this book. To download the matching Excel® spreadsheet, just type the link into your Internet browser, starting with the *http://dx.doi.org* prefix, or click on the link from the e-book edition.

Acronyms and abbreviations

AAC	Agrarian Credit Corporation
AIFC	Astana International Financial Centre
APG	Associated petroleum gas
BAT	Best available techniques
BIS	Bank for International Settlements
BP	British Petroleum
BRI	Belt and Road Initiative
CEO	Chief executive officer
CFC	Convertible foreign currency
CIS	Commonwealth of Independent States
COP	Conference of Parties
CPI	Consumer price index
DBK	Development Bank of Kazakhstan
EBRD	European Bank for Reconstruction and Development
EDF	Entrepreneurship Development Fund
EECCA	Eastern Europe, Caucasus and Central Asia
EGDI	E-government development index
EIA	Environmental Impact Assessment
EITI	Extractive Industry Transparency Initiative
ELV	Emissions limits values
EQS	Environmental ambient quality standards
ETS	Emissions Trading Scheme
FAIR	Financial Advisory Industry Review
FDI	Foreign direct investment
FOFA	Future of Financial Advice
FSSA	Financial System Stability Assessment
GDP	Gross domestic product
GEC	Green Economy Concept
GEL	Green Economy Law
GHG	Greenhouse gases
GIS	Geographic information systems

GQBE	Общесоюзный классификатор отраслей народного хозяйства (Soviet classification of "Branches of the economy")
GSPP	Graduate School of Public Policy
HS	Harmonised System
IAIA	International Association for Impact Assessment
ICOR	Incremental capital-output ratio
ICT	Information and communication technologies
IEA	International Energy Agency
IETA	International Emissions Trading Association
IFK	Investment Fund of Kazakhstan
IFRS	International Financial Reporting Standards
IMF	International Monetary Fund
INDC	Intended Nationally Determined Contributions
IPO	Initial public offerings
IPPC	Integrated Pollution Prevention and Control
ISIC	International Standard Industrial Classification
IT	Information technology
ITF	International Transport Forum
JSC	Joint-stock company
KASE	Kazakhstan Stock Exchange
KazETS	Kazakhstan Emissions Trading Scheme
KEGOC	Kazakhstan Electricity Grid Operating Company
KIDI	Kazakhstan Industry Development Institute
KREMZK	Комитет по регулированию естественных монополий и защите конкуренции (Committee on Regulation of Natural Monopolies and Protection of Competition)
KZT	Kazakhstani Tenge
LIBOR	London Interbank Offered Rate
LTE	Long Term Evolution
MBO	Management buy-out
MCI	Monthly calculation index
MDCR	Multi-dimensional Country Review
MID	Ministry of Investment and Development
MMT	Million metric tonnes
MNE	Ministry of National Economy
MUV	Manufacturing unit values
NACE	*Nomenclature statistique des activités économiques dans la Communauté européenne* (Statistical Classification of Economic Activities in the European Community)
NADLoC	National Agency for the Development of Local Content

NAP	National Allocation Plan
NATD	National Agency for Technological Development
NBK	National Bank of Kazakhstan
NEA	Nuclear Energy Agency
NFRK	National Fund of the Republic of Kazakhstan
NGO	Non-governmental organisation
NMH	National Managing Holding
OECD	Organisation for Economic Co-operation and Development
PCI	Product Complexity Index
PEEE	Public Environmental Experts' Examination
PMR	Product Market Regulation
PPL	Public Procurement Law
PPP	Purchasing power parity
PSOE	Partially state-owned enterprises
RCA	Revealed comparative advantage
RFE	Radio Free Europe
SEEE	State Ecological Expertise Examination
SITC	Standard International Trade Classification
SME	Small and medium-sized enterprises
SOE	State-owned enterprises
SPAIID	State Programme of Accelerated Industrial and Innovative Development
TJ	Terajoules
TPES	Total primary energy supply
UNCTAD	United Nations Conference on Trade and Development
UNECE	United Nations Economic Commission for Europe
UNFCCC	United Nations Framework Convention on Climate Change
UNIDO	United Nations Industrial Development Organization
WTO	World Trade Organization
ZHSSBK	Жилстройсбербанк (Housing Construction Savings Bank)

Executive summary

Kazakhstan has embarked upon an ambitious reform agenda to realise its aspiration of becoming one of the top 30 global economies by 2050. As documented in Volume I of the *Multi-dimensional Country Review (MDCR) of Kazakhstan*, the country's economy and society have undergone deep transformations since the country declared independence in 1991. Gross domestic product (GDP) increased 2.8-fold between 2000 and 2014 and living standards improved for most Kazakhstanis, with the proportion of the population living on income below the subsistence minimum falling from 32% to 2.5%.

The period of accelerating growth from 2000 to 2010 owed much to exploitation of Kazakhstan's natural wealth. The oil and gas sector, generated 26% of GDP at its peak and still dominates exports, and generates about a third of public revenues. External conditions, and especially the rapid fall in oil prices, have had a significant impact on the country's economy.

The next stage of economic transformation will be more challenging, with weaker external conditions and the need for productivity gains to make a larger contribution to growth. The government has laid out an ambitious programme to modernise how the Kazakhstani state operates and works with the private sector. The president's "100 Concrete Steps" and associated programmes target the way the state operates, more than the scale or scope of its action. Efforts to expand the operating space of the private sector, ensure markets are contestable, reduce administrative burdens, and strengthen the rule of law can bring well-documented benefits to Kazakhstan. Continuing reforms to civil service and competition law can help address key constraints on development in Kazakhstan.

This report is the second volume of the MDCR of Kazakhstan. It analyses four key issues for the country's development on the basis of the constraints identified in Volume I, and provides concrete recommendations to address those constraints.

Diversification and resilience

Kazakhstan's economy grew increasingly concentrated during the 2000s, in terms both of exports and production. Diversification is an imperative for Kazakhstan's future development, to reduce its exposure to external risk as well as furthering job and value creation domestically. It has been a major policy objective for Kazakhstan since the mid-1990s but the implementation of industrial policy only came into being in earnest in 2010. Between 2010 and 2014 the process of relative deindustrialisation stopped and new major non-natural resource export products were discovered.

To increase its efficiency and ability to adapt to a rapidly changing environment, industrial policy should seek sources of flexibility in its implementation. A number of programme measures should be moved from programme to policy settings, where they can be predictable over time for economic actors. Flexibility can also be found by implementing more indirect instruments. Experience in Kazakhstan has shown that the involvement of private sector banks in project selection can lead to more diverse sectoral allocation, enhancing opportunities for discovering new avenues to diversify. The functions of industrial policy should be expanded to include non-financial instruments that allow the economy to increase its anticipation and adaptation capacity. Finally, instruments and programmes should be rigorously evaluated and monitored for continuous improvement.

Success in diversification will also require continuous improvement in complementary inputs, especially a skills system that adequately prepares the workforce, a more developed logistics system that capitalises on the ongoing efforts to upgrade physical infrastructure, and innovation systems that link research and business more effectively.

Mobilising finance to transform the economy

Kazakhstan's financial sector is unusually shallow, which limits firms' investments and operations and impedes the economy's diversification. Scarce funding constrains bank lending. This shallowness is partly attributable to transitory factors, including the economic cycle, the legacy of unsustainable use of international credit, and a period of an unsustainably high exchange rate. Structural factors, such as uncertainty over property rights and the judicial system, and perceptions that financial statements lack integrity, also impede financial deepening.

Schemes to support firms' access to finance through interest rate subsidies and loan guarantees were effective during the financial crisis, but have limited benefits in the long term. Strengthening banks' ability to access wholesale funding would generate sustained improvements in their ability to provide credit. In the short run improved access to international wholesale financing can address this, requiring that the state maintain a good sovereign rating. Joint ventures and equity sales to international banks can also improve banks' access to international financing while strengthening their management. Other efforts to develop domestic savings need to continue, with priority given to improving the management and long-term investment strategies of the pension fund. In the longer term, the financial sector's institutional environment must become stronger to provide investors with greater confidence in their ability to protect their investments and in the reliability of financial information.

Privatisation and the role of the state in the economy

State involvement in the economy in Kazakhstan stands out among comparable and OECD countries. State-owned enterprises (SOEs) are the dominant form of state control in the economy, although price controls are also widespread. SOEs in Kazakhstan are present in a wider range of sectors compared to OECD countries. Kazakhstan has embarked on a major privatisation programme with the aim of reducing the size of the state in the economy, with close to 800 entities up for privatisation including a set of large enterprises (the "Top 65").

The privatisation programme should clearly state its objectives and be monitored on the basis of appropriate indicators. Offices responsible for privatising assets should be given adequate time and resources to prepare the assets, including due diligence, but also adjustments in the capital structure of the entity and the identification and costing of any public service obligations. The privatisation programme should be controlled ex-post by an independent body to ensure a maximum requirement of transparency and accountability, ultimately increasing credibility for investors.

The governance and management of SOEs in Kazakhstan departs in several ways from OECD best practice. The privatisation programme is an opportunity to bring ownership policy and practice more into line with OECD guidelines by developing an ownership policy defining the rationale for state ownership and the role of the state and its agents in corporate governance, centralising SOE ownership functions which are currently scattered, separating ownership and regulation functions, and developing a consistent system of reporting on state ownership.

Towards better environmental regulations

The expeditious reform of a basic environmental regulatory framework could unlock vast opportunities for green growth in Kazakhstan. Today, the country is one of the most energy-intensive economies in the world. Uncoordinated implementation of environmental requirements together with the high volume of complex environmental regulations based on unrealistic assumptions have resulted in a regulatory environment that is complicated, burdensome and costly to both the administration and industry. What is more, the evidence suggests that it does not lead to actual environmental improvement. Moreover, environmental liability in Kazakhstan remains focused on calculating and collecting monetary compensation rather than on preventing and correcting damage, reducing emissions over time and incentivising the use of best available techniques (BATs).

To improve the effectiveness of environmental quality regulation, environmental quality standards need to be revised in the light of international best practices and domestic capabilities to technically feasible and enforceable levels. The focus should shift from "end-of-pipe" solutions to integrated pollution prevention and control. Integrated environmental permits are one of the most effective ways in achieving better pollution control since the permit is linked to techniques associated with lower emissions. Furthermore, Kazakhstan should adopt the strict liability/polluter-pays model and abandon fault-based concepts for damages. Finally, Kazakhstan should be applauded for taking steps toward better use of market-based environmental policy instruments to reduce its carbon footprint, and should step up implementation efforts.

Multi-dimensional Review of Kazakhstan
Volume 2. In-depth Analysis and Recommendations

Chapter 1

Overview: Overcoming constraints to fulfilling Kazakhstan's development vision

Kazakhstan has adopted an ambitious vision for the year 2050, aiming to become one of the top 30 global economies. For that to happen, the country's impressive economic growth of the first decade of the 21st century will need to find new drivers that allow development to be more robust and resilient. This in turn requires a commitment to structural reforms that have the potential deeply to transform the Kazakhstani economy and society. This report is the second output of the Multi-dimensional Country Review (MDCR) of Kazakhstan. The goal of the MDCR of Kazakhstan is to support the country in achieving its development objectives by identifying the key constraints, providing practicable policy recommendations, and supporting the implementation of these recommendations. This second report analyses in depth four key issues for Kazakhstan's mid-term development success: diversification, financial sector development, the role of the state in the economy, and the effectiveness of environmental regulation. This chapter examines the increasingly challenging external environment, revisits key conclusions of the first volume in its light, and presents the key findings and recommendations of this report.

Kazakhstan's development objectives and performance since 2000

Kazakhstan is undergoing reform to realise its aspiration of becoming one of the top 30 global economies by 2050. It aims to have a competitive and diversified market economy that can respond and adapt to the changing global environment, and to provide a high standard of living for its citizens. Its goal is to be an open and integrated global player in the international community, as well as a prominent regional actor, seizing opportunities for export and trade with its neighbours. To benefit from strong sources of domestic growth driven by private enterprise, Kazakhstan will display an efficient financial sector, a favourable business environment, well-developed institutions, and an effective civil service that delivers high-quality public services. Kazakhstan as a major global economy will aim to deliver for citizens, and enable high levels of well-being with good quality jobs, an active social policy, and a vibrant and inclusive Kazakhstani culture.

The country has achieved remarkable progress since 2000 towards realising its long-term development ambitions. Gross domestic product (GDP) increased 2.8-fold between 2000 and 2014. Average monthly salaries rose from the equivalent of USD 101 to USD 565 in 2015, pensions quadrupled, while the proportion of the population living on incomes below the subsistence minimum fell from 31.8% to 2.5%. However, this rapid economic growth has only partly translated into improvements in other aspects of citizens' well-being. To sustain economic progress, overcome recent difficulties, and drive improvements in well-being to realise its 2050 aspirations, Kazakhstan will need to address a number of challenges to ensure its economy becomes more productive and diverse, and is sufficiently flexible and resilient in the face of an ever-shifting external environment.

The next stage of economic transformation will be more challenging, with weaker external conditions and gains in productivity needing to contribute more to growth. External conditions in the second half of the 2010s are likely to be less supportive than they were between 2001 and 2014. Most relevant to Kazakhstan, commodity prices, and especially energy prices, are expected to remain at significantly lower levels than those achieved during that period, in view of the availability and falling marginal cost of new supply and slower growth in demand. External financing will also remain scarcer for markets such as Kazakhstan than was the case during the mid-2000s given ever stricter prudential requirements and the weakening in the country's debt sustainability. Kazakhstan has been more affected than most countries by the decline in foreign direct investment (FDI) inflows. While debt levels have stabilised, and the country has taken some action to address its debt servicing needs, these remain at a relatively high level.

To raise productivity growth and improve resilience in the face of global shocks, Kazakhstan will need to transform the structure of its economy and diversify it away from resource extraction. The country will need to reduce the intervention of state in economic activity. It can achieve this through privatisation, improving the business environment by enhancing the contestability and transparency of markets, carefully implementing reforms to the labour market, and improving the attractiveness of Kazakhstan as a destination for foreign investment. Reforming the financial sector to improve access to finance for all private enterprises will be important to allow the private sector to realise new opportunities and to grow, and for it to invest to raise its efficiency and international competitiveness. The state can change its role from driving structural transformation through its investment programme to creating a supportive, transparent and stable operating environment for private actors to make these investments.

Continuing economic diversification and structural change require a changed approach to state support and regulation. Many programmes of state support are framed around target structures of economic activity or approaches to particular issues, rather than in terms of the underlying outcome that is desired. The prescriptive approach can restrict the flexibility in how economic agents behave, or can allocate resources to areas that do not offer the greatest returns or long-term opportunities. Better and more effective outcomes could be achieved by framing regulations and support towards generating an environment that allows independent actors to work towards achieving desired outcomes along the path of their choosing. An approach that better supports structural transformation and productivity growth is one that provides economic agents with an environment that is transparent and stable and with incentives to behave in ways that generate the outcomes that are desired. This approach also allows regulations and intervention programmes to be simplified. The benefits of this approach are evident across the topics addressed in this volume. Framing various targeted investment programmes and subsidy schemes more neutrally across the economy may support the emergence of unexpected areas of activity and competitiveness for the Kazakhstani economy. It would allow agents to find efficient mechanisms to manage their environmental impacts while limiting the regulatory burden for firms. And it would ensure that the state maintains a presence in the economy sufficient to meet its economic and social objectives.

Perceived weaknesses in the transparency of the business and investment climate can be addressed through an approach to state support and regulation that is less prescriptive and more focused on outcomes. Kazakhstan has recently undertaken many steps to improve the quality of the investment climate through, among other measures, administrative simplification, changes to the regulatory process, and efforts to reduce corruption. These efforts have earned Kazakhstan a substantial improvement in their World Bank *Doing Business* ranking with a rise of 16 places, up to 35th position. The business and investment climate continues, however, to be considered to lack transparency. The benefits of reforms to formal rules and processes over recent years are undermined by a widening disconnection between policy and practice, and actions by the state which some actors may perceive as being unexpected. Enduring growth and diversification require improvements in the business environment that allow operators to emerge and flourish in ways that targeted support programmes rarely achieve. Some of the state's investment and financing programmes have led to further concentration of economic activity in natural resource extraction. In some cases these interventions have been necessary to ensure that investment projects go ahead and generate revenues for Kazakhstan entities. However, these interventions have also diverted scarce finance and other resources from entrepreneurs with business ideas that might generate significant returns but are in non-targeted sectors, notably domestic consumption services.

Accelerating structural reforms will help reinvigorate economic development

To achieve Kazakhstan's development aspirations and the country's continued development and economic transformation, the country needs to improve the investment and operating environment, the efficiency of public spending, and the provision of public goods and services. The government has laid out an ambitious programme to modernise how the Kazakhstan state operates and works with the private sector in the president's "100 Concrete Steps" agenda. This agenda, and its associated programmes, can help the country generate its next stage of growth in the face of weaker economic conditions. Much of the programme can be implemented in spite of the reduced outlook for fiscal space, as it targets *how* the state operates, rather than the scale or scope of *what* it does. Further, the agenda includes actions that expand the operating space of the private sector, from efforts to ensure markets are contestable, that reduce the burden of obtaining permits or passing goods through customs, or that provide a greater role for private providers in areas such as health care. The programme includes efforts to strengthen the rule of law, which brings well-documented benefits for long-term growth while having limited fiscal cost.

Civil service reform is central to changing how the state works with the economy at large, to improving the quality of public spending and as part of a wider modernisation process. Reforms to professionalise and raise the integrity of the civil service have been ongoing since independence and are a major component of the "100 Concrete Steps" programme. Reforms to the management of public servants include the creation of a specialised civil service management agency housed in a relevant ministry. The reforms shift civil service recruitment and promotion to a career-based system, rather than allowing open recruitment even at senior levels from those outside the civil service. This is seen as leading to appointments for reasons related to factors other than the candidate's merit. Those entering the civil service are subject to a more exhaustive selection process. Throughout, the reforms seek to strengthen professional ethics, through a new ethics code and "ethics commissioner".

Well-executed civil service reforms can contribute to a higher quality of governance and a strengthening of the rule of law, addressing important obstacles to economic diversification. The civil service reform programme is intended to address well-recognised weaknesses involving corruption, and to strengthen integrity and the perception that the civil service is based on merit. Greater civil service integrity can improve the value for money in public procurement. (These issues are discussed in Volume 1, Chapter 5 [OECD 2016b]). Progressive reform efforts to improve the civil service's regulatory framework, training and recruitment and its management structures are important. However, their effectiveness is dependent on organisational stability. Reform efforts are weakened if there is a perception that the reforms will be reversed or substituted a short time later. This appears to be a concern in Kazakhstan given the rapid efforts to modernise the nation since the 1990s. Effective civil service reform also requires substantive changes in behaviour and work cultures that go beyond formal regulations and organisational structures. This is a long-term process.

Making markets more readily contested by outside actors will be fundamental to diversifying the economy, increasing competitiveness and attracting investment. Although there have been large advances recently in the contestability of local markets and the effectiveness of anti-monopoly policies, Kazakhstan markets remain highly concentrated and the competition framework is in need of fundamental reform (OECD, 2016a). Current enforcement practice focuses on observed cases of parallel pricing rather than on practices with proven harm to competition. Kazakhstan has committed itself to eliminating price controls in 2017, as well as the State Register for Dominant Undertakings which has acted as a *de facto* system of price and profit controls for all undertakings defined as dominant. Further reforms should ensure that the remit of the competition authority, the Committee on Regulation of Natural Monopolies and Protection of Competition (KREMZK), is clearly defined and that it has effective detection and enforcement instruments which also provide for predictability and transparency for the business community. By completing these reforms Kazakhstan should strengthen the judicial system and the rule of law. Effective competition policy needs technically competent judges who have some specialisation in the topic area.

Productivity and competitiveness can be increased by allowing private actors to compete in sectors currently reserved for state actors. Kazakhstan's World Trade Organization (WTO) membership and the changes in the state's involvement in the economy through privatisation of state owned enterprises (SOEs) have the potential to improve the competitiveness of many sectors where the state is active, by ensuring competitive neutrality across bidders. This can support private-sector providers and improve value for money for the state.

Labour law reforms have reduced regulation, shifting power towards employers from employees and are likely to reduce labour costs, not without controversy. The revised labour code became effective on 1 January 2016, with probation periods extended, overtime allowances reduced, and dismissal of workers made easier. The reforms also make collective bargaining more difficult. These reforms have not been uncontroversial. External observers have raised concerns about the laws' practical effects on the freedoms of association and assembly, while some domestic actors have sought greater consultation. The arguments for these reforms centre on their stimulation of employment by reducing the cost of labour and increasing flexibility for employers. In practice, during a period of economic slowdown, the reforms are likely to reduce employment costs and real incomes in those sectors where skills are relatively available, with less of an impact for employees with the scarcest skills. In the longer term, as workers face greater uncertainty over their incomes without having the safety net of a solid social security system, they are likely to cut spending and build a buffer of precautionary savings in case they lose their income.

The contribution of the MDCR to the realisation of Kazakhstan's 2050 development aspirations

The MDCR is a timely contribution to planning the policies and actions for the next stage of Kazakhstan's progress toward its 2050 development aspirations. This second phase of the three-phase MDCR provides detailed analysis of key constraints on Kazakhstan's ongoing economic transformation, and recommends how they can be addressed. The analysis presented in this volume has been prepared as Kazakhstan navigates a turning point in the global commodity price cycle, and incorporates these changed conditions into its analysis and recommendations. The analysis is also timed to inform the government's preparations of its 2025 strategy. It highlights the areas where policy interventions are likely to do most to unlock Kazakhstan's development potential. It provides deeper analysis and makes recommendations to improve economic diversification, accessibility of finance, environmental regulation, and the role of the state in economic activity. It also seeks to identify factors that are common to these limitations and that need to be addressed to achieve sustained progress in development.

This report tackles four of the seven most significant obstacles to multidimensional development identified during the first phase of the MDCR and detailed in the first report (OECD, 2016b). Beyond the four issues addressed in this report, the first phase of the review also identified three further key issues: widespread corruption that hinders the business environment and undermines meritocracy; limited implementation capacity to fulfil certain government functions, leading to mediocre service delivery in certain sectors, including public service delivery; and the inadequacy of the skills system vis-à-vis the needs of the labour market. A number of parallel OECD reviews address these issues in depth. Their preliminary results are taken into account when available and pertinent.

Figure 1.1. **The MDCR of Kazakhstan and constraints to development**

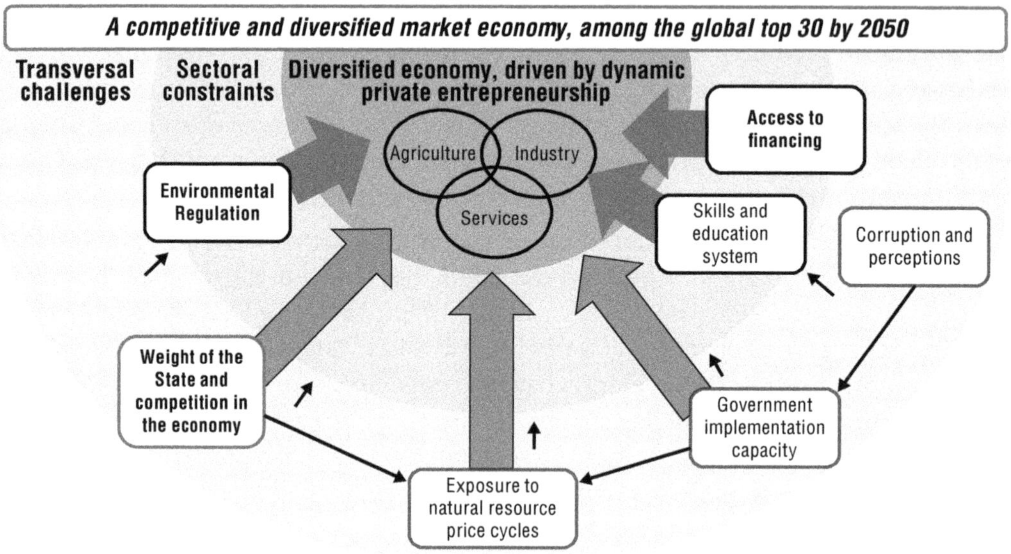

The analysis and recommendations of the MDCR are based on OECD experience and standards. They draw extensively on analyses based both on trends that are global and on those that make specific reference to the group of benchmark countries that were presented in detail in Phase 1 of the MDCR. It applies various specialised tools developed by the OECD and other bodies to diagnose the impediments to development progress and to identify the most effective policy responses. For example, the Product Market Regulation tool presents an objective assessment of the scale and implications of the state's control of the economy.

The recommendations presented in this report will be further refined and contextualised during the third and final phase of the MDCR. This process will draw on further consultation with local stakeholders, to support the specifics of the action plan and to ensure that it fully accounts for the context, in particular the features of the institutional landscape and priorities and resources of the various actors involved in reforms.

Recent external economic developments have created new challenges

External economic conditions have deteriorated significantly and are likely to remain weaker

Kazakhstan's external economic environment shifted from a driver of economic transformation to a drag on growth, as prices of Kazakhstan's exports and demand for them became unexpectedly weaker. The global economic environment turned sharply negative for Kazakhstan as the "100 Concrete Steps" were being prepared in early 2015. Growth of Kazakhstan's major export destinations weakened and underperformed forecasts.

Economic growth in China diminished and became less reliant on heavy investment and more on consumption of domestic services, while advanced economies' recovery from the 2008-09 global financial crisis continued to be less strong than expected. Reflecting these developments, global growth underperformed projections, which major forecasters repeatedly revised downwards (Figure 1.2). As demand underperformed, overall production of many of Kazakhstan's major commodity exports continued to grow, leading prices to fall sharply. For example, in the two years to March 2016, world prices of crude oil fell by two-thirds, copper by one-quarter and wheat by 35%.

Figure 1.2. **Global growth disappointed in the mid-2010s**

OECD World Real GDP Growth Forecasts

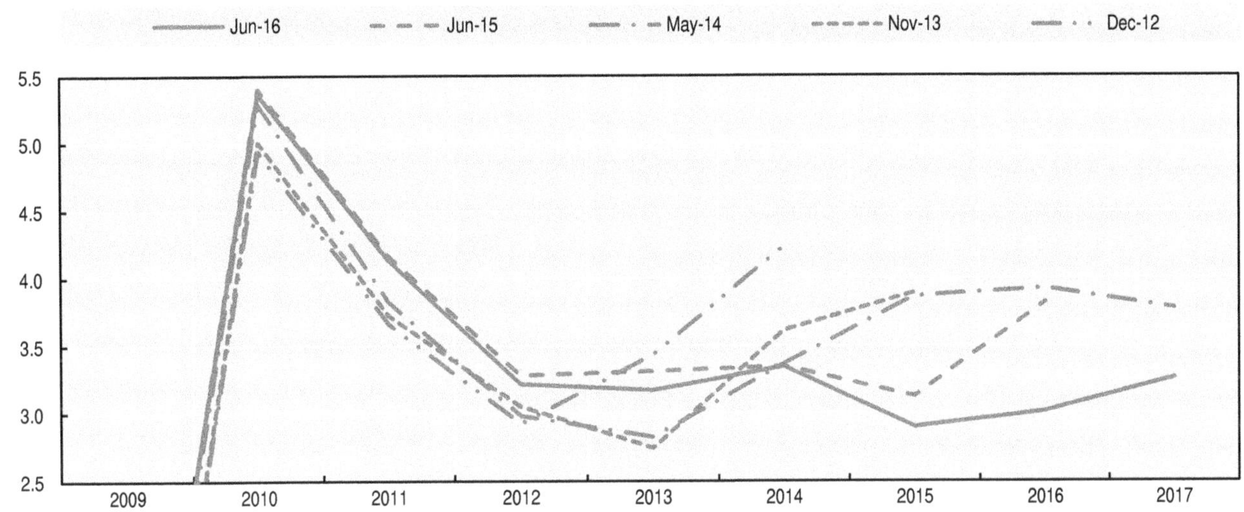

Source: OECD *World Economic Outlook* (2012, 2013, 2014, 2015, 2016c) and authors' calculations.

StatLink http://dx.doi.org/10.1787/888933445263

External developments sharply slowed the Kazakhstan economy. Weakening external conditions reduced inflows of receipts from exports and tax payments, and also of investments in future production (Figure 1.4). Kazakhstan's trade surplus and inwards FDI contracted. The eventual depreciation of the tenge (KZT) (discussed below) compressed domestic consumption by raising the local price of imported items. A large fiscal stimulus package, financed by drawing down offshore funds, provided some offsetting support. Overall real GDP growth slowed from 6.4% between 2010 and 2013 to 0.6% projected over 2015 and 2016. That growth remained positive at all is remarkable given the scale of the negative external shocks: for example, the Russian economy is expected to contract by 5.5% between 2014 and 2016. The fall in oil prices halved the value of 2015 crude oil exports compared with 2014, falling from USD 53.6 billion to USD 26.8 billion: the exported volume fell from 68.2 million metric tonnes to 63.6 million metric tonnes. Overall, mining output volumes fell by 2.4%. A 1.7% decline in household production illustrated the effects of price inflation and the devaluation of the tenge on household incomes. Support to the economy came from the public infrastructure and housing investments within the Nurly Zhol economic stimulus programme, which were evident in the 4.4% increase in construction activity despite weaker investment in mining. Meanwhile agricultural activity also grew solidly, by 4.6%, despite the weakening of wheat export values.

Figure 1.3. **In the mid-2010s, international prices of Kazakhstan's main exports all fell to the real levels of a decade earlier**

Quarterly average price of a barrel of oil and metric tonne of copper and wheat respectively, constant 2016 USD, deflated by interpolated manufacturing unit values (MUV).

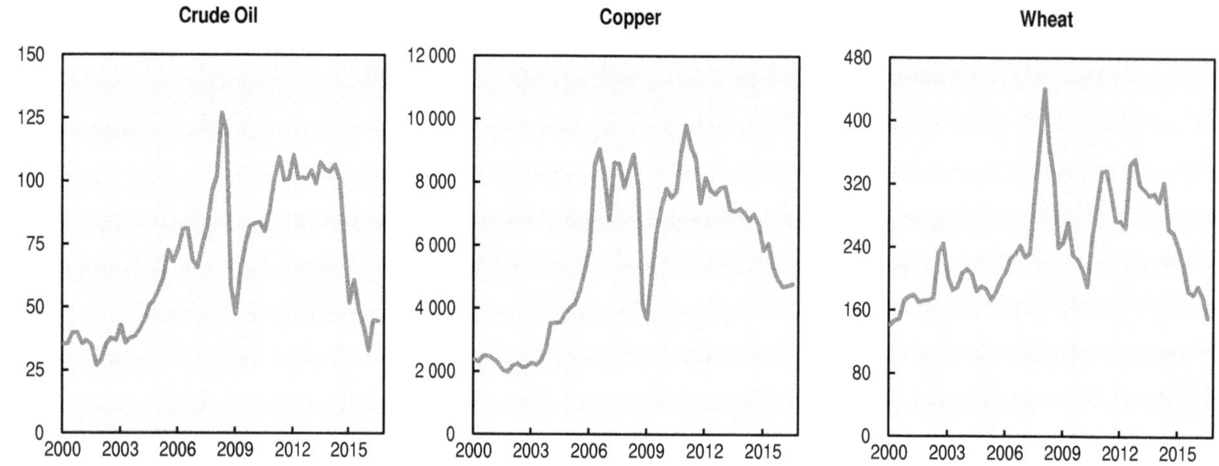

Sources: World Bank Global Economic Monitor (2016) and authors' calculations.

StatLink http://dx.doi.org/10.1787/888933445279

Figure 1.4. **Exports and inward investment weakened, and shifted the current account to deficit**

USD billions, four-quarter rolling total value

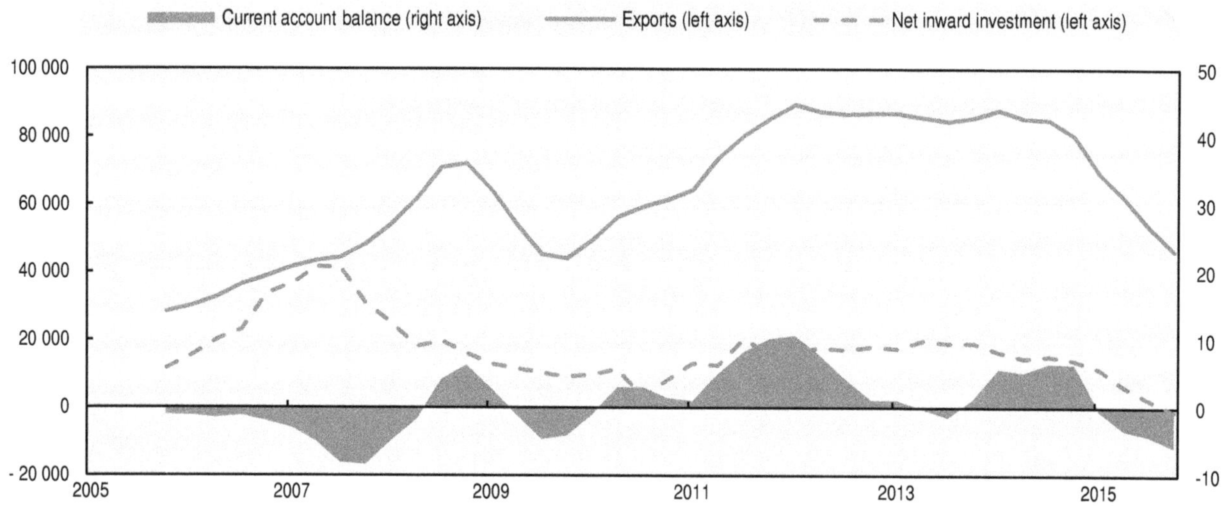

Source: NBK Statistical Bulletin (2016) (NBK, 2016) and authors' calculations.

StatLink http://dx.doi.org/10.1787/888933445281

Monetary and exchange rate policy have been adjusted for the weaker structural conditions

Deteriorating external conditions made Kazakhstan's pegged exchange rate increasingly unsustainable. After the 2008-10 crisis Kazakhstan's formal monetary policy tool to achieve economic and price stability was a stable exchange rate. This policy was sustainable while external conditions were supportive – rising export prices and solid growth of trading partners and strong investment inflows – and while reconsolidation of the domestic financial sector eased credit growth and domestic demand. These developments allowed external accounts to be in surplus and for these surpluses to be accumulated in foreign reserves, while domestic inflationary pressures were moderated by the strong real exchange rate and slow credit growth. As conditions first stabilised and then started to deteriorate, efforts to maintain the exchange rate peg would ultimately prove to be unsustainable and costly. Pressures became acute when countries with similar export baskets as Kazakhstan allowed their exchange rate to depreciate to absorb weaker prices and activity, meaning that the Kazakhstan tenge effectively appreciated, further undermining the economy's competitiveness and domestic production and receipts. Among these depreciations, the most significant was the halving in value of the Russian rouble against the dollar between mid-2014 and early 2016, as its external position weakened with oil prices and the ramifications of its various foreign policies. This represented a particular loss of competitiveness for Kazakhstan, given the two countries' membership of the Eurasian customs union and similarities in their domestic production sectors.

Figure 1.5. **Depreciating competitor currencies made the fixed exchange rate untenable, in due course leading to a sharp adjustment of the tenge**

KZT per USD and exchange rate index level; KZT/USD devaluations indicated

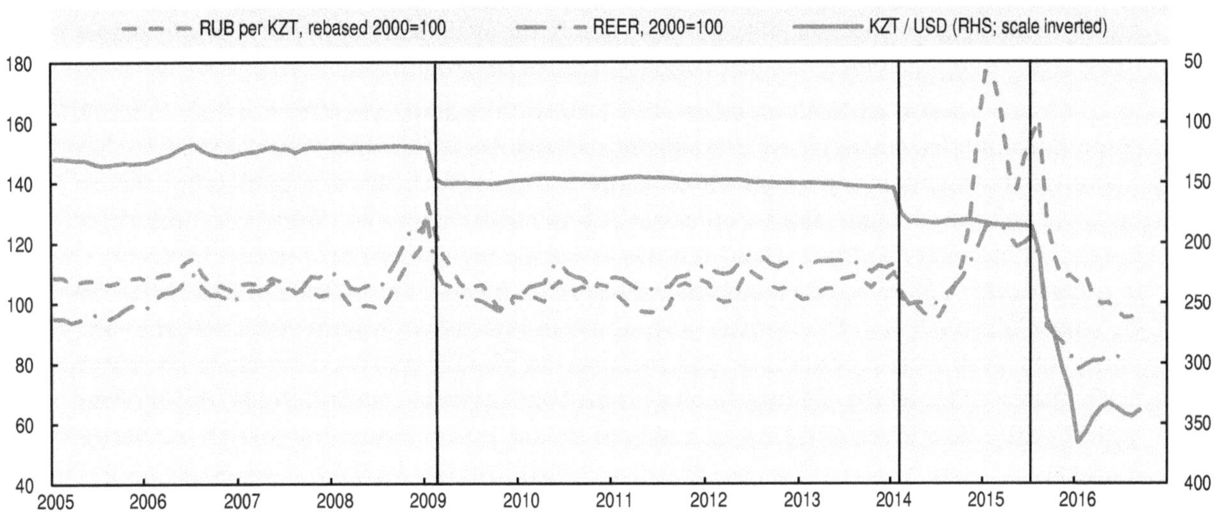

Sources: NBK Statistical Bulletin (NBK, 2016), World Bank Global Economic Monitor and authors' calculations.

StatLink http://dx.doi.org/10.1787/888933445290

Maintaining the tenge's peg undermined the government's wider economic stabilisation and diversification goals. Foreseeing that the central bank would eventually allow the exchange rate to depreciate, economic actors switched from tenge to foreign currency for deposits and transactions. This reduced the pool of tenge in the domestic banking system, shrinking the money supply, while increasing the demand for foreign currency. It created short-term liquidity pressures for banks, as the pool of tenge deposits decreased while borrowers continued to prefer credit in tenge, leading to sharp spikes in interest rates on short-term tenge funds (see Chapter 3). The National Bank of Kazakhstan (NBK) attempted to maintain the tenge's stability against the dollar through both rhetoric and its regular auctioning of foreign exchange, as well as providing banks with instruments such as long-term currency and interest rate swaps. It also sharply increased borrowing interest rates, from around 10% to 19%, depending on the term and borrower. These measures assured liquidity and reduced instability in the tenge market, but also offered banks greater profitability than their usual financial intermediation role of taking deposits and lending to businesses, and added to domestic firms' difficulty in accessing credit for investment and working capital.

Monetary authorities responded to weaker conditions by shifting to an inflation-targeting regime, better adapted to Kazakhstan's macroeconomic challenges. Shifting monetary policy to inflation targeting allows the exchange rate to cushion the domestic economy and will deepen the domestic financial system. In August 2015 NBK specified the monetary policy goal of achieving annual inflation of 3% to 4% by 2020, and the shift in its instrument to a policy interest rate, allowing the exchange rate to float. NBK reserved its right to participate in foreign exchange markets to offset volatility unrelated to fundamental factors and which may threaten financial stability, and started publishing monthly data on interventions as part of an effort to increase transparency around the conduct of monetary policy. The stabilisation of external and domestic monetary conditions will enable real interest rates to return towards levels consistent with international markets. This will encourage more funds to remain in tenge, and so deepen the domestic monetary system. The shift in the policy instrument allows the NBK to set the short-term price of money by acting in the domestic money markets to adjust the base interest rate. This activity has the aim of influencing savings and lending behaviour of commercial banks with the real economy. It allows movements in the exchange rate to help absorb fluctuations in Kazakhstan's export prices, reducing the volatility in interest rates and in the availability of credit. This will enable more stable and predictable domestic inflation and GDP growth.

The full benefits of these policies are likely to take some years to emerge. Initially, controlling inflation during a period of substantial negative supply shocks and a depreciating exchange rate requires higher short-term interest rates, with the aim of slowing capital outflows and the exchange rate's depreciation, while reducing inflationary pressures. After the tool of monetary policy shifted from the exchange rate to the new policy interest rates in August 2015, NBK raised its benchmark policy rate from its initial level of 12% to 16% in October 2015 and 17% in February 2016. As the economic environment stabilised, the new policy approach gained credibility, and the rise in inflation proved to be temporary and expectations of the exchange rate stabilised, the base rate was reduced to 13% by July 2016 and 12.0% by November, and NBK was able to reduce its activity in the foreign exchange markets.

The likely persistence of weaker conditions has put public finances on an unsustainable path

The plunge in oil receipts and the fiscal stimulus significantly weakened Kazakhstan's public finances, an effect partly offset by the depreciation of the exchange rate. Weaker oil prices and overall economic conditions in 2015 cut government revenues, although not as sharply as the 2009 global financial crisis and associated policy measures. Revenues reached a low point in September 2015 at 8.6% below their peak (in 12-month rolling terms),[1] largely because of a 28% decline in oil-related revenues, but also a 9% decline in non-oil revenues related to domestic activity (IMF, 2014, 2015). These trends reduced public revenues to their lowest levels relative to GDP since the early 2000s. The government sought to offset weaker private demand by maintaining public spending. Nominal spending grew very strongly in 2013 and somewhat more moderately in 2014, before broadly stabilising as economic conditions and revenues deteriorated in 2015.[2] Current spending on wages and purchases of goods and services led the surge while other capital and other current spending were stable and transfers grew at their trend rates. These developments raised spending to

21.6% of GDP, its highest level since the 2009-10 global economic downturn. Indeed, this effort to support the economy contrasts with the global financial crisis, when nominal expenditure fell by 7% in 2009, before rapidly recovering. After accounting for financing transactions, these revenue and spending trends shifted the budget from a surplus of 5% of GDP in 2013 to an estimated deficit of 5.3% of GDP in 2015 and projected deficit of 4% in 2016. This represents a fiscal impulse of 4.5% of GDP or KZT 3.8 trillion (USD 21 billion at annual average exchange rates) over two years.

Figure 1.6. **Public spending on wages and goods and services surged ahead of the economic slowdown**

Realised spending, trillions of KZT

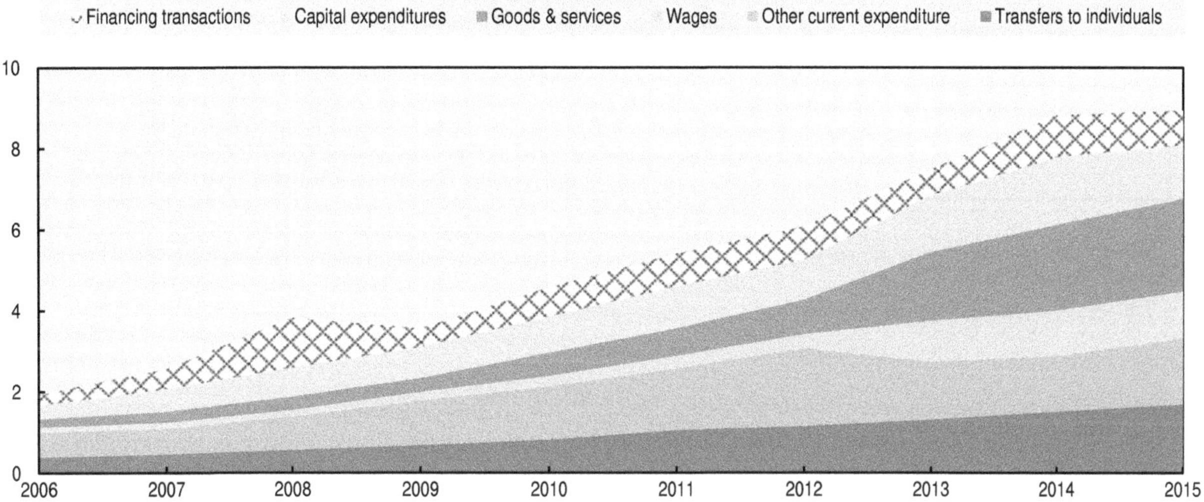

Sources: Ministry of National Economy (2006-2015), IMF (2016) and authors' calculations.

StatLink http://dx.doi.org/10.1787/888933445304

The government's various economic support programmes quickly drew down the state's financial assets. Total public offshore financial assets fell by USD 14.9 billion from their peak in 2014 before stabilising in early 2016, while the government also raised USD 6.3 billion through foreign debt sales, and also expanded domestic debt. By early 2016 the assets in the National Oil Fund had fallen by USD 13.7 billion from their historical peak in mid-2014 of USD 77.3 billion, while the government's holdings of convertible foreign currency (CFC) fell by USD 2.7 billion over the same period. These drawdowns complemented the government's return to international sources to finance its deficit. The government restarted issuing dollar-denominated bonds and tapping multilateral lenders from 2014.

The government's stimulus efforts extended to programmes implemented through public entities. Economic support programmes were also implemented by state-owned entities outside of the budget. The 2015 and projected 2016 budget deficits required USD 14 billion in financing, while over USD 22 billion were raised through various sources. Examples of these programmes include the subsidised credit and entrepreneurship schemes or directed investment programmes implemented by companies within the Baiterek and Samruk-Kazyna groups, such as Damu or the Development Bank of Kazakhstan (discussed elsewhere in this report). These schemes contributed to domestic spending, expanded productive capacity, and supported demand for tenge in foreign exchange markets.

Figure 1.7. **The mid-2010s slowdown had a larger impact on Kazakhstan's public finances than the 2009 global economic crisis**

Central government revenues and expenditure, trillions of KZT, and budget deficit, as a percentage of GDP, excluding financing transactions

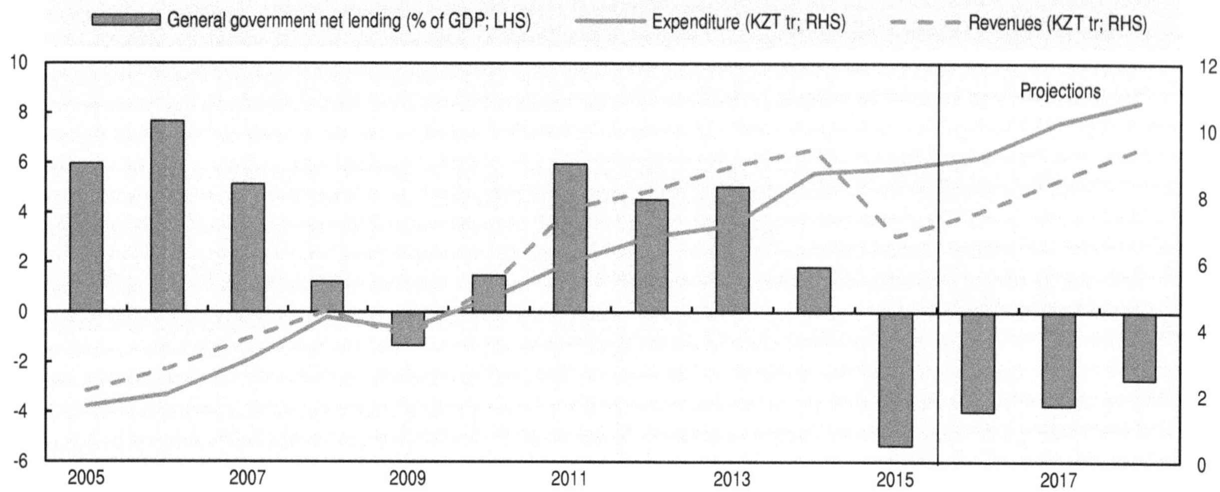

Notes: Revenue and expenditure are adjusted for financing transactions to be consistent with the Global Financial Statistics, following the IMF presentation.

Sources: IMF (2016), adjusting national data sources, and authors' calculations.

StatLink http://dx.doi.org/10.1787/888933445313

Kazakhstan's sovereign debt rating has felt the impact of the drawdown in sovereign foreign assets and increased debt issuance and their implications for the sustainability of the national oil fund and its role as a source of macroeconomic stability. Within the international context of weaker growth among resource-exporting countries, the use of the National Fund assets to support countercyclical fiscal policy, weaker flows into the fund with lower oil prices, and the issuance of offshore public debt, have prompted agencies to cut their sovereign credit rating for Kazakhstan. This reduces the demand for offshore debt for the government as well as for private bodies, and increases the cost of issuing it. In early 2016 Kazakhstan's overall gross external debt was equivalent to 92% of GDP, slightly lower than the 2009 peak of 98%, although approximately half of this is inter-company debt and has been stable in per capita nominal terms for a decade. Meanwhile the debt maturity profile appears to have been lengthened, with reserve assets now over four times the value of short-term external debt, reducing repayment risks. Rating agencies have cited the rapid drawdown of the reserves held in the National Oil Fund during 2014-16, given that these reserves represent an important buffer against weaker revenues and economic volatility. Relaxing the drawdown rules of the national fund so that it is more easily exhausted may undermine the quality of the stabilisation, savings and inter-generational equity objectives of such funds. Indeed, consistency in the application of inflow and drawdown principles is essential if sovereign wealth funds are to play their role as sources of stability and robustness for economies exposed to the natural resource cycle. This role of providing stability is central to funds' contribution to national economies, acknowledged in the "Santiago" Generally Accepted Principals and Practices for Sovereign Wealth Funds, and in the OECD Guidance.[3]

Weaker external economic conditions have also challenged monetary policy, and the adoption of a simple, clear and stable goal is likely to benefit development and economic diversification into the longer term. Monetary authorities are seeking to reduce inflation while other factors are not supportive. The decline in the international prices of Kazakhstan's leading exports effectively constitutes a negative supply shock, reducing the value of the country's production and national income. Allowing the exchange rate to depreciate can absorb part of this, and effectively reduces real incomes by raising prices of imported items relative to domestic goods and services. But this is only effective to the extent that domestic production can substitute for imports. Further, these developments challenge the longer-term goal of making finance more readily available to support economic diversification. When it shifted its inflation management policy tool from the exchange rate to the new policy base rate, the central bank increased the costs of funds. Higher lending rates combined with weaker external conditions and lower expected returns on domestic investments to slow lending, reinforcing the weaker trends in economic activity. By reducing the expected returns to investments, these developments also make external finance less available for Kazakhstan entities. Since the early 2000s, there has been a positive relationship between the growth of lending to the economy and economic activity, although the relationship changed before and after the 2008-10 financial crisis, and does not show statistical causality. The relationship between lending and activity varies considerably between economic sectors, which suggests significant segmentation of the credit markets (IMF, 2015).

Weaker conditions are likely to persist, reducing space for development spending

Weaker external conditions are likely to persist into the longer term. Many forecasters have lowered their assessment of long-term sustainable growth rates for both advanced and emerging economies. In the longer term this is associated with a slowdown in productivity growth, which is explained by various developments. One analysis attributes it to a smaller contribution from new information and communications technologies compared with the innovations of the late 19th and 20th centuries. Productivity growth also appears to have slowed in emerging economies and the convergence of emerging economies with high-income countries is not occurring at the rates that were earlier expected. Finally, and of particular significance for Kazakhstan and its commodity exports, China's economic model is adjusting to more moderate growth and a stronger role for consumer demand rather than heavy industrial investment.

The international climate change agreement reached in Paris in December 2015 represents an opportunity for Kazakhstan to improve the economy's energy efficiency. To achieve the long-term temperature goal set out, the parties to the United Nations Framework Convention on Climate Change (UNFCCC) aim to reach global peaking of greenhouse gas emissions as soon as possible and then undertake rapid reductions of them, with the aim of limiting the rise in global temperatures. This presents challenges for Kazakhstan, by weakening expected global demand for the country's fossil fuels, while requiring it to adapt its relatively emissions-intensive economy. Long-term cuts in global demand for fossil fuels will rely on major technological advances, including large improvements in reducing emissions or in capturing and storing carbon, while rapid gains in energy efficiency are likely to diminish demand for fossil fuels. This adaptation represents an opportunity to raise the efficiency and competitiveness of Kazakhstan's industrial structure. Large investments and industrial adaptation will be required to raise the efficiency and competitiveness of Kazakhstan's economy.

The government's economic support measures are prudent responses to a temporary downturn, but cannot be sustained while weak conditions persist. The extent and likely duration of the weakening in economic conditions was not expected. Between 2013 and

2015, projections of total government revenues for 2016-18 fell by 28%, or KZT 10 trillion, or 3.5% of revised GDP[4] (IMF forecasts of nominal GDP). The likely protracted weakness in outlook makes drawing down reserves and borrowing to offset weaker revenue unsustainable, even if resources remain robust. The weaker revenue outlook suggests that spending must be reduced and revenues strengthened to return public finances to a sustainable path (Behar and Fouejieu, 2016). This adjustment should also apply to spending by off-budget publicly owned entities that are able to draw on offshore funds, where these drawdowns have financed the economic support and directed investment programmes implemented by various state-owned entities. Achieving this requires mobilising revenues from the domestic non-resource economy more efficiently while stabilising overall spending. Overall spending can be adjusted with limited impact on the delivery of public goods and services by spending more efficiently, for example by adjusting the directed investment and subsidised credit programmes.

As conditions stabilise, the benefits of a floating exchange rate and of an inflation-targeting regime will start to be realised. By mid-2016 commodity prices and Kazakhstan's terms of trade, as well as the exchange rate and foreign reserves had stabilised, albeit at significantly lower levels than the preceding decade. As the real exchange rate reaches its new equilibrium, market participants will no longer expect further exchange rate depreciation or intervention by the NBK, thus reducing the incentive to shift funds out of tenge. The central bank can build its credibility by remaining committed to reducing inflation while ensuring its interventions in foreign exchange markets are directed at maintaining market liquidity rather than delaying the exchange rate's movement away from medium-term equilibrium. Given that perceptions about exchange rate movements can be self-fulfilling in the short term, changed perceptions and stronger clarity and credibility on the part of the central bank around its goals can help entrench stability in the exchange rate and the conditions affected by it, allowing the NBK to rebuild its buffers of foreign reserves. This stability also reduces inflationary expectations and the cost to the economy of reducing inflation. By mid-2016 the central bank was able to lower its benchmark interest rate. Fiscal policy can support this process by credibly moving back to a sustainable path, by improving the efficiency of spending and by reducing financing needs. This will stabilise Kazakhstan's country risk outlook, improving access to external finance for the private sector. All of these developments would help rebuild domestic tenge liquidity, supporting lending by banks, and the long-term goals of developing and diversifying the domestic economy.

Assessment and recommendations

Diversification and resilience in Kazakhstan

The period of growth acceleration in Kazakhstan (2000-10) was characterised by an increasing reliance on natural resources, in particular oil. The oil and gas sector, including extraction and associated activities, generated at its peak 26% of GDP in 2012. Despite its relatively small weight in terms of employment, oil dominates exports (64%) and generates about a third of public revenues. As observed in Volume I of the MDCR (OECD, 2016b), oil exports are also concentrated in terms of their destinations. The pattern of concentration was largely, but not solely, led by the increase in oil prices.

Kazakhstan's natural wealth has largely contributed to its economic take-off but has not been exploited to its full potential. Not only does Kazakhstan hold 1.8% of global oil reserves, it is also a major gas producer – although most of the gas production is used in oil extraction –, and is the world's leading uranium producer. Reserves and production in metals – copper, iron, chromium, magnesium, zinc, gold and silver – are also significant. Mineral and metal production, however, remains largely dependent on outdated and inefficient equipment and as a result is not very competitive internationally, a state of affairs that has resulted in volatile iron and steel exports and a loss in the sophistication of exports among mineral products – with unrefined ores gaining share at the expense of refined products.

Production also became increasingly concentrated between 2000 and 2010. The economy's reliance on individual sectors fell dramatically in the 1990s, as the economy recovered from the disruption of the transition phase and agriculture's weight in GDP fell from 34% to 11.4% by 1997. However, concentration increased gradually from the late 1990s to the early 2010s. In particular manufacturing in Kazakhstan is much more concentrated than in many emerging economies, although it is comparable to other Central Asian countries. Concentration in production shows that export concentration was not merely a reflection of changes in terms of trade, but that those changes affected the allocation of capital.

Diversification is an imperative for Kazakhstan's future development, to reduce its exposure to external risk as well as to further job and value creation domestically. Commodity-dependency exposes Kazakhstan to external shocks and can hinder long-term development prospects. There are multiple channels through which natural resource wealth can negatively affect long-term development prospects, offsetting the undeniable opportunities that it offers. One major channel through which natural resource wealth affects growth across countries is the volatility that it imposes in the economy. Oil is one of the commodities with the most volatile prices: oil prices not only have high-frequency volatility, but are also subject to large cyclical fluctuations. Price shocks affect Kazakhstan through multiple channels, most notably through shocks to the real foreign exchange rate and through shocks to public revenues.

The National Fund plays an important role in reducing the impact of oil price volatility and has also managed to limit "Dutch disease" effects. A fixed nominal exchange rate made it possible to limit some of the high-frequency volatility effects – especially given the level of price rigidity. Although the National Fund can help smooth public expenditure, its implementation has not altered the budget's reliance on oil revenues. During the 2008-10 crisis, the National Fund played a major role in sustaining countercyclical stimulus. However, in the medium term, over-reliance on oil revenues to finance public expenditure is likely to limit the degree to which Kazakhstan can have countercyclical fiscal policy.

Diversification has been a major policy objective since the mid-1990s but its implementation only came into earnest in 2010 with the implementation of the first State Programme on Accelerated Industrial-Innovative Development (SPAIID). SPAIID suffered from a number of limitations, including the dispersion of effort, which gave rise to a large number of instruments and institutions and significant co-ordination problems. Essential lessons have been learned and incorporated into the design of the next phase of industrial policy, as described in the Concept of Industrialisation and the second SPAIID programme. The SPAIID 2015-2019 programme focuses actions more through the selection of a smaller number of sectors and clusters, incorporates private sector and regional representatives into the decision-making process, and consolidates actions across sectors that were previously scattered.

Since 2010, the process of relative deindustrialisation has stopped, and new major non-natural-resource export products have been "discovered". Measures of concentration in production also exhibit a slight decline. Investment in fixed assets in manufacturing increased in real terms by 8% per annum between 2010 and 2014, after stalling for the five preceding years and grew from 8.9% to 11.1% of total investment in fixed assets. Unfortunately, evaluations of industrial policy are based on very aggregate indicators and do not follow a rigorous impact evaluation method, and therefore these successes cannot be unambiguously attributed to SPAIID. One of the key instruments of industrial policy, the Map of Industrialisation, is a tool for monitoring large industrial projects which are eligible for individualised state support. While criteria for inclusion in the Map of Industrialisation also make the projects eligible for significant state support, their inclusion also serves to co-ordinate logistic and financial support and to provide a picture of key industrial projects in the country. Its direct effects (in terms of job creation and investment) are significant. Indeed, a large share of investment in fixed assets during the first SPAIID programme went to the oil and gas sector, above and beyond the sector's weight in the economy.

Despite recent improvements, industrial policy in Kazakhstan is largely reliant on direct financial support and depends on the selection of key sectors and projects by implementing agencies. Implementing agencies remain scattered, despite ongoing consolidation and rationalisation efforts. Particularly in what concerns monitoring and transparency, there is a wide diversity in the availability of information regarding the activities of the various actors concerned, and no uniformity in how this information is provided. Within financial support alone, sources typically report investment project sizes or credit or support, which makes comparing different programmes and their relative efficiency a very arduous task.

The number of priority sectors was narrowed down in 2016. The government decided in mid-2016 to trim the list of priority sectors from the wide set of 14 sectors originally considered in SPAIID 2015-2019 to eight branches in five sectors. They are ferrous and nonferrous metallurgy, oil refining, petrochemicals and agrochemicals, food processing, automotive and electrical engineering. These sectors were selected on the basis of their export potential. It is expected that companies in other sectors that engage in exports or in improving productivity will also receive support, but current normative texts and practice do not specify what instruments will be available to firms in non-priority sectors. Companies in the eight priority branches are expected to receive support in the form of infrastructure, and long-term and concessional finance, among others.

The reliance on the choice of predefined sectors can be a risky strategy in a rapidly evolving environment. With these sectors being predetermined for a relatively long period of time (five years), the ability of agencies implementing industrial policy to adapt to changing circumstances can be called into question. The recent announcement of a narrowing down of the list of priority list from 14 sectors to eight branches is one symptom of this lack of flexibility, as it happened a year after the significant structural shift that were the change to a floating exchange rate and subsequent fiscal tightening measures. The sector selection criteria are not fully transparent, which is not to say they are misguided. The sectors selected appear reasonable in the light of Kazakhstan's position in the product space, its prospects to move up the value chain in sectors related to its natural resource extraction activities, and the ambition to develop a number of sectors where it already has a presence (chemistry, petrochemistry and vehicle manufacturing).

Main recommendations for the implementation of industrial policy:

- Consistent objectives and clear principles of implementation should be set for industrial policy. The key guidance document, the Concept on Industrialisation, sets a number of core principles, but is silent on how balance will be achieved between sector-specific and horizontal support, or on what the basis is for selecting sectors for specific support.

- Align monitoring and evaluation with the objectives and with best practices. Current publicly available information on industrial policy is scattered and not comparable. There should be a role for independent actors in evaluation, given the very significant sums involved. Evaluation functions should overall be strengthened both in terms of the evaluation framework and the evaluating agency.
- A number of measures in industrial policy and especially complementary measures determining the framework conditions should be moved from a programmatic to a policy setting. There is merit in certain forms of support being time-bound, but those measures that constitute the conditions of operation in a sector should be predictable over longer periods to attract foreign and domestic investment, especially when SOEs play an important role in those sectors.
- Seek sources of greater flexibility in implementation to allow industrial policy to adapt to changes in circumstances. Sources of flexibility can be found in the institutional and programmatic framework itself, by setting principles that allow objectives and key implementation issues to evolve over time. Flexibility can also be found by implementing more indirect instruments, which give a greater role to private sector actors – both entrepreneurs implementing projects and financial institutions providing finance – in identifying profitable opportunities.
- Re-examine the key functions of industrial policy and the responsible bodies. Functions should be expanded beyond traditional finance and co-ordination to include also strengthening the anticipation, adaptation, embeddedness, interconnectedness and learning capacities in the economy. Public-private bodies can play an important role in providing these.
- Put greater emphasis on non-financial instruments and increase the direct participation of the private sector based on responsible business conduct principles and standards. Non-financial functions of existing instruments, such as the co-ordination role of the Map of Industrialisation, are also important. They should be recognised in their own right, ensuring they remain, even if and when the financing role of the state diminishes. Private sector participation in decision-making and consultation bodies is an important advance over the command and control basis. Direct private-sector intervention through more indirect instruments can open up new avenues and projects.
- Include other sectors in the industrial policy framework, in particular those industries in agriculture and services that have potential in Kazakhstan. The country has many features that would make it a good candidate for regional service provision in business, information technology (IT), and financial and environmental services. However, their development suffers from lack of appropriate specific infrastructure and a certain disconnect between public and private actors.

Continuous improvement in complementary inputs, especially high-quality infrastructure, and reforms, needs to accompany industrial policy if it is to have an effect. Continuing and recent reforms in the areas of regulatory quality, competition and public service can improve conditions for entrepreneurs and investors across the country but much remains to be done, especially in the areas of human capital formation, finance, and in levelling the playing field between economic actors. Significant efforts in the upgrading of physical infrastructure will need to be pursued, and should be complemented by efforts to develop logistics capacity to facilitate access to markets and the integration of value chains.

Education, training and innovation policies should be further developed in line with structural transformation objectives. This requires mechanisms to anticipate future skills needs and design appropriate training curricula and methods, possibly with the participation of the private sector. Innovation efforts will need to be upgraded if Kazakhstan is to become an innovation-driven economy; this will involve not only an upgrade in research and development (R&D) spending but also efforts to bring the innovation and research system closer to business.

Mobilising finance to transform Kazakhstan's economy

Kazakhstan's financial sector, especially its banking system, is unusually shallow. Whether measured by credit to the private sector or broader measures that include deposits and financial markets, Kazakhstan's financial system is small relative to its GDP. Banks' limited deposit bases and lending are particularly notable. The only countries that have achieved higher income levels with as thin a financial sector as Kazakhstan are even more reliant on narrow resource extraction sectors. Equity and bond markets lack the liquidity needed to provide effective funding, while the structure of the pension system limits its capacity to fund long-term investments.

The shallow banking sector hampers firms' investments and operations and impedes the economy's diversification and the emergence of new sectors. Smaller firms, especially those in domestic services sectors or newer firms, report that access to finance is a major obstacle to doing business. These firms are particularly reliant on banks for financing. International evidence and NBK research suggest that this weakness imperils investment and economic diversification more broadly, and that a robust banking sector is essential for sustained growth. Larger firms, and those with connections to the state, are able to work around these limitations by tapping international sources of finance or through the government's systems of financing its SOEs. Shallow equity and other financial markets are less of a hindrance for economic development and diversification. Cross-country evidence suggests that these markets become important drivers of development for significantly larger economies with higher levels of productivity and diversity.

Both structural and cyclical factors explain the shallowness of finance in Kazakhstan. Banks have limited access to wholesale funding, reflecting the ongoing effects of earlier unsustainable use of international credit flows, as well as the structure of the pension system, and limited domestic savings. Domestic savers are discouraged from holding their savings onshore. The period of an unsustainably high exchange rate encouraged savers to shift their funds out of tenge and into foreign currency. Longer-term uncertainty over property rights and the continuing uncertain status of past transactions has also encouraged wealthy individuals to shift their funds offshore. The NBK's efforts to stabilise the exchange rate also encouraged banks to engage in financial trading rather than business lending. All actors face uncertainty and a lack of transparency around the judicial system, including the protection of investors' rights. Lenders even cite the uncertain integrity of financial statements and auditors' reports as an obstruction to their ability to lend, especially to new firms.

The government's various schemes to support firms' access to finance were effective during the financial crisis, but have limited long-term benefits. The government has introduced a large number of schemes intended to improve access to finance for targeted categories of firms. These avoid some weaknesses of similar schemes by working through second-tier banks. The commercial banks are responsible for identifying borrowers and managing the loans. The schemes subsidise the interest rate or guarantee the loan, and can accompany this support with various efforts to improve the businesses' operations through training and capacity development. The schemes have been funded by drawing on savings in the national oil fund and from Kazakhstan's development partners. They made an important contribution to ensuring that firms could continue to access credit during the depths of the 2008-10 financial crisis. But econometric analysis could not find evidence that they have generated lasting gains in credit growth or investment.

Main recommendations to strengthen the role of finance for economic diversification:

- Strengthening banks' ability to access wholesale funding will improve their ability to provide credit. Banks' lending is constrained by the availability of funding. The pool of domestic savings will remain limited into the medium term, even after the shift of monetary policy regime and the exchange rate stabilisation slowed the outflow of funds. In the short and medium term, international wholesale financing can address the immediate hindrance of shortage of financing. However, accessing these funds is likely to remain challenging for Kazakhstan's financial institutions. The legacy of the stress of the 2008-10 period continues to limit banks' ability to access international wholesale markets, and the recent downgrading of the state's international sovereign credit rating adds to their difficulties. Government actions need to ensure that its sovereign rating is not further downgraded, including through sustainable budget deficits, and transparent and stable management strategies for the offshore reserves, including the National Oil Fund. To circumvent these issues, joint ventures or equity sales to international banks should be supported where they can improve banks' access to international financing and internal management.
- Other efforts need to continue to develop domestic savings. Management of the consolidated pension fund should focus on ensuring the funds are efficiently invested for secure but optimised long-term. Such behaviour usually requires competition between fund managers. The government is developing this policy, including transfer of management to private companies and removing the single accumulative pension fund from the NBK. The shift to a floating exchange rate, inflation-targeting monetary policy should stabilise the outflow of funds, if the policy is seen as credible and enduring. Efforts to improve the rule of law and protection of property rights will also support Kazakhstan investors' willingness to hold funds onshore.
- Strengthen with transparency and continuity the financial sector's institutional environment. Kazakhstan has made significant gains in the quality of its supervisory system since the 2000s, and banks have strengthened their internal management. Converting these gains into improved access to finance will require ensuring that investors can be confident in the protection of their investments, ability to enforce agreements, and reliability of financial information and audits. Especially relevant for smaller enterprises, the capacity of accountants needs to be developed, while misleading audits need to be prevented, for example through credible sanctions. The Astana International Financial Centre may support this process, by providing a model legal and accounting jurisdiction alongside Kazakhstan's institutions.
- The programmes supporting access to finance for targeted categories of firms would be more effective with greater focus. The programmes are effective in responding to short-term crisis situations, when banks cut their lending. They can be effective at helping firms develop their internal management capacity. However, indefinite implementation of the programmes does not appear to accelerate the development of firms or of credit growth,

and can lead to the misallocation of lending to investments that do not offer the highest returns. Further, they may mask the symptoms of deeper institutional weaknesses, at considerable cost for public finances.

Privatisation and the role of the state in the economy

The economy of Kazakhstan is dominated by state-owned enterprises (SOEs) and large private industrial and financial conglomerates. There are close to 7 000 registered state-owned enterprises, of which over 1 000 are considered large as they employ over 250 people. According to data supplied by the Ministry of National Economy, the gross value added by the SOE sector was 8.1% of GDP in 2014. In addition there are about 20 000 state agencies which engage in public administration and do not conduct commercial activity.

SOEs are the dominant form of state control in the economy. An analysis of the degree and mechanisms of state control using the OECD Product Market Regulation Indicators shows that state involvement in Kazakhstan stands out among benchmark and OECD countries. This assessment reflects the heavy involvement of government in network sectors, with full ownership and control of the largest firms in the gas sector, in several transport sectors, the post, mobile services, electricity distribution, supply and generation and the ownership of majority stakes in firms in other sectors. This scope of presence is larger than in OECD economies.

The extent of state involvement in the economy is such that even large-scale privatisation is unlikely to lower state involvement much unless the state relinquishes significant control over key firms. Beyond SOEs, price control is much more prevalent in Kazakhstan than in OECD member countries or major emerging economies. Price controls are applied across a wide range of sectors; plans to abolish price regulation from January 2017 have been announced and offer an opportunity to bring Kazakhstan into line with conventional OECD approaches that rely on prices for the provision of market signals. Regulation in Kazakhstan stands out for taking a coercive rather than an incentivising approach. Current efforts to reduce the amount of regulation through Regulatory Impact Assessment should be accompanied by efforts to change the nature of regulations in some sectors.

Kazakhstan has set a target to reduce the share of the state in the economy to 15% by the year 2020 from the present level, which represents its most ambitious privatisation programme since independence. There is significant support for the notion that privatisation can bring about significant increases in the profitability, output and efficiency of companies. The use of that particular target, based on book value to GDP, as the key measure of privatisation efforts is debatable. The ongoing privatisation programme is very ambitious, with close to 800 entities up for privatisation including the "Top 65", a set of large enterprises whose privatisation has been given priority.

The legal framework for privatisation has been reformed in advance of the launch of the comprehensive privatisation plan. Public firms which operate in markets where private enterprises exist should be privatised or exit the market. The Law on State Property was amended in view of the new privatisation programme, setting out the possibility of carrying out privatisations by auction, tender or direct sales. The January 2016 reform has also simplified procedures to make them more agile: following the reform, only the price is decisive in auctions and tenders with or without the existence of conditions. Direct sale of state assets to "strategic investors" are now allowed, following the recent amendments to the law. To limit the risk of corruption, requirements have been included for independent pricing for assets worth over KZT 5 billion and for the participation of independent external advisors in all directed sales.

Following the examples of KazTransOil and KEGOC, which were the object of initial public offerings in 2012 and 2014 respectively, a number of firms are expected to have part of their equity sold in the stock market. In both cases, minority stakes of 10% minus one share have been sold to the public. While benefits in terms of increased transparency can be expected, strategic decisions will remain in the hands of the state as a shareholder. In strategic companies, foreign buyers can purchase stakes after approval by the government.

The governance and management of SOEs in Kazakhstan departs in several ways from the OECD Guidelines on Corporate Governance of State-owned Enterprises. While some encouraging recent measures have been taken to improve the governance of individual SOEs, Kazakhstan does not have an ownership policy that would define the rationales of state ownership, the role of the state in the governance of SOEs and the roles and responsibilities of government offices involved in the implementation of the policy. The Kazakhstan authorities point out, however, that in their opinion the Law on State Property and the recently promulgated Entrepreneurial Code form together an ownership policy. Moreover, the playing field is not level between private firms and SOEs. Enterprises with foreign ownership have experienced that SOEs often enjoy better access to resources, markets, credit and licences. Access to finance is challenging in Kazakhstan, but SOEs have explicit or implicit state guarantees and can tap in some cases internal funds from national managing holdings.

There is no single ownership entity in charge of exercising ownership on behalf of the state. The Committee of State Property exercises authority on behalf of the government and has property rights on all republican entities. The committee has, by government decisions, delegated the rights of use and possession to a number of responsible sector ministries, which exercise the owner's rights over the entities. In addition, there is a structure of legally independent national managing holding companies, which are outright owners of dozens of enterprises, including the most important industries. All this deviates from the principle of unified ownership. Moreover, no emphasis has been put on separating ownership and regulation functions. The Ministry of National Economy, the Ministry of Finance and the Ministry of Agriculture exercise ownership of SOEs and are responsible for regulation in relevant sectors (taxation, industrial policy, competition, public procurement). The corporate governance of national management holdings involves high-level officials, which increases political control. At the same time, these organisations control significant public wealth without direct parliamentary oversight.

Main recommendations:

- The privatisation programme is an opportunity to bring ownership policies and practices more into line with the OECD Guidelines. This entails developing an ownership policy, which is particularly important in countries like Kazakhstan that have high state participation in the economy. Kazakhstan should also reduce the dispersion of the organisation of SOE ownership, clearly identify the body exercising ownership rights and separate ownership from regulatory functions to ensure the playing field is even between SOEs and private enterprises.
- A centralised ownership entity would be appropriately located in the Office of the Prime Minister, given the importance of SOEs in the economy of Kazakhstan. It should also have shareholder powers over the boards of national managing holdings. These boards should

be reorganised with professional corporate leaders taking over from political decision makers. The ownership entity should be held accountable to parliament and develop a consistent system of reporting on state ownership and publishing an aggregate report at least annually.

- The ultimate objective of privatisation should be clearly stated and monitored. A dashboard of indicators could be developed to improve upon the objective set in terms of book value to GDP (all the more so, given the recognised overvaluation of certain assets included in the privatisation programme). Since privatisation efforts aim to revitalise the private sector in Kazakhstan, reform of state ownership is of major importance for privatisation efforts because of the need to ensure that the playing field is even and that SOEs with private equity participation strive to meet objectives of all shareholders.
- The privatisation process should be controlled *ex post*, by an independent body reporting to the parliament. The requirement of maximum transparency and accountability in all aspects of the privatisation process is essential. The appointment of a single co-ordinating unit would help reduce the dispersion of privatisation. Its accountability would also limit political interventions which could damage credibility for investors and ultimately reduce privatisation revenues or thwart privatisation plans. Progress in the privatisation process should be regularly disclosed to parliament and the general public.
- Owners, or the office responsible for privatisation, should be given adequate time and resources to prepare the assets for privatisation. Such preparation entails due diligence, but also adjustments to the capital structure of the entity, on one hand to ensure its viability and on the other hand to strip out excess cash holdings. Concerns over the viability of the companies should be addressed. A number of enterprises (e.g. Kazakhstan Temir Zholy) have public service obligations. The obligations and any compensation should be disclosed in connection with the listing or privatisation, which would otherwise compromise minority shareholders' rights. Environmental liabilities should also be identified and costed.
- Identifying buyers will prove challenging in the current conditions. When direct sales take place under conditions – e.g. for strategic investors to agree to specific undertakings, investments, or operations – those conditions, their method of monitoring and the consequences of non-observance should be clarified. For smaller entities, which are more likely to find buyers in the domestic market, the possibility of management buy-outs should be introduced and encouraged, as they can lead to more favourable outcomes for smaller firms, given the specific knowledge of managers.

Towards better environmental regulations in Kazakhstan

Notwithstanding the recent global financial crisis, Kazakhstan's gross domestic product (GDP) doubled over the past decade while export earnings increased correspondingly over the same period. Yet, much of this growth was based on the extractive and heavy industries and on the use of electricity which is produced mostly from coal. Consequently, Kazakhstan today is one of the most energy-intensive countries in the world and the energy intensity has not improved during the last decade. The environmental damage inherited from the Soviet era was exacerbated by the impacts from energy production, pollution from heavy industry, accelerated extraction of oil, gas and other mineral resources, as well as from agriculture and from growing road traffic in urban areas.[5]

Kazakhstan has undertaken steps to move towards a more sustainable mode of development which were outlined in two key strategic documents: the 2012 "Kazakhstan 2050 Strategy" and the 2013 "Green Economy Concept" (GEC) which outlined the path to long-term growth based on climate-friendly technologies, energy efficiency measures, and the restoration and sustainable management of natural resources. The GEC, in particular, envisaged modernising deteriorating environmental infrastructure, and set ambitious environment-related targets for the power generation, mining, industry and agriculture sectors and for energy, soil and water use. It stated that "...by successfully achieving these targets, the country will recover its water and land resources by 2030, and its resource productivity will largely be on par with the average indicators of the OECD members and other developed countries".

However, the implementation of the GEC faces serious challenges, including:

- "top-down" and "command-and-control" approaches based often on the Soviet standards or regulation, combined with frequent incidents of corruption to avoid heavy handed non-compliance response,
- limited use of market-oriented, compliance promotion and information-based instruments to incentivise companies to invest in pollution reduction and technology modernisation,
- lack of willingness by local authorities to implement green reform because of fear of the reallocation of revenue from environmental payments away from local budgets; and
- strong vested interests in the energy-intensive sectors, such as domestic electric power, mining or chemical industries not to allocate their own resources to the improvement of their environmental performance.

In order to meet its ambitious targets, Kazakhstan urgently needs to develop and implement a set of measures and policies defined in the GEC and other key policy documents. Among many, one of the most important steps that could unlock vast green growth opportunities is the expeditious reform of a basic environmental regulatory framework. Despite recent progress, the uncoordinated implementation of environmental requirements together with the high volume of complex environmental regulations based on unrealistic assumptions have resulted in a regulatory environment that is complicated, burdensome and costly to both the administration and industry. What is more, the evidence suggests that it does not lead to actual environmental improvement. To address these fundamental flaws, further efforts to streamline and simplify these requirements are needed in a way that realistic objectives are set and environmental ambitions are not compromised.

Extensive preparations by the government of Kazakhstan for the upcoming EXPO 2017: Future Energy, the emphasis on green technologies and the overall business case for a green economy are promisingly timed for new policy breakthroughs.

Main recommendations include:

- Environmental quality standards need to be revised in the light of international best practices and domestic capabilities to technically feasible and enforceable levels, striking a balance between what is desirable from an environmental point of view and what is feasible from a technical and economic standpoint. The government should make the best use of limited technical capacity and prioritise the provision of the financial and human resources to regulate effectively those polluting substances that pose the greatest risk to human health and/or the environment.

- The present environmental permitting and compliance control requirements need to shift the focus of environmental requirements from "end-of-pipe" solutions to integrated pollution prevention and control. For the largest and "high impact" polluters there should be a shift away from the mentality of command-and-control regulation, which just penalises non-compliance, and re-incentivise it through integrated pollution prevention and control. Integrated environmental permits are one of the most effective ways of achieving better pollution control since the permit is linked to best available techniques (BATs) which are associated with lower emissions.
- Building on the reform and improvements of Environmental Impact Assessments (EIA) and State Environmental Experts' Examination (SEEE) there is a further need to simplify and shorten the procedures for medium and small-scale projects. Where possible the EIA/SEEE procedures should be combined with integrated environmental permitting. Further efforts are also needed by the public authorities to open the procedures to the public's active participation, especially at the regional and local levels. This should assist in building the procedures for more regular reporting on environmental pollution (and their impacts) in a consistent and standardised format.
- The OECD country experience shows that Kazakhstan should abandon fault-based concepts for damages that tie liability to exceeding a pre-determined limit in an emissions permit and instead adopt the strict liability/polluter-pays model based on evidence of actual harm to the environment. By contrast, environmental liability for pollution in Kazakhstan applies only if the emission permit limits have been breached (the fault standard), even in the absence of proof of environmental damage.
- Although some important legal changes are being introduced, environmental liability in Kazakhstan remains focused on calculating and collecting monetary compensation for the state (essentially serving as a revenue-raising penalty) rather than on preventing and correcting the damage, reducing emissions over time and incentivising the use of BATs. Credibility in the regulatory system needs to be restored by reforming the laws governing environmental taxes, fines and damages so that they are aligned exclusively and transparently with environmental policy objectives and the international commitments Kazakhstan has made. The state should eliminate discrimination against specific industrial sectors, set rates for taxes and fines which are uniform for all industry sectors and set rules for assessing damages which are also non-discriminatory. The rates applicable to taxes and fines should be realistic and consistent with international practice. Enforcement should also be transparent and even-handed. More regulatory guidance should be provided on how to assess the extent of the damage, needs and costs of remediation, and how to select clean-up measures
- Kazakhstan should be applauded for taking steps toward better use of market-based environmental policy instruments, e.g. in relation to the reduction of greenhouse gases (KazETS) and making commitments under international treaties to reduce its carbon footprint. Implementation will be critical to modernising the country's economy and integrating it into the international community of developed countries. Consistent with the trend across all environmental reform initiatives in Kazakhstan, the state should match its ambitious commitments with real legislative reforms. Authorities should work jointly with relevant stakeholders to clarifying the regulations. The competent authority in charge of the KazETS should be strengthened in order to provide adequate training, clarification and guidance to entities regulated under the KazETS.

Anticipating trends and preparing for future challenges: Scenarios for the future of Kazakhstan

This chapter has so far detailed some of major challenges that Kazakhstan faces in realising its goal of becoming one of the world's 30 most developed countries by 2050. It has also detailed the severe and long-lasting impact of shocks in the global economy on Kazakhstan's economy and growth prospects. Kazakhstan's exposure to the external environment, because of the reliance of its economy on natural resource extraction, means it needs to be prepared for major shifts or shocks that could have an impact on its prospects for development.

The pace and composition of the global economy is changing rapidly, and many economic, social, environmental, political and technological trends will shape development opportunities in the future. Identification of these trends and anticipation of their impacts should be integrated into policy planning to enable decisions that will make the Kazakhstani economy more resilient. To ensure that the recommendations in this report are relevant in the face of these trends, scenarios were developed to test those recommendations against global developments, and foresee their consequences in terms of policy contexts, incentives and trade-offs.

This section details four scenarios for Kazakhstan developed with a time horizon of 2030. The scenarios aim to anticipate different contexts and challenges which Kazakhstan could face in 2030, based on trends in the global economy and Kazakhstan that have been identified today. In the light of Kazakhstan's recent growth and development patterns, the scenarios were specifically developed to consider and test recommendations against trends and assumptions related to the economic diversification and dependence on natural resources.

Recommendations detailed in each of the following chapters in this report are discussed in the light of these scenarios. The scenarios aim to illustrate how shifts in the policy context may affect incentives as well as scope for reform, and the economic incentives of pursuing different strategies relating to diversification, finance mobilisation, privatisation and the move toward better environmental regulation in Kazakhstan.

Box 1.1. Why use scenarios?

Strategic foresight and scenario-based approaches are used as a fast and flexible method to analyse alternative plausible futures to traditional forecasts. They are often used to complement forecasting exercises, by integrating unquantifiable trends (political, social, behavioural), "shocks" to the system (e.g. financial crises or environmental disaster), or as a means of reducing the complexity of multiple interactions to explore the implications of a specific trend or combination of trends.

While scenarios often use data-based research and quantifiable trends, they are not constructed by means of projections. However, like projections, scenarios are explained by means of a storyline. Scenarios are stories, developed by considering how different trends can combine to create a different context, and thinking through the policy implications, be it in terms of policy options, new policy incentives or trade-offs, that emerge which could affect implementation.

Scenarios are a useful tool when formulating recommendations. They are user-driven, so account for stakeholder perspectives and assumptions, and ensure that a wider array of policy contexts is considered in the formulation of recommendations.

These scenarios were elaborated in consultation with an array of local stakeholders in Kazakhstan, from the public and private sectors as well as academia and civil society. The selected trends used are the following:

- ***Shifting wealth:*** *Continuing increase in the relative contribution of emerging economies to global GDP growth (especially India)*: this trend was selected as emerging economies are expected to drive global growth in the next decade and affect demand for natural resources.
- ***Sluggish growth:*** *Global growth slowdown continues, driven by modest growth in developed economies*: this trend was selected as uncertainty surrounding global growth and the composition of the global economy may affect decisions surrounding diversification for the economy as well as the make-up of the region's trade networks.
- ***Increasing Chinese investment and partnerships on its Western borders:*** *China increases its focus on Central Asia and the old Silk Road*: this trend was selected as it opens new economic opportunities and partnerships for Kazakhstan, and impacts on its infrastructure, trade and territorial development.
- ***Increasing pace of innovation in green technology:*** *Increased investment and innovation in green technology*: this trend was selected as it could affect demand for natural resources but also decisions regarding economic diversification, investment, innovation, education and skills.

Box 1.2. **Scenarios for the future of Kazakhstan 2030**

Scenarios with a 2030 horizon were developed for the Kazakhstan MDCR to highlight the implications of endogenous and exogenous shocks on the policy context in which Kazakhstan will pursue its developmental strategy. The scenarios were developed following strategic foresight approaches in a series of participatory workshops in Astana in December 2014, hosted by the Ministry of National Economy, and in November 2015 hosted by the Ministry of National Economy and Nazarbayev University.

Over the course of these workshops participants carried out a visioning exercise and trend analysis, to identify the assumptions underpinning Kazakhstan's development model, and various exogenous and endogenous shocks which could affect the country's development strategy. The scenarios were subsequently developed in consultation with local stakeholders from different backgrounds including government officials, representatives from the public and private sectors, academia, think tanks, and civil society, and discussed in the light of emerging recommendations on diversification, financing development, privatisation, and environmental regulation. Four scenarios emerged from the exercise:

1. The New Commodity Super-cycle

The rise of India creates a large new source of increased demand for oil and other commodities, and prompts a new global commodity super-cycle. The oil sector attracts foreign investment, and financial and human resources flow to petroleum and away from the sectors that produce other tradeable goods and services such as agribusiness or manufacturing, which also suffer from reduced competitiveness in the Eurasian Economic zone and other export markets. Kazakhstan accelerates the development of its financial service centre and Astana becomes a financial services hub for the region. However, as the exchange rate appreciates with increased investment export inflows, Kazakhstan's strong revenues from oil create symptoms of "Dutch disease" for the larger economy and the oil and financial sectors create only limited employment, mostly high-wage, creating pressures around the inclusiveness of growth. To counter this, the government considers various income transfer schemes, which in turn support household spending and domestic consumption. Investment is focused on Astana, as the new financial hub, which accelerates urbanisation. An international agreement to curb emissions is ratified and Kazakhstan's increased revenues need to support its adaptation to a lower carbon economy. However, this means Kazakhstan is not eligible for financial aid to facilitate the transition.

Box 1.2. **Scenarios for the future of Kazakhstan 2030** *(cont.)*

2. The Great Dissipation

Global growth is weaker than projected and below the pace achieved over the last decade. Demand for oil and other commodities stagnates, while trade in manufactures and services also weakens. Regionalism takes hold and global economic integration recedes. While global interest rates are low, investors' risk appetite is also subdued, with continued uncertainty about the trajectory of the global economy. This translates into weaker export receipts, income and investment for Kazakhstan, constraining fiscal space for public investments and services. However, the associated weakness in the exchange rate makes it easier for Kazakhstan's non-resource exports to compete with its oil sector for investment and domestic financial and human resources. This allows for a strategy to stimulate dynamism in other sectors of the economy, targeting the Eurasian Economic Zone as an export destination. Kazakhstan's relative stability and ongoing improvements in the quality of governance and the business environment make the country an attractive island for foreign investors looking to access the domestic market and the Eurasian Economic Zone.

3. The New Silk Road and Central Asia Resurgence

As the centre of global of economic activity continues to shift eastwards, China formalises and expands its "Belt and Road Initiative" (BRI), strengthening economic and cultural ties in East and Central Asia and beyond. Kazakhstan's stability and good co-operation make it an ideal partner as a transit country for the BRI. This draws Kazakhstan into deeper association with China, which is accompanied by investment but also stronger cultural ties. Kazakhstan engages more with the economic take-off occurring to its south in Kyrgyzstan, Tajikistan, Uzbekistan, and Turkmenistan. The opportunities along the BRI railway and the areas bordering the emerging countries to the south support a series of towns and secondary cities. This favours policies pursuing regional integration. Intra-regional trade and institutional reforms improve the business environment and attract foreign direct investment (FDI) for industries catering to the regional market. While wages in Kazakhstan are higher than elsewhere in the region, it can compete with the skills, expertise and productivity of its workforce and through the relative quality of its institutional environment.

4. New Green Technology Solutions

An international agreement on climate change is ratified, which generates a market for significant investment in green technologies. These investments result in revolutionary improvements in green energy storage and other green technologies, reducing demand and prices of hydrocarbons (although significant carbon taxes increase the cost of using high-emission fuels). These developments raise global demand for low-carbon and energy-efficient goods and support new growth in mature economies. Demand for oil weakens but is stronger for other commodities, including agricultural goods, and for services. Overall these developments maintain export and fiscal revenues for Kazakhstan, but support the non-oil tradeable goods sectors. This supports investment, employment and economic activity across more of the country, although the competitiveness of Kazakhstan's non-resource exports remains under pressure.

Notes

1. Ministry of National Economy, State Revenue Committee monthly revenue data.
2. The rate and composition of spending growth various between data sources, particularly with respect to the treatment of financing transaction. To facilitate comparison with other economies, this report follows presentation that are consistent with the International Financial Statistics where possible.
3. The OECD Guidance documents around sovereign wealth funds are collected at: *http://www.oecd.org/daf/inv/investment-policy/oecdguidanceonsovereignwealthfunds.htm*
4. IMF Country Reports and authors' calculations.
5. For a detailed description of environmental challenges in Kazakhstan see OECD (2016), "Multi-dimensional Review of Kazakhstan - Vol. 1 - Initial Assessment".

References

Behar, A. and A. Fouejieu (2016), "External adjustment in oil exporters: The role of fiscal policy and the exchange rate", *International Monetary Fund Working Paper* WP/16/107, Washington, DC.

IMF (2016), *World Economic Outlook* (database), *http://www.imf.org/external/pubs/ft/weo/2016/01/weodata/index.aspx*.

IMF (2015), *2015 Article IV Consultation Staff Report*, International Monetary Fund, Washington, DC.

IMF (2014), *2014 Article IV Consultation Staff Report*, International Monetary Fund, Washington, DC.

Ministry of Finance of the Republic of Kazakhstan (2006-2015), "Статистические бюллетени" [Statistical bulletins], *www.minfin.gov.kz/irj/portal/anonymous?NavigationTarget=ROLES://portal_content/mf/kz.ecc.roles/kz.ecc.anonymous/kz.ecc.anonymous/kz.ecc.anonym_budgeting/budgeting/reports_fldr/statistical_bulletin_fldr* (accessed 15 December 2016).

NBK (2016), Statistical Bulletin, National Bank of Kazakhstan, various editions, *www.nationalbank.kz* (accessed December 2016).

OECD (2016a), *Competition Law and Policy in Kazakhstan: A peer review*, OECD, Paris, available at *www.oecd.org/competition/competitionlawandpolicyinkazakhstan2016.htm*.

OECD (2016b), *Multi-dimensional Review of Kazakhstan: Volume 1. Initial Assessment*, OECD Development Pathways, OECD Publishing, Paris. *http://dx.doi.org/10.1787/9789264246768-en*.

OECD (2016c), *OECD Economic Outlook*, 2016(1), OECD Publishing, Paris, *http://dx.doi.org/10.1787/eco_outlook-v2016-1-en*.

OECD (2015), *OECD Economic Outlook*, 2015(1), OECD Publishing, Paris, *http://dx.doi.org/10.1787/eco_outlook-v2015-1-en*.

OECD (2014), *OECD Economic Outlook*, 2014(1), OECD Publishing, Paris, *http://dx.doi.org/10.1787/eco_outlook-v2014-1-en*.

OECD (2013), *OECD Economic Outlook*, 2013(1), OECD Publishing, Paris, *http://dx.doi.org/10.1787/eco_outlook-v2013-1-en*.

OECD (2012), *OECD Economic Outlook*, 2012(2), OECD Publishing, Paris, *http://dx.doi.org/10.1787/eco_outlook-v2012-1-en*.

World Bank (2016), *Global Economic Monitor* (database), *http://go.worldbank.org/MMW0XOJVG0*.

Multi-dimensional Review of Kazakhstan
Volume 2. In-depth Analysis and Recommendations

Chapter 2

Diversification and resilience in Kazakhstan

Economic growth in Kazakhstan between 2000 and 2014 was impressive. During this period the economy also grew increasingly dependent on natural resources, and oil in particular, setting up the economy for challenging times when the commodity cycle ended. This chapter examines the role that industrial policy plays in encouraging diversification in Kazakhstan. It examines the pattern of concentration in the economy using trade and industrial production data as well as the product space. While diversification has been prominent in the policy agenda since the mid-1990s, industrial policy has been much more developed since 2010, with the implementation of the first State Programme on Advanced Innovative-Industrial Development (SPAIID). This programme introduced a large number of actors and instruments of industrial policy, with the aim of halting deindustrialisation and creating the basic conditions for the emergence of strong industrial entrepreneurship, although with disappointing success in promoting diversification in the short run. Industrial policy can help the Kazakhstani economy to be more resilient, but to that end it needs to become more flexible and adaptable and mobilise market forces rather than act as a substitute for them.

Kazakhstan achieved remarkable economic growth between 2000 and 2014, thanks to favourable external conditions and a steadfast commitment to reform. This period saw the emergence of a number of dynamic sectors in Kazakhstan, leading to massive job creation. However, during this period the country's economy grew increasingly concentrated on natural resources, limiting the employment content of growth and its capacity to distribute the proceeds of growth widely. Fulfilling Kazakhstan's objectives for 2050 will require not only economic growth but the structural transformation of the economy.

The reliance on the oil and gas sector during the growth spurt of the 2000s led Kazakhstan to be overly dependent on oil. The oil sector has generated a much smaller share of growth since the mid-2000s (OECD, 2016a) and especially since 2010. Oil extraction made up 13% of gross domestic product (GDP) in 2014, but when other oil and gas activities are included, the figure rises to 20% in 2014, down from a peak of 26% in 2012. Oil also generates 60% of export proceeds and is the source of a third of general government revenues.

Diversification can help buttress a more stable and resilient growth path. High degrees of concentration of activity in natural resources expose the economy to external shock. Kazakhstan has adopted instruments to manage the volatility that comes with its industrial structure. However, moving to a higher-quality development path requires that the conditions are put in place for structural transformation to happen. While diversification has been a policy priority in Kazakhstan since the mid-1990s, industrial policy – aimed at developing specific sectors and encouraging the productive transformation of the economy – has been implemented in earnest since 2010, with mixed results.

This chapter analyses the motivation for diversification policy in Kazakhstan, with specific reference to the role of economic concentration in increasing volatility in the economy. It goes on to analyse the instruments and institutions of industrial policy in Kazakhstan, to examine the relevance of the identification of priority sectors, and provides recommendations for Kazakhstan to increase the effectiveness of industrial policy.

Kazakhstan's dependency on natural resources: Exposure to risk and opportunities for growth

The extractive sector has been a force for growth since Kazakhstan gained independence

Since independence the extractive sector has been the central pillar of the economy in Kazakhstan. Making the transition to a market economy was initially difficult and was complicated by low commodity prices and the weak Russian economy, to which Kazakhstan was still tied. Between 1991 and 1999 GDP contracted annually by an average of 4.8%. However, natural resources still attracted attention from foreign investors, including Chevron's efforts to develop the Tengiz field, first agreed upon in 1990 and finalised in 1992. By 2000 rising commodity prices created a boom in Kazakhstan's economy. GDP growth averaged 7.7% between 2000 and 2014. Rents[1] from the extractive sector helped drive that growth, with resource rents constituting 30% of GDP in 2013, and averaging almost 41% of GDP between 2000 and 2013, with a peak of 51.4% in 2005. Of the total natural resource rents, oil rents made up an average of 31.7% of GDP (or 78% of total resource rents) during that period (World Bank, 2015). Mineral rents made up a much smaller portion during that period, with an average of 3.23% of GDP (or 7.94% of total resource rents), with a peak of 5.7% in 2007. These numbers are significant, even compared to other natural resource-based economies in the area. For example, over the same period (2000-13), resource rents contributed an average of 28.76% of Russia's GDP, down to 18.2% in 2013.

Hydrocarbon exports continue to represent the majority of Kazakhstan's exports by trade value, but have contributed little to GDP growth since 2010. Crude oil and other petroleum liquids were responsible for approximately 71% of total exports in 2014 (United Nations, 2016). That year, Kazakhstan was the 18th largest oil producer in the world, with approximately 1.7 million barrels per day (bpd) and 1.9% of total global production, and the second largest producer among the former states of the Soviet Union after the Russian Federation (EIA, 2015). Kazakhstan had an estimated 30 billion barrels of proven, recoverable reserves, 1.8% of the global total and the 12th highest in the world, giving it a production horizon of approximately 50 years at current production levels (BP, 2015). However, growth in oil production has slowed as major fields have matured, and the rapidly declining price of oil has reduced its ability to contribute to economic growth. New discoveries, including the massive Kashagan offshore field[2] in the Caspian Sea will help Kazakhstan expand oil production, offsetting production declines in more mature fields.

Kazakhstan is expanding its oil transportation options to increase capacity and diversify export routes. As a landlocked country, it currently relies on a variety of methods to transport crude out of the country, including pipelines, exports across the Caspian Sea, and shipments by rail. It has been increasing the capacity of some of these existing routes and constructing new ones. The Tengiz-Novorossiysk pipeline, which connects the Tengiz field to the Russian Black Sea port of Novorossiysk, is currently undergoing construction and aims to more than double its capacity from 28.2 million tonnes (MMT) to 67 MMT per year, with 52.2 MMT of oil from Kazakhstan. The Kazakhstan-China pipeline, which first carried oil in 2006, currently transports 12.2 MMT, and will be expanded to 20 MMT (Ernst and Young, 2014; EIA, 2015). The Kazakhstan Caspian Transportation System, currently under construction, will help export oil from the Kashagan field as it becomes fully operational. The project is a mix of a pipeline from the Kazakh city of Yeskene (near the Kashagan field) to Kuryk, where tankers will transport the oil across the Caspian Sea to Baku for loading on to the Baku-Tbilisi-Ceyhan pipeline. Initial capacity will be 23 MMT per year, expandable to 56 MMT (Ernst and Young, 2014, EIA 2015). Rail is also a major shipper of oil in Kazakhstan, moving 9 MMT of oil in 2013. The oil-exporting infrastructure helps shape the end markets for Kazakhstan's crude. In 2013, Europe received 70% of Kazakhstan's crude, and China received 15%. As export capacity increases, China may begin receiving a greater proportion of Kazakhstan's oil (United Nations, 2016).

Kazakhstan consumes approximately 15% of its crude oil production domestically, exporting the remaining 85%, and meets approximately 70% of its gasoline and diesel demand from three domestic refineries, two of which are fuelled mainly by domestic crude. The three refineries together produced a total of 345 093 barrels per day of distilled petroleum products in 2014 (EIA, 2015). The Kazakhstani government is currently implementing a refinery modernisation and expansion programme that, when complete, aims to allow the country to meet 100% of its domestic demand and raise the quality of the fuels it produces to meet EU Euro-4 and Euro-5 fuel standards. As private vehicle ownership becomes more popular in Kazakhstan, demand for transportation fuel has also increased, and part of the refinery programme aims to shift capacity into transportation fuel (Lee, 2015).

Natural gas production in Kazakhstan has increased, supporting a reduction in imports and an increase in oil production through the reinjection of gas into existing reservoirs.[3] Between 2000 and 2013, natural gas production rose from 354 597 terajoules (TJ) to 1 428 235 TJ – a four-fold increase (IEA 2015). Kazakhstan has estimated recoverable reserves of 1 500 billion cubic metres[4] (bcm), 0.8% of the world's total and enough to continue production at current rates for the next 78 years (BP, 2015). Kazakhstan has enough gas to meet domestic demand, but because of a lack of infrastructure connecting the more populated east of the country with its gas producing west, continues to rely on imports. In 2013, it imported 201 109 TJ and exported 398 355 TJ, for a total domestic supply of 1 182 292 TJ. Much of the gas that is produced in Kazakhstan's oil fields is re-injected on-site to pressurise the oil fields and increase oil production. The energy sector accounted for 78.19% of total domestic use in 2013 (Figure 2.1). Kazakhstan has two main outlets for gas exports, both of which are part of the Caspian export infrastructure pipeline system. From the northwest Kazakhstan exports through the Central Asia Centre pipeline, which passes through Uzbekistan and Kazakhstan on its way from Turkmenistan to Russia. The other main export route is the Central Asia-China gas pipeline, which also originates in Turkmenistan. Once completed the Beineu-Bozoi-Shymkent pipeline will connect with the Central Asia-China gas pipeline (EIA, 2105), increasing potential for exports to China and other neighbouring countries. There has also been continuing interest in establishing gas-exporting capabilities across the Caspian Sea for shipment on to Europe. The Trans-Caspian Gas Pipeline has been a subject of discussion since 1996, when it was initially proposed to bring gas from Turkmenistan through Azerbaijan and Georgia to Turkey, for further shipment through either the Mediterranean or a gas line to Central Europe. Kazakhstan would potentially benefit from being able to export natural gas to European markets through this alternative route.

Figure 2.1. **Kazakhstan natural gas production, imports, exports, and use by energy industry**

(2000-13)

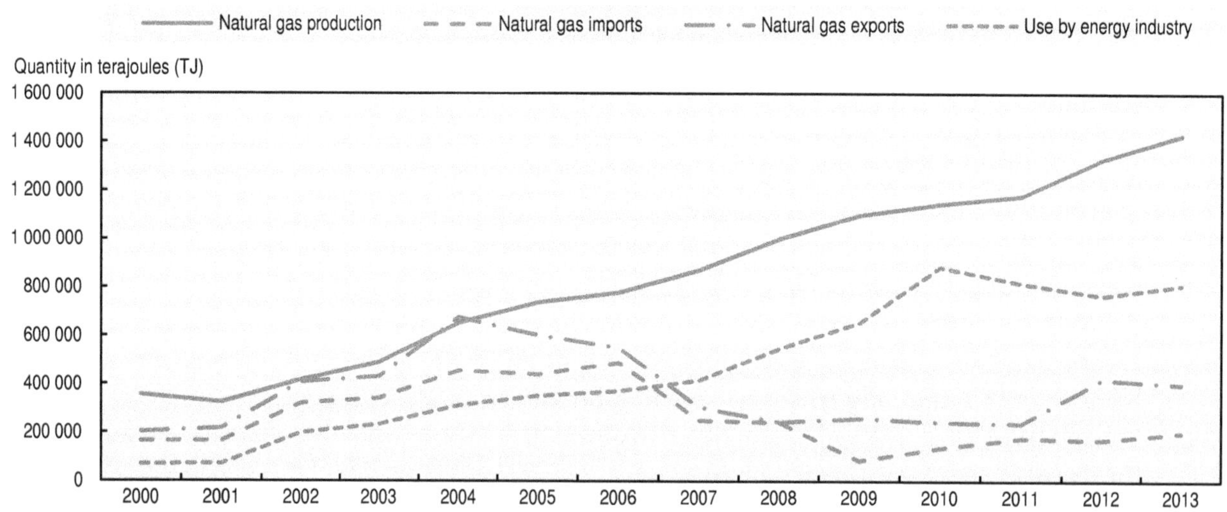

Source: IEA 2015a, Statistics, Kazakhstan, *https://www.iea.org/statistics/*.

StatLink *http://dx.doi.org/10.1787/888933445320*

Kazakhstan had a significant mining and metallurgy sector during the Soviet Union era, and is currently working further to develop and modernise the sector. The country has approximately 12% of global uranium reserves, and since 2009 has been the world's leading producer, responsible for 41% of global production in 2014. Kazakhstan's ferrous and non-ferrous metal reserves are also substantial, including copper (5% of total global reserves), chromium (18%), magnesium (5%), and zinc (8%), as well as substantial quantities of gold and silver. Copper is a major extractive commodity in Kazakhstan, with potential to expand: in 2014, refined copper, copper ores and copper concentrates together accounted for 3.2% of total exports, worth approximately USD 2.53 trillion. Kazakhstan is also a major producer of iron and steel (ferroalloys), responsible for 4.26% of exports in 2014, as well as iron ore (1.39% of exports). Although it only generates 0.3% of world steel output, Kazakhstan is in the top ten for iron ore deposits. However, as in other mining sectors, there is substantial reliance on outdated and inefficient equipment (KIDI, 2015a). Most companies are operating assets that were constructed before the dismantling of the Soviet Union. While production levels over the past 15 years have increased, non-energy minerals and metals have declined as a proportion of exports. In Figure 2.2, that trend is visible in a comparison between the dollar value of iron and steel exports (rising) and as a proportion of total exports (declining).

Figure 2.2. **Mineral oil compared to iron and steel exports from Kazakhstan**

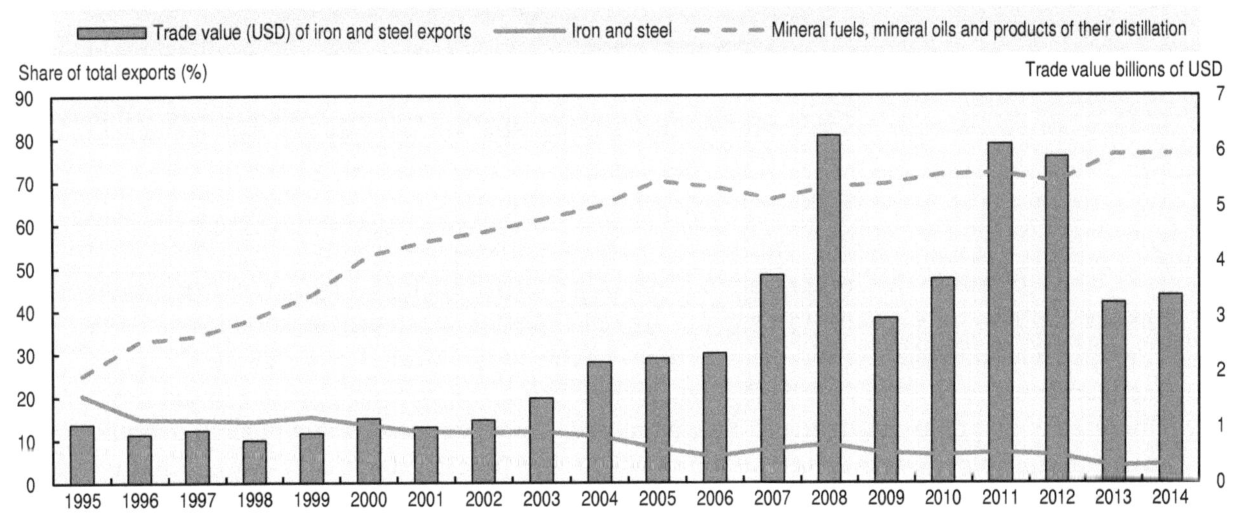

Source: UN COMTRADE (database), United Nations (2016).

StatLink http://dx.doi.org/10.1787/888933445334

Kazakhstan has grown increasingly dependent on oil revenues

Kazakhstan's economy has become increasingly concentrated on the natural resource sector. In 2014, 68.55% of Kazakhstan's export earnings came from crude oil. If gas and other hydrocarbons are included, that number rises to 76.56% of export earnings, followed by uranium (2.44%), refined copper (2.19%), ferroalloys (1.99%) and iron ore and concentrates (1.41%). The only product in the top ten that is not an extractive commodity is wheat (1.23%).[5] The increasing concentration of the economy is visible in metrics such as the Herfindahl-Hirschman Product Concentration Index[6] score, a measure of the dispersion of trade value across an exporter's products. A country with a perfectly diversified export portfolio will have an index of zero, whereas a country which exports only one export will have a value of 1 (World Bank, 2015). The trend of Kazakhstan's economy as a whole is towards greater concentration – between 2000 and 2014, the concentration index went from 0.48 to 0.67. By way of comparison, during that same period the index for Russia, another regional commodity-exporting economy, went from 0.28 to 0.37 (UNCTAD, 2016). The concentration of exports when measured on the basis of SITC 4-digit product sub-groups was 0.41 in 2014, up from 0.06 in 1993 (Figure 2.3).

Figure 2.3. **The concentration of Kazakhstan's exports has increased notably since 1990**

Herfindahl index calculated over SITC 4-digit product groups

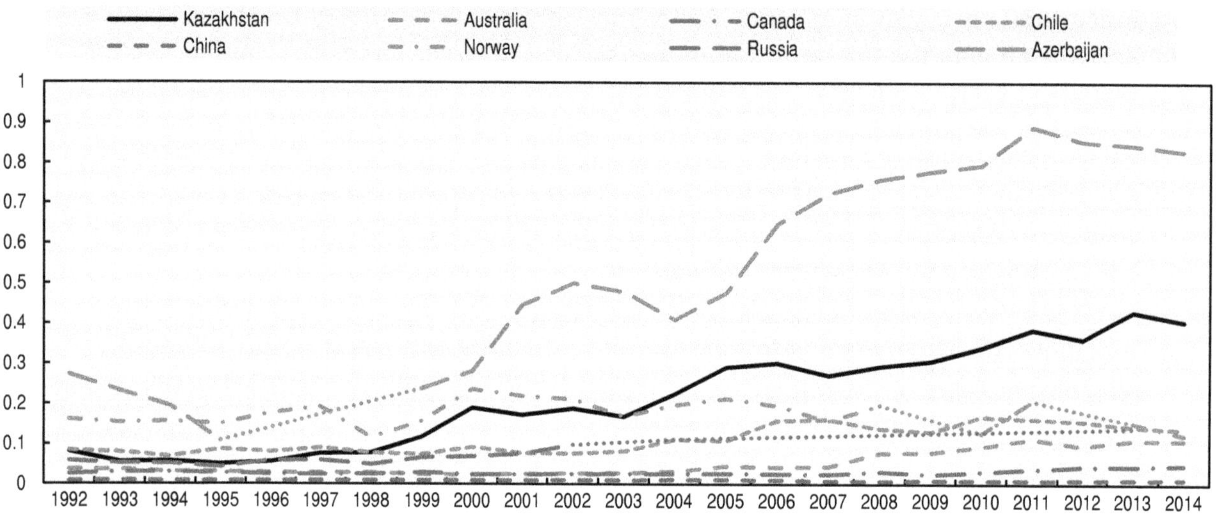

Note: dotted lines indicate that data coverage is below 80% of total exports.

Source: Calculations based on UN COMTRADE (database), UN (2016).

StatLink http://dx.doi.org/10.1787/888933445347

The increase in the concentration of exports was driven largely by the increase in oil prices. If prices for Kazakhstan's exports are held constant at their level in the year 2000, the increase in concentration of exports is much more modest and a downward trend appears from as early as 2010. Like many oil producers, the volume response to the rapid increase in oil prices during the 2000s was muted. Given the major share of oil in exports, any concentration index is largely determined by the share of oil in total exports, whether in nominal or deflated terms.

Production also became increasingly concentrated between 2000 and 2010, but the trend has been reversed since. In 1990, given the large disruption to the economy, agriculture contributed 34% to GDP. The fall in concentration during the 1990s shown in Figure 2.4 is attributable to the very significant fall in the share of agricultural value added, down to 11.4% in 1997. The steady rise in concentration between 1998 and 2009, on the other hand is largely attributable to the increase in importance of the extractive sectors. It is possible to establish an international comparison of concentration for manufacturing sectors, for which comparable data exist for a number of countries. Manufacturing output in Kazakhstan is rather concentrated and is comparable to other countries in the region. The level of concentration is, however, significantly higher than that of more advanced economies, including some with significant natural resources.

Figure 2.4. **The increase in concentration was driven mainly by price effects**

Herfindahl index over SITC 4-digit product groups, deflated by unit prices

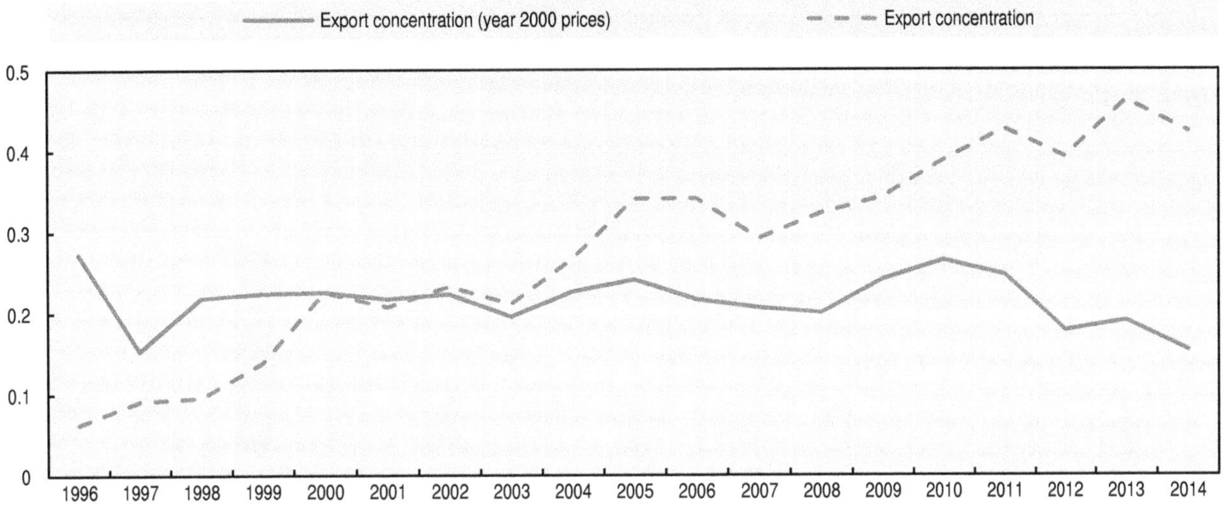

Note: The series in year 2000 prices was built on the basis of unit value series from Kazakhstani data. Products with insufficient quantity data are entered in nominal terms.

Source: Calculations based on COMTRADE (database), *http://comtrade.un.org*, United Nations (2016).

StatLink http://dx.doi.org/10.1787/888933445359

The increasing concentration in Kazakhstan's production structure runs counter to the historical experience of developed economies. Empirically, countries' production structures tend first to increase diversification as multiple sectors develop and large sectors produce commodity products. This is then followed by a second stage in which countries specialise (Imbs and Wacziarg, 2003). Evidence from cross-country regressions suggests that the "resource curse" – the negative impact of natural-resource dependency on development – works through the concentration of the export basket rather than through natural resource abundance (Lederman and Maloney, 2008)

Figure 2.5. **Production became more concentrated between 2000 and 2010**

Herfindahl index of concentration over 1-digit GQBE (1990-1997) and 1-digit NACE (1998-2014)

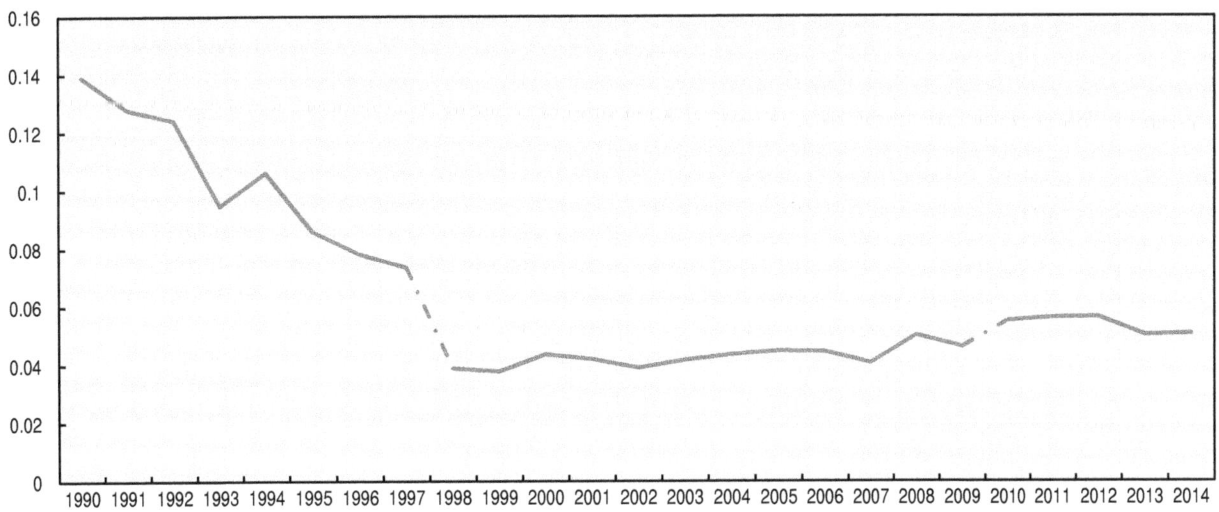

Note: The figure shows the normalised Herfindahl index of concentration of value added by sectors. Dotted lines show breaks in the series due to changes in the classification.

Source: Committee on Statistics of the Republic of Kazakhstan (2016) Official statistical information published in *www.stat.gov.kz/*, accessed July 2016.

StatLink http://dx.doi.org/10.1787/888933445362

Figure 2.6. **Kazakhstan's manufacturing sector is highly concentrated**

Normalised Herfindahl index for ISIC Rev 3 3-digit manufacturing sectors, selected countries

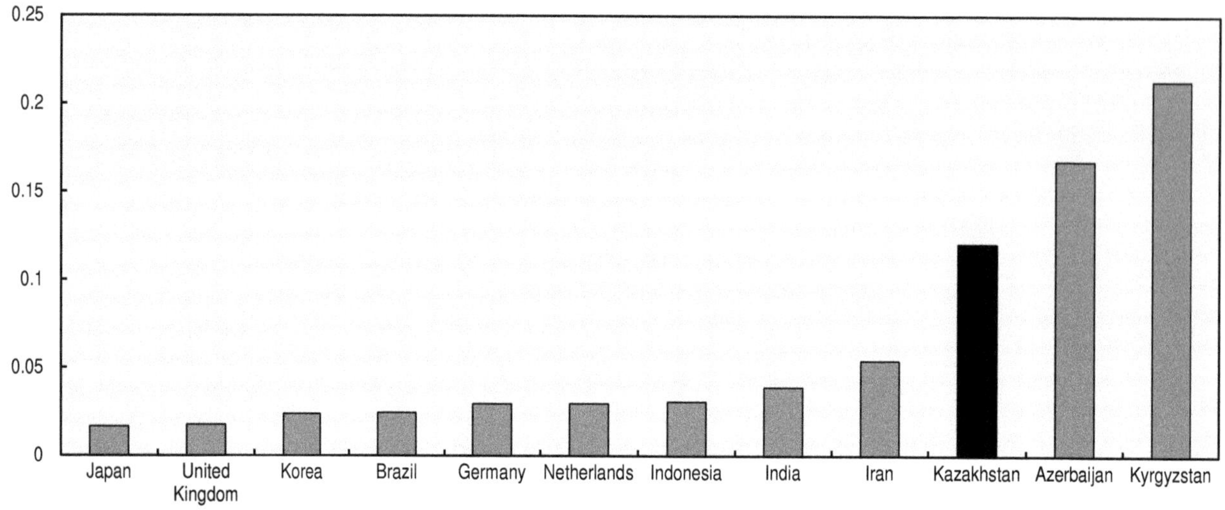

Source: Calculations based on INDSTAT4 database (UNIDO, 2014).

StatLink http://dx.doi.org/10.1787/888933445379

Dependency exposes Kazakhstan to external shocks

The weight of commodities in Kazakhstan's export basket exposes Kazakhstan to external trade shocks. Commodity prices are highly volatile, and those of oil and gas are among the most volatile of all. Given the concentration of exports in Kazakhstan, volatility in commodity prices translates into high volatility in terms of trade (Figure 2.7). A number of academic studies single out the volatility of terms of trade as the channel through which resource dependency lowers long-term growth (Frankel, 2012; Blattman, Hwang and Williamson, 2007; Hausmann and Rigobon, 2002). There are multiple channels through which volatility itself can have an effect on the growth path of a country: volatility in the terms of trade can lead to volatility in the real exchange rate, depressing investment in tradeables; it can also lead to repeated reallocations of capital and labour, which entail costs. Volatility in commodity revenues can also compromise critical investment when both revenues and investment are made by the public sector.

The establishment of the National Fund has equipped Kazakhstan with a key instrument to manage volatility. By sterilising a large part of oil revenues on the one hand and by stabilising government revenue on the other, the National Fund contributed to limiting the impact of terms of trade volatility on the economy of Kazakhstan (OECD, 2016a; forthcoming c). Indeed, the accumulation of assets in the National Fund in the first half of the 2000s allowed Kazakhstan to implement a major stimulus package in the face of the severe crisis of 2009. While the National Fund has allowed Kazakhstan to manage volatility over the commodity cycle, the recent reversal in the commodity super-cycle – that is the reversal in the decade-long increase in commodity prices – has tested the limits of its efficacy.

Fiscal policy has not been sufficiently counter-cyclical in spite of the establishment of the National Fund. While the National Fund allowed Kazakhstan to smooth the share of oil revenues in the budget, overall reliance on oil has increased notably since the turn of the century. Fiscal consolidation was timid following the 2009 crisis and the degree of fiscal space provided by the National Fund has shrunk with the fall in oil prices. At the end of 2014,

National Fund assets stood at around 34% of GDP, close to the minimum of 30% set out by the National Fund rules. The significant nominal contraction that followed the floating and depreciation of the tenge has increased this margin somewhat. As a result of this reliance of public finances on oil, fiscal policy has been acyclical in the current downturn, with fiscal consolidation taking place in a moderate growth environment.

Figure 2.7. **Export concentration exposes Kazakhstan to terms of trade volatility**

2000 - 2014

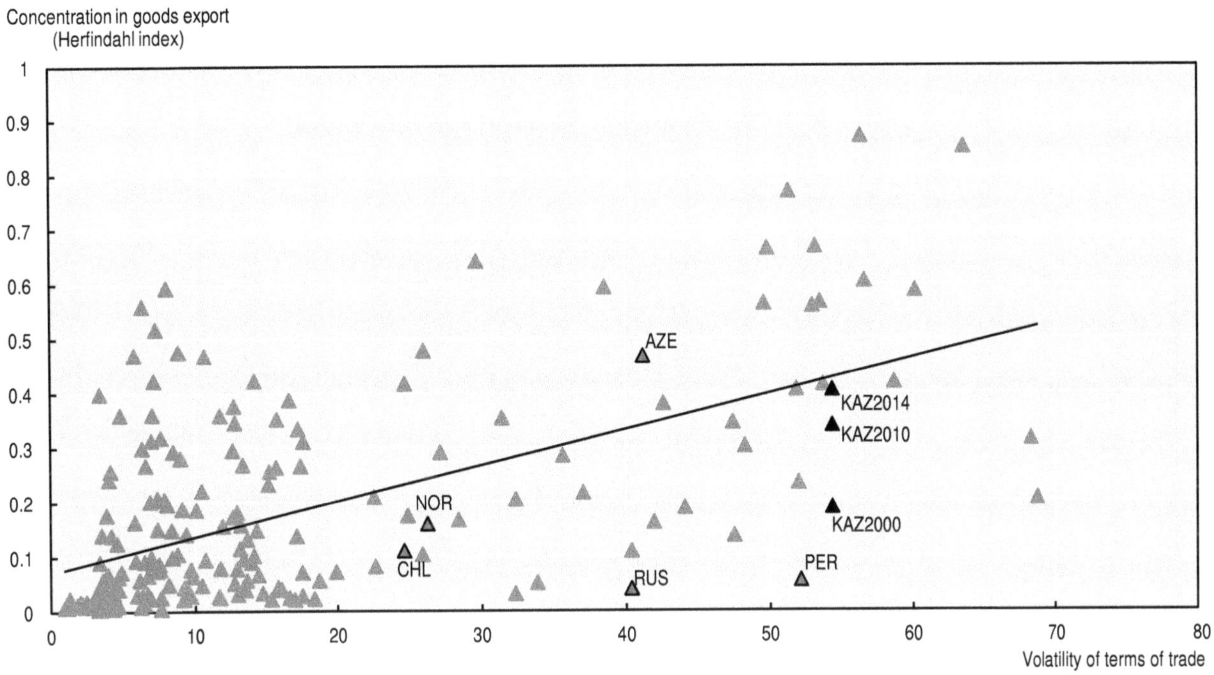

Note: Volatility is calculated as the standard deviation of a terms of trade index in the period 2000-14. Export concentration is the normalised Herfindahl index over the value of exports for 2014 (or nearest available date). Data for Kazakhstan for 2000 and 2010 depict volatility over the whole period and concentration for the specified year.

Source: Calculations based on World Development Indicators (database) (World Bank, 2015) and UN COMTRADE (database) (United Nations, 2016).

StatLink http://dx.doi.org/10.1787/888933445383

Kazakhstan needs to diversify its export basket to reduce volatility in the long run. Possible reforms of the National Fund and the ongoing transition towards an inflation-targeting monetary policy regime with a free-floating exchange rate will probably allow Kazakhstan better to weather volatility (Frankel, 2013). In the long run, however, high real exchange rate volatility can still have negative effects on long term growth. Likewise, over-reliance on oil revenues for public expenditure is likely to limit the degree to which Kazakhstan can have a countercyclical fiscal policy stance in the medium term with current prospects for oil prices.

The legacy of the past and current challenges

Kazakhstan's extractive sector is largely focused on the production and export of primary products. There is some evidence of backward linkages developing in the oil and gas sector and in mining, supported by the Law on Subsoil and Subsoil use, which sets out requirements for local employment and purchase of goods and services by enterprises operating in that sector. According to Kazakhstan's 2014 Extractive Industries Transparency

Initiative report, both the mining sector and the oil and gas sector spent approximately 50% of their total spending on goods, works and services on local content. As part of Kazakhstan's accession to the World Trade Organization, by 1 January 2021 all local content regulations that are inconsistent with WTO rules will be eliminated (WTO, 2015). Already, on 9 November 2015 the Law on Subsoil and Subsoil use was amended to lessen (in the case of services and personnel) or totally remove (in the case of goods) local content requirements for new contracts (Dentons, 2015). How this will impact existing suppliers in Kazakhstan remains to be seen. There has not been significant development of downstream or forward linkages, with Kazakhstan's main exports remaining raw or primarily processed extractive products.

Figure 2.8. **Public finances are overly reliant on oil**

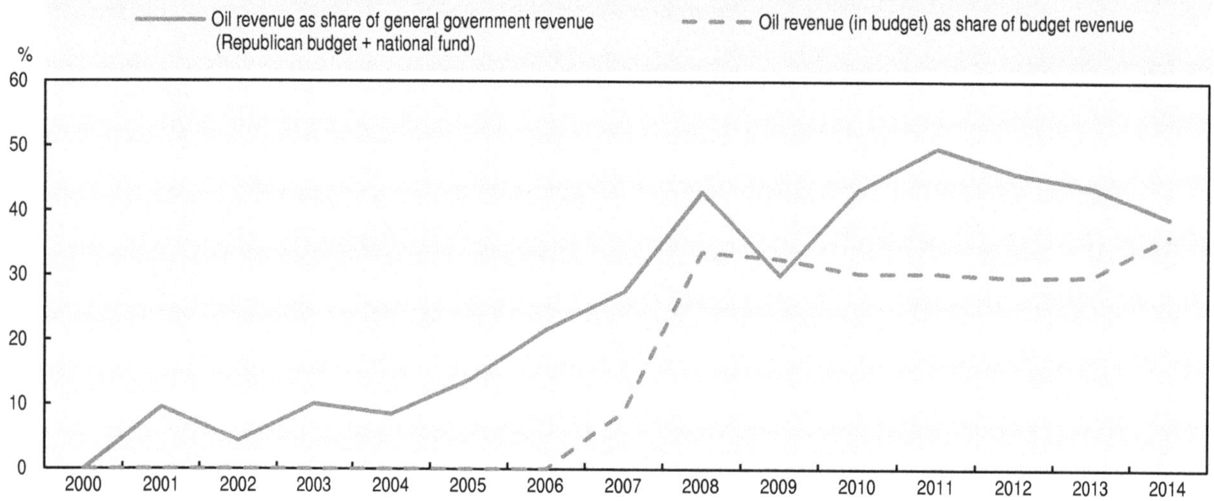

Source: Calculations based on data provided by the Ministry of National Economy.

StatLink http://dx.doi.org/10.1787/888933445394

Although primary products were always dominant in Kazakhstan's economy, in the years since independence the technological complexity of Kazakhstan's exports has declined. (Figure 2.9).This decline in export technological sophistication may be due to the loss of the planned economy of the Soviet Union, and with it high-tech manufacturing such as the military and aerospace sector, as well as the increased importance of manufacturing powerhouses such as China. Within mining and metals, some areas are also seeing increases in exports of less refined products. For example, Figure 2.10 shows the increasing export share of less-refined copper products – while exports of copper have been rising as a general trend, exports of copper concentrate and copper ore have become an increasingly substantial part of that. This trend is likely due to the rapid expansion over the past 15 years of China's smelting and refining capacity in ferrous and non-ferrous metals. China has the largest copper refining capacity in the world, and the largest steel-producing capacity.

There has not been substantial exploration of new resources since independence, nor have any major new mines been constructed. According to the government's Programme for Geological Exploration, the sector suffers from a weak research base and a shortage of qualified specialists, which will potentially worsen when the last generation of Soviet-trained technicians and engineers retires. From a technological standpoint, these issues are exacerbated by the use of outdated equipment in exploration and a lack of modern laboratories for testing samples, of collaborative industrial research institutes to develop new techniques, or of a developed network of local service companies to support exploration (Government of the Republic of Kazakhstan, 2014). While the quality of ore is declining, no major new mines have been developed for over three decades. In 2008 the average crude ore copper grade was 1.18%; in 2011 it declined to 1.01%, and by 2012 had fallen to 0.95%. At the same time, copper illustrates the potential for the mining sector to attract foreign investment. UK-based Rio Tinto, one of the largest mining companies in the world, began conducting copper exploration activities in Kazakhstan in August 2015 as part of a joint venture with Kazgeology (MID, 2015). The exploration agreement was originally announced in 2012, when Rio Tinto said it would spend USD 100 million on exploration work in Kazakhstan in agreement with the state-owned enterprise Tau Ken Samruk (Antoncheva, 2012).

Figure 2.9. **Technological sophistication of Kazakhstan's exports over time**

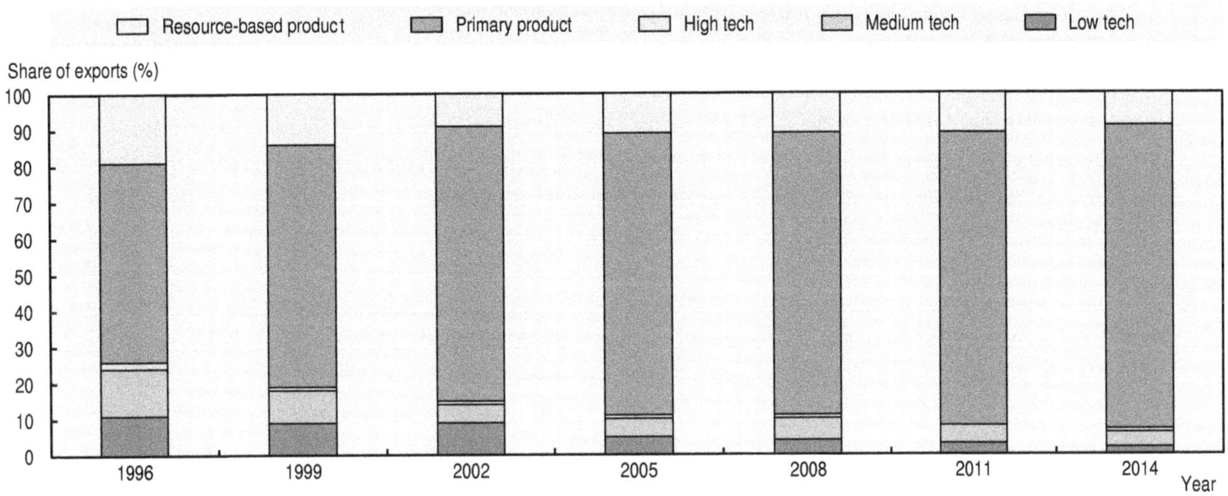

Source: World Integrated Trade System, UN COMTRADE (United Nations, 2016).

StatLink http://dx.doi.org/10.1787/888933445403

Figure 2.10. **Kazakhstan copper exports in trade value (USD) and net weight (kg)**

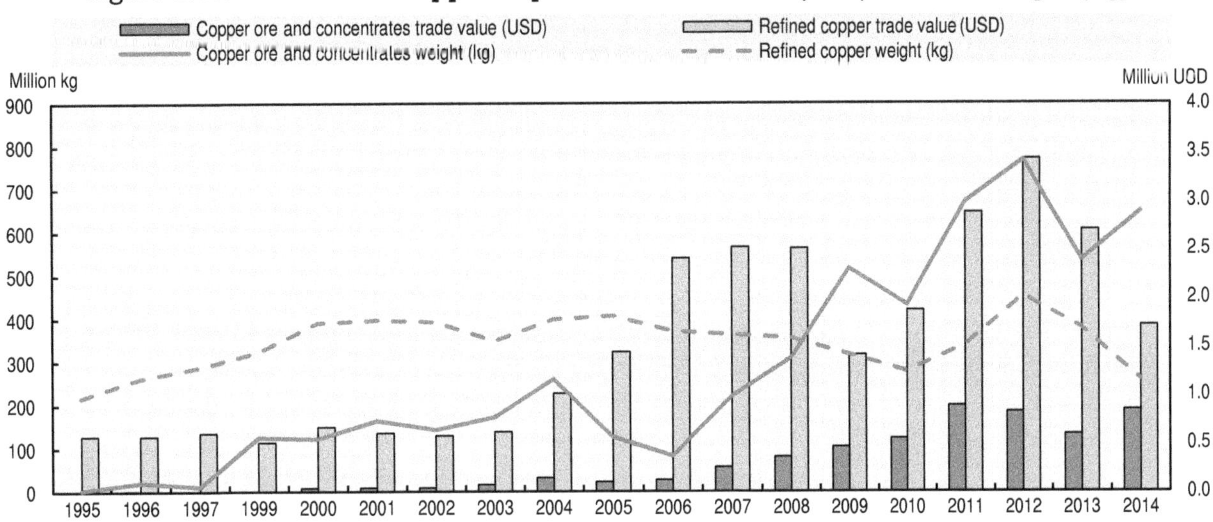

Source: UN COMTRADE (United Nations, 2016).

StatLink http://dx.doi.org/10.1787/888933445416

Revenue from the extractive sector is a major input to the government budget, but the booms and busts make long-term government planning difficult. In 2014 government revenue from the extractive sector amounted to almost USD 27 billion (EITI, 2015), and USD 30 billion in 2013, constituting approximately half of total government revenue. In 2015, declining oil prices led the government to revise the budget twice. The budget for 2015-17 was initially based on an expected oil price of USD 80 per barrel. In January 2015, it was revised to an expected price of USD 50 per barrel (RFE, 2015). In October 2015, President Nazarbayev said that the continuing decline in commodity prices had reduced government revenues by 40%, and warned that Kazakhstan was on the brink of a crisis more dangerous in scope than the global economic downturn of 2007-2009 (Farchy, 2015c). In February 2016, the budget was revised to reflect an estimated cost of USD 30 per barrel (Reuters, 2016).

Kazakhstan subsidises fossil fuel use and production, although since independence subsidies have been reduced. While lower oil prices will help reduce the amount that the government is spending on subsidies in the short term, subsidies ultimately promote inefficient use of energy, benefit the already wealthy more than those most in need, and are an expensive drain on the government's budget (OECD/IEA/NEA/ITF, 2015). Subsidies in Kazakhstan take a broad array of forms, going to both consumers and producers. For consumers, that includes price caps on diesel fuel to keep it affordable for farmers. For producers, that includes investment support for the extraction of oil and gas, direct transfers from the National Welfare Fund Samruk Kazyna to KazMuniGas, and potential tax concessions to producers (OECD, 2013). In 2014, the government spent USD 2.6 billion on fossil fuel subsidies, up from USD 2 billion in 2013, and USD 1.6 billion in 2012. At the same time, total energy subsidies[7] have been declining over that same period, from USD 7 billion in 2012 to USD 5.3 billion in 2014. Overall, fossil fuels are subsidised by an average of 31.9%, meaning consumers pay 68.1% of the total cost (IEA, 2015b).

Diversification in Kazakhstan since the turn of the century

Kazakhstan's product space has evolved little since the mid-1990s. The product space network map is a map of all possible products that a country could export. It is a depiction of the set of products exported with comparative advantage where the proximity between nodes is an indication that the product groups utilise shared productive capabilities (Hausmann et al., 2014). The network is stable, and calculated on the basis of trade data. A depiction of a country's product space sheds light on its productive capabilities and the potential for developing capacity to be a significant exporter of a given product of goods. Figure 2.11 depicts Kazakhstan in the product space in the years 1996, 2000, 2010 and 2014. Over time, the number of products exported with revealed comparative advantage (RCA) in Kazakhstan fell from 96 in 1995 (in the SITC classifier) to 49 in 2010, before rising again to 68 in 2014. Since the measure of revealed comparative advantage compares the share in a country's trade to the share in global trade of a given product, this fall is partly explained by the increase in oil prices. However, as shown in this section, the concentration in exports is also visible in real terms. More remarkably, while products in the periphery of the network have remained, products closer to the core are no longer exported with RCA. Products in the core of the network have more or closer links to other products. The population of the core of the network therefore signifies the development of productive capabilities in a country that matter for the production of a larger variety of goods.

The position of Kazakhstan in the product space reflects the weight of natural resources and connected activities in the economy. The group of products in the northeast of the product space corresponds to hydrocarbons (crude and non-crude oil are the large circles), metals and connected activities (base metals, copper wire, ferroalloys and metallurgy products form the northward branch next to the petroleum products. Other clusters to the north, west and south of the figure correspond to individual metal productions while the production of key agricultural commodities (wheat, barley, seeds) is in the south-eastern quadrant of the product space. There are remarkably few products close to the centre of the product space for Kazakhstan, the exceptions being medicinal plants (the rightmost point in the 2014 figure), tobacco products, and construction materials (in the middle of the figure). Product complexity can be measured by the Product Complexity Index (PCI), which is based on how common it is for countries to export a product and how diverse their export portfolios are (Hausmann et al, 2014). The three main export products of Kazakhstan are crude petroleum, copper and other chemical materials. The first is the product with the lowest complexity in the PCI ranking. On the other hand, despite very low complexity ratings for raw copper products, manufactured and other copper products are well ranked in terms of complexity (within the top 100 in terms of ranking and in most case exhibiting a PCI score in excess of 2). This signals that downstream activities in the mineral value chain have significant potential as stepping stones to diversify the economy. In practice, however, low margins on semi-fabrication combined with competition from China make the further development of the industry a challenge.

The concentration of exports in raw materials shows slight signs of reversal. The composition of the competitive export basket of Kazakhstan became not only increasingly concentrated, but also increasingly concentrated in raw materials during the first decade of the 2000s. However, since 2010, a number of other products have entered the export basket, increasing its complexity. This development corresponds to developments in terms of production. Indeed, from 2000 to 2010, the share of manufacturing in total value added suffered a significant decline, which was stopped, but not reversed from 2010 (OECD, 2016a).

Export product discoveries in Kazakhstan also show an incipient trend towards a more complex export basket. Table 2.1 lists "discoveries" of export products in Kazakhstan since 1996. Discoveries are products that constitute major exports of a country and the date of discovery is set at the time where they became significant exports,[8] following Klinger and Lederman (2004). The literature shows that discoveries are important steps in diversification across countries regardless of their level of development (Klinger and Lederman, 2004, Lederman and Maloney, 2012). Table 2.1 omits "traditional" exports of Kazakhstan (products for which exports were sizeable since independence in 1991) as well as a number of agricultural commodities and products that became prominent in the first half of the 1990s. Early discoveries are dominated by semi-processed natural resources and further natural resources following exploration (e.g. uranium). However, since 2010 discoveries have been much more complex, fully processed products, which draw on Kazakhstan mineral resource wealth.

Figure 2.11. **Kazakhstan's product space, 1996-2014**

Figure 2.11. **Kazakhstan's product space, 1996-2014** *(cont.)*

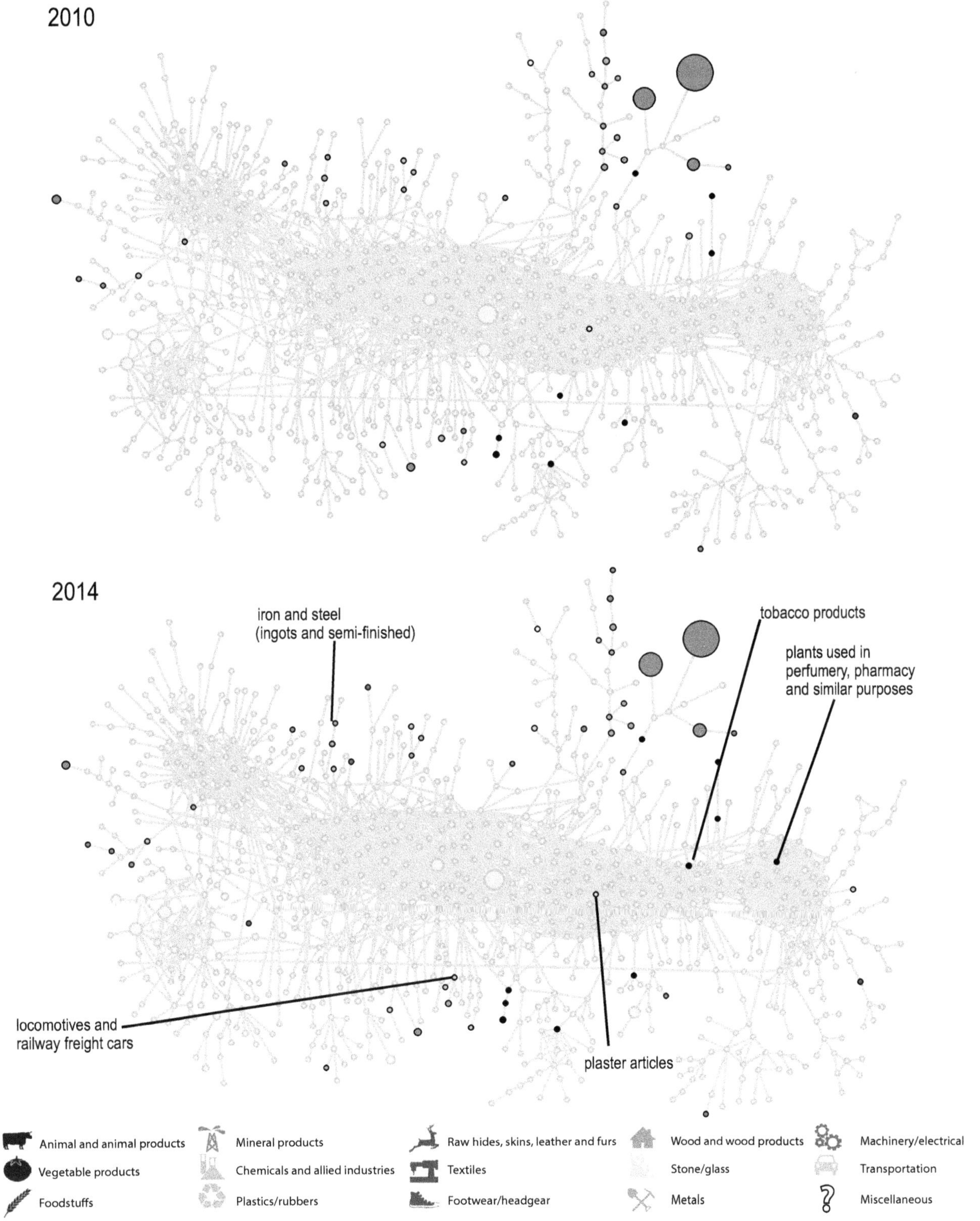

Note: Coloured notes with black outline represent product groups (in the HS classification at 4-digit product groups) that Kazakhstan exported with Revealed Comparative Advantage in the corresponding year. Product groups not exported with RCA are represented as grey nodes with grey outlines. Node sizes indicate the share of the product in world trade.

Source: The Atlas of Economic Complexity, *http://atlas.cid.harvard.edu/* (database).

StatLink http://dx.doi.org/10.1787/888933445424

Figure 2.12. **Number of products exported with revealed comparative advantage by product type**

1995 - 2014

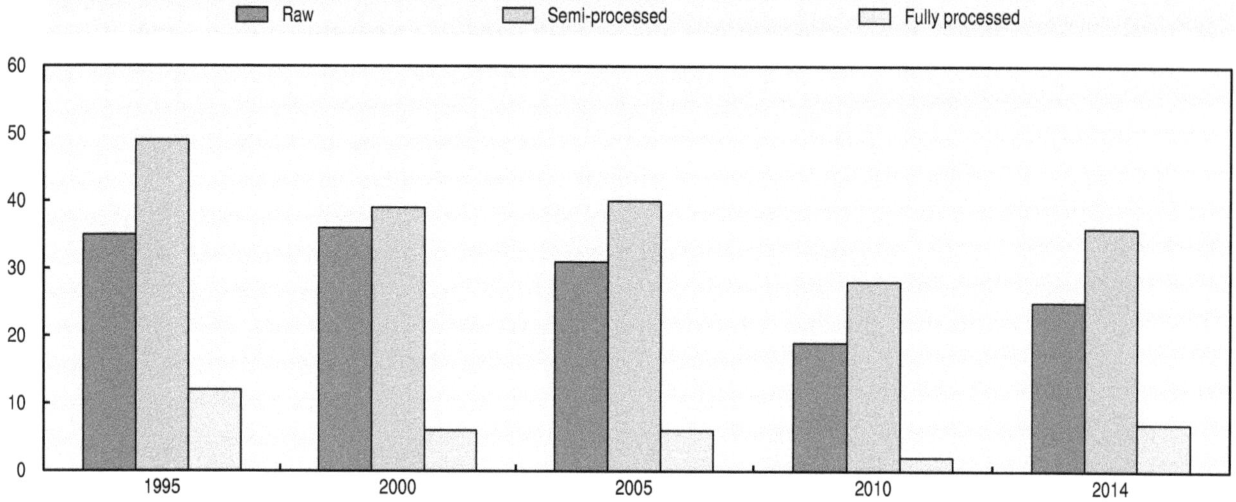

Source: Author's calculations based on COMTRADE data (United Nations, 2016).

StatLink http://dx.doi.org/10.1787/888933445431

Table 2.1. **Export product discoveries in the period 1996-2012**

Year of discovery	Product class (SITC Rev 3, 4-digit)	Type of good
1997	Ingot/primary iron/steel	Semi-processed
	Semi-finished iron/steel	Semi-processed
	Liquefied propane	Semi-processed
	Construction and mining machinery	Fully processed
1999	Liquefied butane	Semi-processed
2002	Quartz, mica, feldspar, fluorspar, cryolite and chiolite	Unprocessed
	Precious metal ores and concentrates	Unprocessed
2003	Non-alcoholic beverages	Fully processed
2007	Lead ore and concentrates	Unprocessed
2008	Uranium ore and concentrate	Unprocessed
	Linseed	Semi-processed
2011	Digital automatic data-processing machines	Fully processed
2012	Electromechanical tools for working in the hand, with self-contained electric motor	Fully processed
	Electrical apparatus for switching or protecting electrical circuits, or for making connections to or in electrical circuits.	Fully processed

Note: Discoveries are identified as products for which exports are greater than USD 10 million (in 1985 prices) over three consecutive years. Discovery years are set at the time where exports first exceeded USD 1 million (in 1985 prices).
Source: calculations based on COMTRADE (database) (United Nations, 2016).

The state's role in promoting discoveries has also evolved over time. While some of the developments, in particular in some raw material sectors (gas, uranium) and in heavy industry, are closely linked to the intervention of the state or state-owned enterprises, more recent discoveries in manufacturing products are more linked to the efforts of Kazakhstan to attract foreign direct investment (FDI). In a sense, the discovery patterns in Table 2.1 conform to the finding that diversification in natural resources and raw materials can favour diversification in other sectors (Rieländer and Traore, 2016). This can be interpreted as suggesting that cross-cutting capabilities to produce and trade play an important role in developing new competitive products.

Instruments and institutions to foster diversification

Diversification features prominently as a major policy objective in strategic documents

Diversification has been a major policy objective in Kazakhstan since the mid-1990s. Strategy 2030 was laid out in a speech by President Nazarbayev in 1997. The strategy noted that progressive concentration of the productive structure in raw materials posed a risk for the sustainability of growth. It set out several sets of industries that were of paramount importance and indicated that the focus should first be on labour-intensive industries including agriculture, timber and timber-processing, light industry, agri-food, tourism and construction. Strategy 2030 also called for the establishment of an industrial policy able to bring about structural transformation.

The Innovative Industrial Development Strategy for 2003-2015 was a landmark document in establishing industrial policy in Kazakhstan. The strategy set out the principal target of fostering sustainable development through the development of non-extractive industries. It also specified export competitiveness as the test of success. While the strategy recognised the role of extractive sectors in the economy of Kazakhstan, it left the development of those sectors to state intervention through specific sectoral programmes. The strategy also set out a number of numerical targets: growth in excess of 8% in manufacturing sectors, a tripling of labour productivity and a reduction by half in power intensity, as well as an increase in the share of research and innovation activities to 1.5% of GDP by 2015. One of the salient features of the strategy was to enumerate other policy areas that would work to support diversification, ranging from trade to capital market development to regulatory policy.

The current strategic framework document focuses on the creation of incentives for diversification and the development of the manufacturing sector. The Concept of Industrial and Innovation Development of the Republic of Kazakhstan (Government of the Republic of Kazakhstan, 2013) is the basis for the development of industrial policy in Kazakhstan. The concept draws lessons from the implementation of industrial policy since the turn of the century and sets out a number of principles for the design and implementation of industrial policy: i) balance between industry and cluster priorities and sectoral and general support; ii) the proactive role of the state; iii) continuity and flexibility; iv) commitment to results; v) partnership with business; vi) a larger role for regions and vii) a balanced funding model.

Kazakhstan has created a complex network of institutions to advance diversification

A number of "development institutions" provide finance or assistance to finance investment. The development institutions were established to implement Strategy 2030 and intervene with different instruments in investment promotion. The Development Bank of Kazakhstan provides direct finance for large projects, the Investment Fund of Kazakhstan was set up to support non-extractive industries via non-controlling equity stakes,[9] KazExportGarant provides export credit guarantees against credit and political risk, the National Agency for Technological Development (NATD) provides support to innovation projects and to the innovation infrastructure, while the DAMU entrepreneurship development fund provides support to small and medium-sized enterprises (SMEs) and Kazyna Capital Management is a fund of private equity funds.

Other national development institutions have roles in implementing actions in industrial development. They include the Kazakhstan Institute of Industrial Development (KIDI), the National Agency for the development of local content (NADLoC), and the investment and export promotion agency (KAZNEX INVEST). These are completed by a number of state-owned enterprises (SOEs) with specific roles in the implementation of industrial policy, including a number of "socio-entrepreneurial" corporations, which act as implementers of regional industrial policy. The multiplicity of institutions and the generality in their mandate in relation with industrial policy makes it difficult to establish accountability for the performance of industrial policy as a whole.

The large network of SOEs plays a pivotal role in the implementation of industrial policy. Kazakhstan has a sizeable SOE sector (see Chapter 4) with activities across economic activities, including large operators in the oil and gas sector, uranium extraction, the energy sector and in network industries (transport and telecommunications in particular). Major state assets are managed under the national management holding Samruk-Kazyna, which acts as a sovereign wealth fund.

Regional institutions play an increasingly important role in the implementation of industrial policy. Regional authorities (*akimats*) have duties both in the definition of the objectives of industrial policy at the regional level, in accordance with the national plan, and in the attraction of investment to their specific regions.

Financial development institutions were consolidated under the National Management Holding Baiterek in 2013. Baiterek includes national development institutions which provide finance (the Development Bank of Kazakhstan, Kazyna Capital Management, the Investment Fund of Kazakhstan, KazExportGrarant and the Center for State and Private Partnership Projects Support). It also includes the DAMU fund and NATD. Baiterek also encompasses national companies involved in the implementation of public projects in real estate, savings for construction and regional development.

The functions of certain institutions in implementing industrial policy are at odds with their main mandate. The sovereign wealth fund, Samruk-Kazyna has multiple objectives that include increasing the value of the assets it manages and supporting the diversification of the economy. However, given the weight of oil and gas in Samruk-Kazyna's portfolio, these objectives are potentially at odds with each other. Moreover, as discussed in Chapter 4, diversification objectives, like other public service obligations, are likely to be incompatible with maximising shareholder value once the subsidiaries of Samruk-Kazyna, and KazMunaiGas in particular, are open to private capital.

The evaluation functions should be better defined and attributed. Currently, the Kazakhstan Institute of Industrial Development (KIDI) is the institution that is better positioned to carry out an evaluation of industrial policy programmes since it has the necessary knowledge base and access to data on firm performance. However, KIDI is also responsible for the design of industrial policy and in particular for issues of sector selection, and has an implementation function in certain areas of industrial policy, albeit relatively small ones.

The implementation of industrial policy accelerated in 2010

The State Programme of Accelerated Industrial and Innovative Development 2010-2014 (SPAIID) was initiated in 2010 with the aim of providing an umbrella programme for industrial policy in implementing the 2003-2015 strategy. SPAIID selected a number of sectors for specific support: the oil and gas sector, petrochemistry, ore mining and metallurgy, chemical industry, atomic industry, machinery, pharmaceutical industry, construction engineering and construction materials, the agroindustry complex, light industry, tourism. It also identified a number of sectors for future development: information and communication technologies

(IT), biotechnology, space activities and nuclear energy. Following the 2003-2015 strategy, SPAIID lists a number of transversal actions to support diversification.

The creation of a state programme on industrial and innovative development signals the importance the authorities give to industrial policy. Kazakhstan's planning architecture is a hierarchical set of strategic documents, with the long-term Kazakhstan 2050 plan at the apex, followed by ten-year national plans. State programmes and sectoral programmes are multi-year strategy and policy documents to be implemented by multiple agencies. Among the various programmes, state programmes are those with the highest level of priority. At the time of writing, there are ten state programmes in implementation, of which SPAIID is arguably the largest and most important.[10]

SPAIID 2010-2014 was a significant financial effort. It mobilised KZT 4.2 trillion (about 20% of 2010 GDP) over the period 2010-15 (Ministry of National Economy, 2015) of which KZT 2.39 trillion from the national budget (Ministry of Finance, 2012a, 2012b, 2013a, 2013b, 2014a, 2014b). Beyond the budget, significant resources were drawn from own funds of public and private enterprises as well as from the funds of Kazakhstan's development institutions. A significant share of the funds was transferred from the National Fund to these institutions. The bulk of the funds were directed to infrastructure projects and to support the institutional infrastructure for critical sectors of the economy: 30% of funds were devoted to transport infrastructure, 10% to the programme to develop the electric power industry and 3% to develop ICT (information and communication technologies).

SPAIID 2010-2014 was implemented via 25 separate programmes. Of these, 14 were sectoral programmes specifying investments and support measures for individual sectors. The remaining 11 so-called "operational" programmes included systemic measures, such as development of competition or development of local content, as well as the establishment of modes of implementation for the sectoral programmes, in particular by the establishment of financial support programmes (Productivity 2020, Business Road Map).

The mode of implementation of SPAIID 2010-2014 into separate programmes led to a scattering of responsibilities and tasks. Although the Ministry of Industry (now Ministry of Investment and Development, MID) played a prominent role, some of the sectoral programmes were administered by other line ministries and operated in part by SOEs under the management of Samruk-Kazyna (itself governed by a board with a number of other cabinet ministers). For example the programme for the development of transport infrastructure was administered by the Ministry of Transportation and operated by KazMorTransFlot, the Ministry of Transportation and Communication, Kazakhstan Temir Zholy (the publicly owned railway company) and by local administrations. Likewise, the programme for the development of the oil and gas sector was administered by the Ministry of Oil and Gas and operated in part by Samruk-Kazyna.

High-level co-ordination bodies were created to oversee the implementation of the programme. The State Commission on the issues of modernisation of the economy was created under the presidency to monitor and assess the measures taken to modernise the economy. The Republican Control Centre for Accelerated Industrial-Innovative Development of Kazakhstan was charged with the responsibility of co-ordinating the implementation of investment projects. Both bodies were put under the presidency of the prime minister, comprised members of the cabinet as well as, in the case of the Control Centre and the Chairman of Samruk-Kazyna, the chairman of the National Chamber of Entrepreneurs.

In practice, however, co-ordination issues remained one of a series of constraints on the implementation of industrial policy. The Ministry of National Economy, in its evaluation of the programme (MNE, 2015), estimated that about 70% of the actions planned had been carried out by 2015, despite a disbursement rate of 96% of the projected budget. Of six headline target indicators, two were achieved (the increase in labour productivity in the processing industry (which increased by 57% over its 2008 level) and the fall in energy intensity.

During the period of implementation of SPAIID, the legal framework for industrial policy was also adapted. The Law on State Support of Innovative-Industrial Activity of 2012, later reformed and subsumed into the Entrepreneurial Code in 2015, set out the implementing agents of industrial policy, the main instruments to be used and the measures available for support. On the occasion of the 2015 reform, the law extended the instruments available to public financial actors by including the power to restructure debt, carry out direct investment in capital, purchase loans extended by development institutions, and develop measures pursuing the recovery of industrial entities. It is expected that these activities will be carried out by the subsidiaries of the National Management Holding Baiterek.

Other institutional reforms were also put in motion by 2010 to ease entrepreneurial activity and reduce the cost of doing business. Among them, significant efforts were put into reducing red tape, especially by cutting the number of licences and turning a number of licences into notices. The development of e-government received significant impetus (see next section), with the possibility of obtaining 100% of licences electronically and dealing with many administrative procedures online.

Performance in manufacturing sectors and in exports improved during the implementation of the first five-year SPAIID. As highlighted in the preceding section, the period 2010-14 saw new products enter Kazakhstan's export basket with revealed comparative advantage. Moreover, a number of indicators of performance in manufacturing sectors improved: labour productivity increased by 30%, and the energy intensity of GDP decreased by 5.4%. Investment in fixed assets in manufacturing increased in real terms by 8% per annum between 2010 and 2014, after stalling for the five preceding years (Figure 2.13). Despite this increase, in 2015, investment in fixed assets in extractive sectors still made up 33% of total investment in fixed assets in the economy.

Figure 2.13. **Investment in fixed assets by sector**

Real, index = 100 in 2003

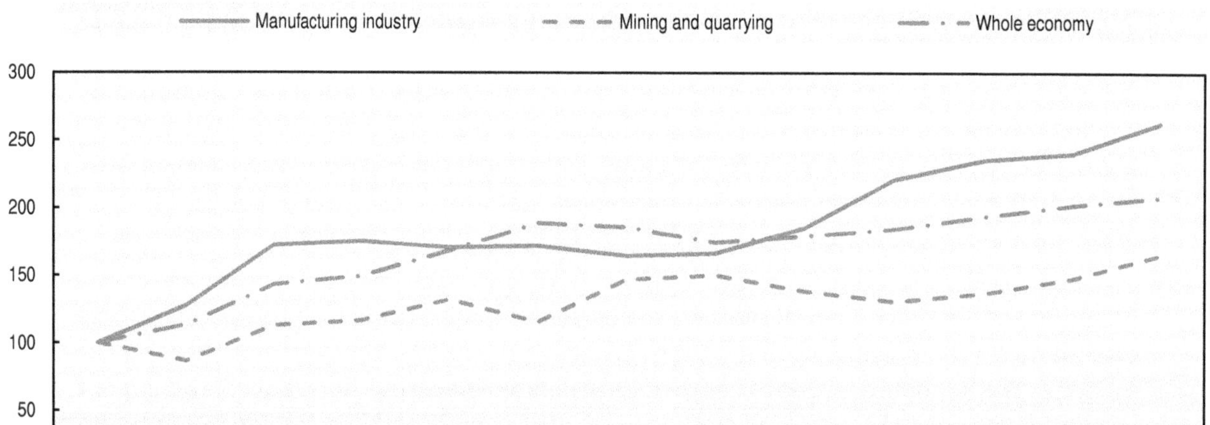

Source: Calculations based on data from the Committee on Statistics of the Ministry of National Economy of Kazakhstan. Official statistical information published in *www.stat.gov.kz/*, accessed July 2016.

StatLink http://dx.doi.org/10.1787/888933445441

It is not straightforward to assess the contribution of SPAIID to this improved performance. Indeed, the evaluations available publicly (MNE, 2015; KIDI, 2015b) largely account for the evolution of a number of indicators of performance of the manufacturing sector and other priority sectors. For all its merits such analysis does not necessarily lead to the attribution of the impact of SPAIID on the performance of the economy. For large investments included in the Map of Industrialisation, which have a significant bearing on employment creation and value generation in critical sectors of the economy, the Ministry of National Economy (2015) estimates significant impacts (of close to one percentage point in GDP growth). However, without a rigorous evaluation analysis, it is not clear whether the programme was essential in bringing such investments about, nor is the contribution of the programme itself considered. Indeed, certain projects included in the Map of Industrialisation also received significant outside funding. While evaluation of a complex programme with significant spillovers such as SPAIID as a whole would be extremely difficult in practice, individual components and instruments should be evaluated rigorously so that lessons can be better learned on their performance (Felipe and Rhee, 2013).

Industrial policy is heavily reliant on financial support instruments and direct investment

The main instruments for the implementation of industrial policy are included in the two phases of the SPAIID programme and are financial in nature. Table 2.2 shows how the envelope of SPAIID 2010-2014 was heavily concentrated on programmes for the support of specific industries, while general support programmes to which any enterprise from the designated sectors could participate (Business Road Map 2020 and Productivity 2020) were significantly smaller. In the design of the second phase of SPAIID the different sectoral programmes were consolidated under a single state programme, in order to overcome the fragmentation that generated problems in implementing SPAIID I. The Concept on Industrialization 2015-2019 includes seven areas in which system-wide measures are necessary: financial sector, human resources, infrastructure, technology and innovation, internationalisation, entrepreneurship and SMEs, industrial regulation. However, SPAIID II largely restates the objectives in these areas, without detailing actions that are to be undertaken. Conversely, the SPAIID II programme document contains a very detailed account of investments to be carried out, citing specific industrial facilities to be built or upgraded.

Direct investment and credit instruments are the most heavily used instruments for the implementation of industrial policy in Kazakhstan. There is no consolidated account of expenditure in industrial policy by programme or instrument. However, collection of data across sources, from the Committee on Statistics reports on SPAIID investment and the reports from Baiterek subsidiaries on their contribution to SPAIID account for KZT 6.2 trn in direct investments over the 2010-14 period, and KZT 2.1 trn in credit instruments. These figures do not correspond to budgetary outlays for several reasons: credit is typically counted in volume of credit and not the corresponding budgetary cost of the explicit or implicit credit subsidy. More importantly perhaps, a significant share of direct investment is made by companies themselves, in particular state-owned enterprises (SOEs) whether from own funds, or financed off budget.

The Map of Industrialisation is a key component of industrial policy. The "Map of Industrialisation" is a list of key investment projects to be implemented with the support of the state in Kazakhstan. Only projects with investments larger than KZT 4.5 bn are included, intended to be for production of world-class products in the priority sectors, of which there were 14 at the enactment of the SPAIID II programme. The inclusion of a project in the Map of Industrialisation allows the establishment of specific support measures. Beyond its communication role, the map supposes that a high-level co-ordination body oversees the location of potential new development clusters and considers their needs for complementary investment, in particular in infrastructure.

Table 2.2. **Main diversification programmes in Kazakhstan (2010-19)**

Programme	Instruments	Total (KZT bn)	
		Planned	Executed
SPAIID 2010-2014, including:		**4 399.1**	**4 194.8**
Business Road Map - 2020		177.6	175.9
Productivity - 2020		26.2	25.6
Oil and gas sector		135.5	135.4
Chemical industry		2.0	2.0
Mechanical engineering		4.0	1.7
Light industry		0.8	1.4
Infrastructure	• Subsidising interest rates on loans or finance leases both for investment purposes and working capital funds in priority sectors • Guarantees on loans of second tier banks in priority sectors, • Grants to attract highly qualified foreign specialists, • Training technical staff abroad, • Leadership training (top managers) of enterprises on improving productivity and energy efficiency, • Instruments for funding projects in the industrialisation map projects are chosen individually.	10.4	10.3
Development of competition		0.2	0.2
Electric industry		436.7	432.3
Development of local content		3.6	3.6
Trade development		1.1	1.1
Mining industry		10.0	10.0
Special economic zones and export promotion		55.8	53.9
Innovation and technological modernisation		23.1	22.5
Development of mineral resources		43.6	42.4
Nuclear industry		14.9	13.6
Tourism		5.3	5.2
Information and communication technologies		100.5	94.9
Development of space activities		129.9	128.8
Development of the agro-industrial complex		995.9	848.9
Development of transport infrastructure		1327.7	1304.3
Expenses not included in sector programmes 2010-2014		894.4	877.4
SPAIID 2015-2020		**6 600**	
Nurly Zhol 2015-2019	Mainly infrastructure finance (a KZT 100 bn tranche is allocated to SME finance)	**1 672**	

Notes: * Nurly Zhol budget is the value of USD 9 billion using the April 2015 exchange rate (185 KZT/USD, as the programme was announced at that time) The programme is expected to also include contributions from international financial institutions of USD 8.97 bn.
Source: Ministry of National Economy of Kazakhstan.

SPAIID provides support both to SMEs and to large investors. Business Road Map 2020, directed at SMEs and managed by the Damu fund, executed about 4% of the total SPAIID budget for the first phase of the programme. Given that many of its instruments are direct credit, credit subsidies and guarantees, the amount of credit covered by subsidies or guarantees was much higher, at over KZT 1 trillion (or USD 3 billion at market rates at the time of writing). At the same time, very significant efforts were made to support large investments contained in the Map of Industrialisation. The Development Bank of Kazakhstan (which supports large investment projects) had provided USD 5.24 billion in credit to projects in the Map of Industrialisation in accordance with the SPAIID programme by the end of 2014, which amounted to financing 16% of these investments.

In practice, a significant share of financial support during SPAIID I went to the oil and gas sector. The selection of priority sectors in the original SPAIID programme was very broad, covering a significant share of manufacturing sectors in Kazakhstan including extractive industries. Given the role of SOEs in carrying out the planned investments and of industry in putting forward investment proposals, as much as 56% of investment into fixed assets undertaken between 2010 and mid-2013 under the umbrella of SPAIID went to the oil and gas sectors. By comparison, the Committee on Statistics estimates that the oil and gas sector generated 26% of GDP in 2012 (when this figure was at its maximum). The concentration of public support in the oil and gas sector, while understandable in a context of beneficial terms of trade, appears at odds with the diversification imperative that was one of the objectives of SPAIID.

Figure 2.14. **Investment into fixed assets through SPAIID has largely gone to the oil and gas sector**

Share of investment into fixed assets, Q1 2010–Q2 2013

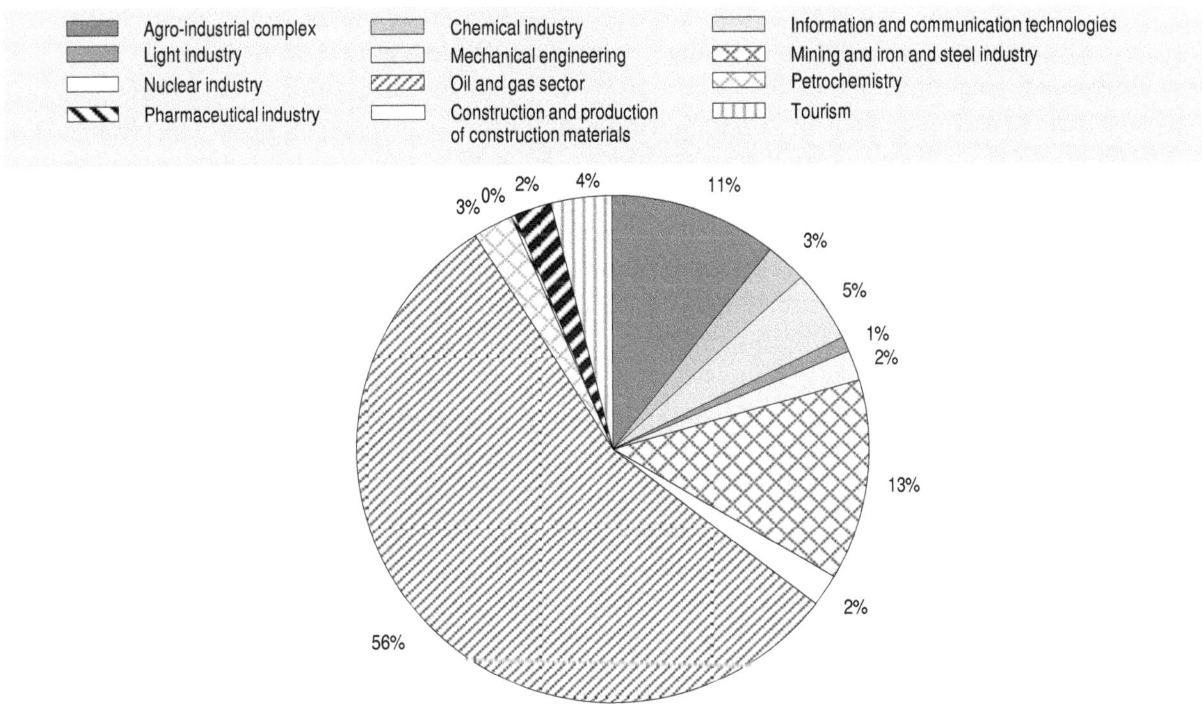

Source: Calculations based on Committee on Statistics of the Republic of Kazakhstan (2016) Official statistical information published in *www.stat.gov.kz/*.

StatLink http://dx.doi.org/10.1787/888933445453

The concentration of resources is partly due to the completion of large greenfield investments and is inflated by reporting by investment rather than support volume. For example, the Development Bank of Kazakhstan's contribution to SPAIID, largely through financing projects under the Map of Industrialisation, included contributions to financing KZT 595 bn of investments in the petrochemistry sector in particular through an integrated chemical complex and a refinery in Atyrau. In both cases, significant shares of finance were provided by subsidiaries of Samruk-Kazyna participating in the project and by ExIm Bank of China.

Efforts are being deployed to rationalise the number of instruments in the implementation of industrial policy. The multiplicity of programmatic documents and of funding sources led, during the first period of implementation of SPAIID, to a proliferation of support programmes and instruments. Even within institutions, there has been a proliferation of programmes. The DAMU Fund for the support of entrepreneurships lists 17 different credit programmes,[11] some with different eligibility and financial conditions, which suggests that the differentiation goes beyond mere administrative programme accounting. Some of these programmes are very small, providing total credit in the hundreds of millions of KZT and with borrowers in the single or double digits. As a response to this multiplicity of activities, the SPAIID II programme considers the standardisation of the support package for all firms, except for projects receiving special assistance through the Industrialisation Map.

Fostering diversification will require adequate skills, infrastructure, and better links between innovation and industrial policies

Diversification will require Kazakhstan further to improve skills in its labour force to respond to the needs of an evolving marketplace. Indeed, growth in new sectors and increased competitiveness in the production of new products require a skilled workforce, all the more so as the sophistication of products and of the production processes used increases. While the labour force in Kazakhstan has levels of education attainment that almost match those of OECD countries, there are significant concerns as to the quality of education and the skill sets of workers (OECD, 2016a). There are indications that the skills mismatch has been alleviated. In 2008 half of enterprises considered an inadequately skilled workforce to be a major constraint on firm growth (Sondergaard and Murthi, 2012). By 2013, only 13% of firms had the same opinion. However, the figure was significantly larger for large firms (21%) and was higher in manufacturing (20%) than services (10%).

Continued efforts in adapting the education and training system will be necessary. Analyses of the obstacles to competitiveness in the Kazakhstani economy highlight skills gaps for the economy as a whole (World Bank, 2013) and for important sectors in Kazakhstan's diversification strategy such as agribusiness and IT and business services (OECD, 2011). Skills needs are particularly acute at technical level, which is surprising given the educational attainment of the Kazakhstani workforce. As a response, Kazakhstan has put in place particular efforts to upgrade its technical and vocational training system, as well as to create sector-specific training centres with linkages to industry (see OECD, 2016a). These efforts can contribute not only to enhancing the skills of the workforce but also to creating an interface between the (largely public) education and skills generation system and the entrepreneurial sector, better to anticipate future needs and design curricula accordingly.

Recognising the challenges that its geography poses to Kazakhstan's diversification, the government has made a very substantial effort to upgrade physical infrastructure. The main focus has been on the upgrade of infrastructure along the Western Europe-Western China road corridor, which alone would have an estimated cost of USD 8 billion (World Bank, 2013). However, these efforts need to be completed by a further development of logistics capacity that can lower the cost of integrating value chains and trading across borders. Despite its stellar performance in *Doing Business* 2017, where it is ranked 35th overall, Kazakhstan is ranked 119th for "trading across borders". This indicates not only high transport costs related to geography, but also burdensome procedures and constraints in terms of logistics capacity. Recognising this, the government is upgrading logistic capacity in the context of the programme supporting services sectors.

Enhancing linkages between innovation and industrial policy will be critical as Kazakhstan approaches the next stage of development. There is a genuine commitment to the implementation of a development model based on innovation as evidenced by policy documents, including the Kazakhstan 2050 strategy. This has translated into efforts in the creation and strengthening of many important components of the research and innovation system (OECD, forthcoming,b). Public investment in research and development (R&D) has increased, but remains too low to support the ambition of an innovation-led development model. Development institutions such as the National Agency for Technological Development (NATD) have created instruments and platforms to link business to innovative activity, including the creation of techno parks, innovation commercialisation offices and centres for international technology transfer. To this day, however, it is difficult to evaluate the effectiveness of these actions. On the other hand, provisions with transformative potential, like the requirement for all subsoil users to invest 1% of annual income in R&D activities, have had little effect because of issues relating to implementation.

Private actors should play a larger role in industrial policy

Among the most important lessons learned from the implementation of the first SPAIID programme was the need to have more direct involvement of the private sector and of the regions. In the institutional design of SPAIID II, private sector involvement is planned in the institutional structures and committees that determine how support is provided, mainly through the participation of the Chamber of Entrepreneurs.

As economies develop and produce more complex products, it is increasingly important that investment decisions be made by informed actors. Kazakhstan's industrial policy remains dominated by a process by which sectors are selected for support and investment projects are supported either by generic instruments or by specific support through the map of industrialisation. Sector participants are more likely than analysts or bureaucrats to be able fully to comprehend the possibilities offered by the market, especially in more complex environments (Felipe and Rhee, 2013). Moreover, private actors' incentives are potentially better aligned to identify profitable investments than those of state-owned enterprises.

Indirect industrial policy, which relies on private sector actors with stakes in the project, should be strengthened. Allowing private actors to identify worthwhile projects, whether for direct investment or for lending, ensures that their knowledge of the sector is put to good use. For such effects to be beneficial, it is critical that they have a stake in the project's success. The use of second-tier banks to disburse finance through the programmes of the DAMU entrepreneurship development fund is an example of such indirect industrial policy. However, their application within a newly narrowed list of priority sectors would defeat the purpose. Indeed, when a sector is identified that has relatively few actors (such as certain activities in metallurgy) project identification is *de facto* left to existing actors, as is support. On the other hand, when activities are more diverse and the potential for profitable entry and upgrade relies more on local and market knowledge (e.g. in food production), the potential for indirect industrial policy is much greater.

A strengthened financial sector would play a major role in indirect industrial policy. Current DAMU programmes do not systematically require that second-tier banks which participate in the selection of projects actually provide part of the loans. Indeed, only about 17% of credit is provided by the banks.[12] Banks channelling DAMU loans without further lending do not contribute to the leveraging effect of public credit and are remunerated through the mandated margin between the DAMU fund loan and the bank loan. Currently, given their focus on SMEs, DAMU programmes are relatively small compared to the financial sector, and have relatively little impact on general credit conditions. Scaling up these programmes to encompass a much larger fraction of total support would require a stronger financial sector (see Chapter 3).

The sector composition of DAMU projects is markedly different from that of SPAIID. Figure 2.15 depicts the sector composition of investments made through Business Road Map 2020, one of the main cross-sectoral programmes implemented under SPAIID and geared towards SMEs. While the sector composition is influenced by the focus on SMEs, the size of support to processing industries and to other sectors conducive to diversification was significantly greater than for the whole of SPAIID. Scaling up such forms of support faces a number of hurdles, including the strength of the financial sector.

Figure 2.15. **Share of sectors in total Business Road Map 2020 investments**

Percentage

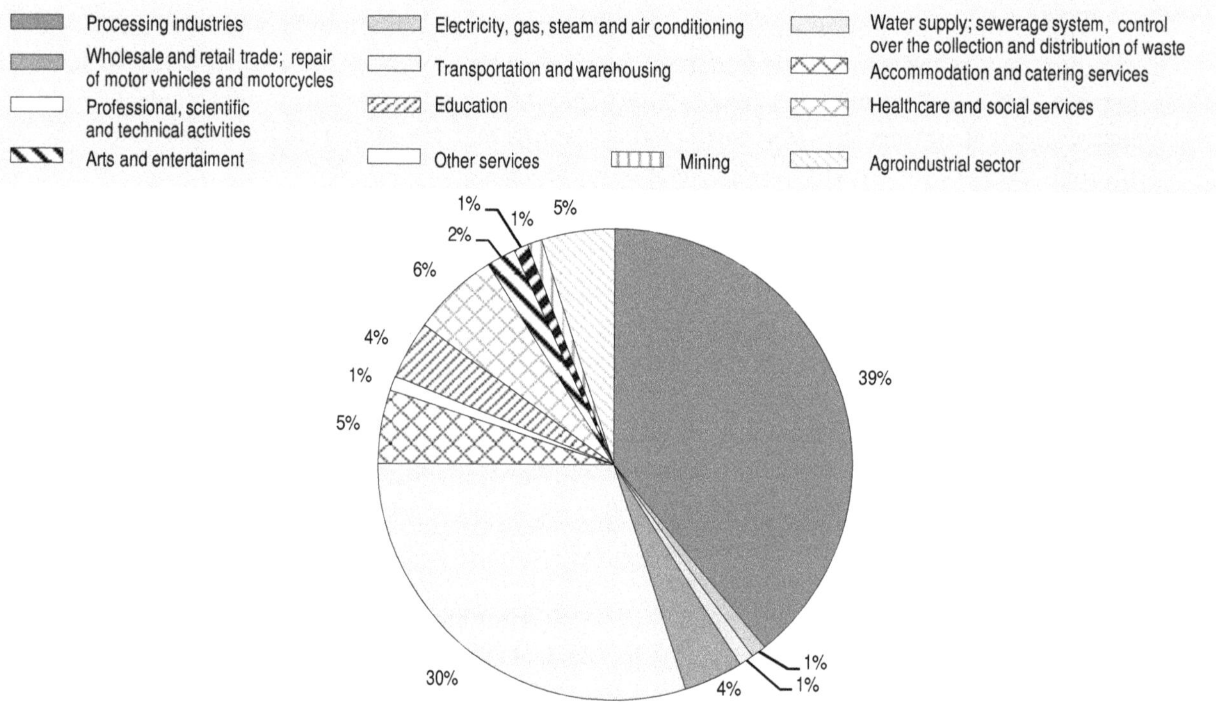

Source: Calculations based on DAMU weekly reports available at (*http://gis.damu.kz*).

StatLink http://dx.doi.org/10.1787/888933445468

For indirect industrial policy to be effective, framework conditions need to provide for opportunities for the private sector. This requires that a number of complementary reforms be implemented so that actors identify opportunities in the market. To the extent that the playing field is not level between private and state-owned firms, the privatisation process under way can play an important role in this regard (see Chapter 4). Ultimately, however, it is the contestability of markets, underpinned by competition policy that is fundamental. Other framework conditions generally conducive to private entrepreneurship can also unleash the effectiveness of industrial policy, including a good business environment and predictable and streamlined sector regulations.

Sector focus and Kazakhstan's economic diversification

Sector selection plays an important role in industrial policy in Kazakhstan

Industrial policy in Kazakhstan focuses on identifying priority sectors for support. The focus on priority sectors in the first SPAIID was very broad, signalling a priority to manufacturing but allowing funds to flow largely to other sectors (see previous section). Attributing the disappointing results of SPAIID to this dispersion, the second phase of SPAIID was designed with a smaller and better defined set of 14 priority sectors and the added condition that 80% of financial support would go to priority sectors. Recently, as a consequence of fiscal consolidation, the number of priority sectors has been further reduced to eight: ferrous and non-ferrous metallurgy, oil processing, petrochemistry and agrochemistry, food production, car manufacturing and electro-technical machine building (Ministry of Investment and Development, 2016). With the reduction in the number of eligible sectors and the concentration of resources, sector selection becomes critical for the success of industrial policy.

The selection of a narrow set of sectors for significant support to the exclusion of others is a risky strategy. Indeed, orienting support to a small number of sectors at the expense of others can limit the potential for diversification. In practice, implementation of SPAIID I contributed very largely to the development of framework conditions that were conducive to development of a large set of sectors. However, current implementation guidelines for example, limit eligibility of financial support to SMEs in some programmes to priority sectors, which would seriously undermine certain manufacturing sectors and is likely to distort credit markets further. The pruning of the originally planned set of priority sectors appears to be driven largely by export potential as well as the availability of interested foreign investors, both of which are acceptable metrics, especially in the current context.

Producers in other sectors that engage in export or in increasing their performance are expected to receive support, but the set of tools available to each group is not clearly specified. Indeed, the normative basis for state support to industrial actors in the Entrepreneurship Code identifies the list of priority sectors as a key instrument but does not specify which tools will be made available to which sectors. The text of the SPAIID 2015-2019 programme allows for non-priority sector projects to receive financial support when they meet a stringent set of criteria (based in rural areas, monotowns [single industry towns] or small towns, led by young entrepreneurs) or, for large projects, on a case-by-case basis, with a limit of 20% of total support provided by the programme. On the other hand, non-financial support measures are made available much more widely. Moreover, the choice and scope of certain incentives are still specified on a case-by-case basis in Kazakhstan via agreements signed by individual investors and the Committee on Investment (OECD, forthcoming, a).

If specific sectors are singled out for support, criteria should be made clear, transparent and accessible. While the selection of sectors in SPAIID II was determined on the basis of in-depth analysis and the list of sectors can be supported by a number of findings, it raises several questions. As mentioned above, it is not clear that analysts are better placed than industry professionals to identify opportunities. Moreover, some of the sectors selected for support involve very few actors. Their singling-out for financial support can therefore raise governance issues. Conversely, some of the sectors selected are much less structured (e.g. food production) and the identification of projects for support on the basis of sectors may lead to subsidising relatively inefficient firms. For the latter, the participation of the financial sector in project selection can mitigate concerns.

A fundamental question for industrial policy in Kazakhstan is the balance between promotion of activities related to natural resources and processing activities in other value chains. A general analysis of the sectors that offer most promise, or that would be expected to emerge in a level playing field, is beyond the scope of this chapter, but the following sections analyse in turn how sectors compare in their placement in the product space and in their domestic linkages, and what specific attention could be devoted to extractive sectors on the one hand, and services sectors on the other.

The product space and indications of product feasibility

The probability of success is an important element in the selection of sectors for support and products to diversify into. The product space can be a useful tool to identify potential products and industries for further diversification. Indeed, proximity of products can be interpreted as indicating lower risk, as the necessary capabilities for producing and successfully exporting the new product are already present. This is the support for the suggestion that Kazakhstan should consider efforts to diversify into a range of products that are close to its product space (Felipe and Hidalgo, 2015; World Bank, 2013).

For Kazakhstan, potential export products that are linked to a greater number of other products are also at greater distance from Kazakhstan's current export basket, and hence potentially riskier. An examination of the relationship between distance to Kazakhstan's network and the potential contribution of individual products to future opportunities for diversification shows a clear positive relationship. That is to say, products which are close to more products – in the framework of the product space – tend to be further away from products that Kazakhstan exports with revealed comparative advantage. This is because the vast majority of products exported with a comparative advantage from Kazakhstan are on the periphery of the product space. The World Bank (2013) has identified seven clusters that are close to existing competitive products, namely: i) oil, ferroalloys and unprocessed aluminium; ii) lead, zinc, manganese, etc.; iii) copper and other non-ferrous metals; iv) metal and non-metal mining; v) iron and steel; vi) cereal grains; and vii) animal skins and leathers, fruits, vegetable oils. However, by and large, these product groups offer less in terms of earning potential than a number of other sectors in value chains in which Kazakhstan is already an important actor: in particular, a number of plastics and plastic products, industrial chemicals, paper and wood products, transport equipment and irons and steel industries.

In terms of distance, the most feasible new products that Kazakhstan can explore are ore-mining and non-ferrous metals, non-natural chemicals, ferroalloy-related products and woven fabrics. Within these product communities, feasible products are liquefied hydrocarbons, nitrogenous fertilisers, dried or shelled legumes, lead ore, paper and paperboard rolls and unwrought nickel, as well as woven cotton and other manmade fabrics. Metals, non-metal mining and manufactured metal products also present opportunities. More complex and strategic value diversification opportunities would build on existing capabilities in machinery and transport equipment, mostly related to large production vehicles and vehicle parts.

Manufactured goods based on metal and metallurgy, although not the closest products in terms of distance, offer large complexity and opportunity gains. Two products could be explored: iron or steel shapes/rods, and iron and steel structures. Iron or steel shapes/rods have a 0.96 complexity index, so their production and export would have a positive impact on the overall complexity of the country. However, aluminium structures (in which the country has a RCA greater than 1 already) are connected to this product. Iron and steel structures have a complexity of 0.36 and are highly connected with other products that Kazakhstan exports albeit with RCA lower than one, again opening the door to enter new markets and product communities. They are connected to some products that Kazakhstan is already exporting with revealed comparative advantage, such as asbestos, aluminium structures, and articles of paper pulp. This proximity indicates that the capabilities needed to export iron and steel structures are close to the set of capabilities that Kazakhstan has, as Kazakhstan is already exporting products with a high proximity to it, meaning that other countries that export these products, also produce these structures.

Kazakhstan's priority sectors in the product space

Priority sectors in the SPAIID 2015-2019 strategy appear aligned with the product space methodology. Basic sectors of industry, iron and steel as well as non-ferrous metallurgy, show strong relatedness to existing products in Kazakhstan's export basket but also present strategy value and opportunity gains in the global market. These products are either within, or highly related to, the set of products that Kazakhstan exports with comparative advantage. Therefore moving into these areas will be easy and will present little risk in terms of reallocation of resources. The manufacture of electrical machinery and apparatus, production of agricultural machinery, production of railway equipment, production of machinery and equipment for the mining industry appear more challenging in the short run given current constraints in productive capabilities, but are not out of reach for Kazakhstan. Although it already exports some metal products, these are mostly unwrought and do not require costly inputs or efficiency in productive capabilities.

Other priority sectors respond to the logic of building capacity to transform competitive advantage. Certain industries have played a key role in sustaining and maintaining industrialisation in other countries in the past. These include electrical machinery manufacturing, motor vehicles and chemical industries, for example (UNIDO, 2013). While Kazakhstan produces some goods in these sectors, it is not a significant exporter. For example, bulldozers, excavators and road rollers are exported with a RCA index of 0.12. Similarly, fork-lift trucks are exported with an RCA index of 0.02. The high transport costs of inputs sourced outside Kazakhstan are a foremost constraint. Long overland distances and inconsistent customs procedures at borders give rise to vulnerabilities in Kazakhstan's supply chain.

Priority sectors and inter-sectoral linkages

The degree of domestic intersectoral linkages is an indication of how much increasing activity in one sector will have multiplier effects domestically. Sectors which make use of domestically produced intermediate inputs have greater potential to develop domestic demand in other sectors and thereby exert a multiplier effect on growth. Inter-sectoral linkages can be measured on the basis of input-output data by calculating the Leontief multiplier, which measures the effect of increased demand for one industry on other industries via derived demand. In the case of the sector with the largest coefficient in Kazakhstan (metal-casting), a 1% increase in demand would increase value added in the domestic economy by as much as 1.71%.

Table 2.3. **Sectors by degree of inter-sectoral linkages, 2014**

Rank	Sector	Leontief multiplier
1	Metal casting	1.71
2	Manufacture of basic precious and other non-ferrous metals	1.70
3	Care services	1.63
4	Public administration and defence; social security	1.61
5	Production of pig iron, steel and ferro-alloys	1.60
6	Water transport	1.60
7	Construction	1.60
8	Electric power generation, transmission and distribution	1.59
9	Manufacture of gas, distribution of gaseous fuels through mains	1.58
10	Arts, entertainment and recreation	1.55
11	Water supply, sewerage, waste management and remediation activities	1.55
12	Mining of non-ferrous metals	1.55
13	Human health activities	1.53
14	Steam and air conditioning supply	1.53
15	Education	1.52
16	Other mining and quarrying	1.51
17	Mining of iron ores	1.50

Note: The table displays the 17 sectors with the highest Leontief multiplier. It is the "direct" multiplier, meaning that it takes into account derived demand from other sectors but not the income effects associated with labour inputs.
Source: Calculations based on Input-Output data from the Committee on Statistics of the Republic of Kazakhstan (*www.stat.gov.kz/*).

A number of priority sectors have high domestic multipliers, while certain non-tradeable sectors that are not eligible for priority funding would also lead to significant multiplier effects. Among priority sectors, manufacturing activities such as metal-casting, metallurgy and mining have high multiplier effects, thanks to Kazakhstan's production of machinery in these areas. On the other hand, certain non-tradeable sectors, such as construction, and a number of services sectors also make use of intermediate inputs from the domestic economy and would help to increase domestic demand.

The role of extractive sectors in industrialisation policy

Despite the challenges it presents, Kazakhstan's natural resource base has provided a strong foundation for growth and can potentially act as a catalyst to modernise the economy and make it greener. The government's interlocking development strategies suggest prospects for future growth, in particular through extending the mining and minerals sector and enhancing green growth and innovation. The most central of those plans is the Kazakhstan 2050 Strategy. In respect of the extractive sector, strategy Kazakhstan 2050 recognises the need for a new approach to managing natural resources, addressing commodity price cycles, technology change and the threat of reduced international demand as a driver to find new exports markets.

The extractive sector remains an important part of SPAIID for 2015-2019, with many of the original 14 priority areas directly or indirectly linked to it. Ferrous and non-ferrous metals are central to SPAIID. The ferrous metal industry is responsible for more than 10% of total manufacturing employment, according to SPAIID 2015-2019, with the outputs both exported and used domestically as inputs in the oil and gas sector, engineering, and construction. Under the previous industrial plan (SPAIID 2010-2014), 27 investment projects were commissioned, including new steel rolling mills and alloying plants. However, SPAIID 2015-2019 takes into account a range of concerns centred around softening demand from China and Russia for Kazakh ferrous metal products, the deterioration of ageing assets, and in some cases a lack of sufficient high grade metals for alloying. Low levels of investment, low productivity, and poor levels of research and skills development are all seen as weaknesses in the area. Non-ferrous metals, including copper, gold, aluminium, zinc, lead, titanium and others, are also substantial employers in Kazakhstan's extractive sector and have linkages with manufacturing and processing. SPAIID 2015-2019 identifies the main strengths of the sector as the availability of raw materials, strong vertical integration of processing, and strong government support for the development of new facilities and products.[13] However, these strengths are contrasted with ageing assets, insufficient investment, shortage of qualified personnel, and the impact of WTO accession on the government's ability to continue providing direct support to the sector.

In tandem with SPAIID 2015-2019, the government is supporting exploration and ferrous and non-ferrous mine development through the State Program on Geological Exploration for 2015-2019. Recognising the mining sector's comparative advantage, the programme aims to increase the attractiveness of the mining sector, and encourage technology transfer and infrastructure development. It sets targets in terms of increased knowledge of probable resources, increased proven reserves of key minerals, the formation of a database of geological information using geographic information systems (GIS), and the liquidation and conservation of oil and gas wells. It encompasses not just geological forecasting, exploration and mapping, but also pilot work on unconventional gas, rare earth elements, and the monitoring and prevention of groundwater and environmental issues. In addition to developing a knowledge base and increasing interest from investors, the programme calls for the creation of a scientific and technological centre of geological studies at Nazarbayev University to develop new techniques, technologies, and software, as well as providing support to public and private actors involved in the sector. It is set to be funded by the national budget as well as by resources from the private sector. The programme lists a total of KZT 119 720 million over 2015-19, beginning with KZT 9 014 million in 2015 and rising to KZT 34 536 million in 2019.

Better natural gas infrastructure can help expand exports and facilitate emission reduction if it used in power generation to replace coal-fired generation. Although Kazakhstan has abundant gas resources, most production and nearly three quarters of its reserves are located in the sparsely populated western area (IEA, 2014). The exceptions to this are the Amangeldy fields in Almaty province in the south, which supply gas for domestic consumption and have been steadily expanding, bringing new wells on line in 2014. The government is expanding the domestic distribution network in an effort to connect the pipeline network in the more populated central and southern areas with the network in the western producing regions, providing gas access to smaller communities along the way. The Beineu-Bozoi-Shymkent pipeline, eventually stretching 1 143 kilometres from Beineu in the west of the country to Shymkent in the southeast, near the Kyrgyzstan border and further pipeline connections to China, will facilitate exports and connect the more densely populated regions of Kazakhstan to its gas production areas.

Local coal basins remain a major advantage for Kazakhstan, but more efficient and environmentally friendly exploitation is necessary to meet environmental and energy-efficiency goals. Environmental standards could provide incentives to the development of better coal-mining practices and cleaner electricity generation. Coal gasification – the transformation of coal to synthetic natural gas – is also a potential source of energy in Kazakhstan, considering its substantial stores of coal. However, current technology is water intensive and may result in greater emissions of CO_2, and projects in China have had higher costs than expected.

Box 2.1. Goals and objectives for ferrous and non-ferrous metals under SPAIID 2015-2019

Ferrous metals

Goal: To stop the downturn in production and support a transition to sustainable development.

Objectives:

1. Utilisation of existing facilities;
2. Modernisation of existing companies in the industry to improve production efficiency;
3. Expand the range and quality of steel and metal products in mass demand sectors;
4. Create new competitive industries in the high-margin segments;
5. Provide the necessary infrastructure for investment projects;
6. Stimulate domestic demand;
7. Promote exports and participation in global value chains; and
8. Provide industry with skilled manpower, including secondary and technical resources management.

Non-ferrous metals

Goal: Increased production of base metals and the production of related products.

Objectives:

1. Expansion of existing businesses' capacity and creation of new production of base metals;
2. Modernisation of existing companies in the industry to improve production efficiency;
3. Expansion of existing production and development of new base metal product outputs for related sectors;
4. Provision of the necessary infrastructure for investment projects;
5. Promotion of demand in the domestic market;
6. Promoting sector exports and participation in global value chains; and
7. Provision to industry of skilled workers and technologists.

Source : State Programme of Industrial and Innovative Development 2015-2019, Government of the Republic of Kazakhstan (2013)

Services sectors have untapped potential for Kazakhstan's diversification

Industrial policy in Kazakhstan apparently disregards the importance of services. Services sectors play an important role as a new driver of economic growth. Not only are services important sectors in their own right, but they can help capture increased shares of trade in value-added, deepen the position of the country in value chains, and reshape the competitive advantage of the country. While Kazakhstan has developed traditional services, services sectors intensive in knowledge and information are underdeveloped in the country. In 2013, the share of business services in added value in Kazakhstan was 5%, almost a third of the 14% level it was in Germany.

Policies to develop the services sector exist but have significantly fewer instruments and resources at their disposal. The Programme for the Development of the Service Sector in the Republic of Kazakhstan until 2020 identifies nine target service sectors (trade, transport and logistics, tourism, real estate, professional services, information and communication, finance and insurance, education, health care). The programme therefore has objectives for a number of critical business services, in particular transport and logistics, which are critical for export performance and one of the areas where Kazakhstan performs less well in terms of the ease of doing business. However, the programme does not appear to have dedicated resources. It contains a number of regulatory proposals but critical achievements in terms of investment in the services industry are linked to programmes under industrial policy, like Business Road Map 2020, which financed the construction of five transport-logistical centres, for example.

Box 2.2. **Digitising Kazakhstan: Investing in the next generation of e-governance technologies**

Kazakhstan has already taken significant strides to improve governmental efficiency through various e-government initiatives. The Public Procurement Law (PPL), enacted in 2007, introduced mandatory e-procurement procedures from July 2012. Kazakhstan launched an e-government initiative in 2004 – the first country in the Central Asian region to do so. E-licensing of certain businesses and electronic state purchases is already operational, an e-notariate (uniform notarial information system) initiated operations in 2011 and regional electronic *akimats* (regional authority system) are under deployment. The "Information Kazakhstan – 2020" state programme, launched in 2013, also introduced an Open Data platform. Kazakhstan's emphasis on digitisation was reflected in its rise in the United Nations e-government development index (EGDI) from 81st in 2008 to 28th in 2014, ranking sixth in Asia and first in Central Asia (OECD, 2016a). Much more remains to be done, however, if Kazakhstan is to converge with benchmark countries.

First, Kazakhstan should focus on broadening access to digital technologies. Developing a highly sophisticated programme of e-government is redundant if citizens cannot access digital services. Kazakhstan has made significant progress over recent years in expanding Internet coverage: 64 % of the population aged 6 to 74 had access to the Internet in 2014. This compares to 84% in Estonia and 70% in Russia.

Second, Kazakhstan should consider following Estonia in its pioneering use of blockchain technologies to further reduce friction in government service delivery and reduce the potential for corruption. A blockchain is essentially a publicly distributed ledger recording digitally occurring transactions. Blockchains are most commonly associated with cryptocurrencies, such as Bitcoin, but can be used to provide digital records of any type of asset. Blockchains provide the triple function of a timestamp, public ledger and digital signature of a transaction (Forde, 2016). Although the ledger is public, details of ownership are secured under cryptographic hashes. As such, people can conduct digital transactions, exchange assets, and register business licences, birth certificates and marriages, without the need for a centralised database.

The Estonian government is partnering Bitnation to provide a public notary service based on blockchain technology (Prisco, 2015). This will enable Estonian e-residents to notarise their marriages, birth certificates and business contracts on the blockchain. The implications of this, and other uses of blockchain technology, are transformative. First, blockchains have the potential to enhance government service delivery through the reduction and elimination of transaction costs (the monetary and administrative costs of maintaining physical notaries, land registries, etc., and the time costs incurred waiting for such transactions to be processed). Second, blockchains can be used to leapfrog stages of development. For example, Honduras has no land registry system. Rather than developing a physical and digital one, it is partnering with Factom to create a land registry based on the blockchain (The Economist, 2015). Third, blockchains can be used to reduce the potential for corruption. If land titles, business licences and other assets are hosted on the blockchain – a public ledger that is digitally verified and timestamped – the possibility of bribes and corruption being used to appropriate or unlawfully exchange such assets is reduced.

Box 2.3. **Gaps in telecommunications market and infrastructure hinder the potential of IT services**

Although the telecommunication sector in Kazakhstan has been privatised and liberalised, there still exist many structural barriers impeding competition within the sector. As a result, the dominant operator in fixed-line telephony and fixed broadband, Kazakhtelecom (KT), which is majority owned by the sovereign wealth fund Samruk-Kazyna, functions in a way similar to a profit-driven monopoly and a universal telecommunications service provider. KT receives a state subsidy to compensate for unprofitable universal provision of telecommunications services.

Kazakhtelecom accounts for an estimated 70% share of the fixed line Internet broadband market. However, as it also fully or partially owns several other Internet backbone and Internet service providers, the estimate is likely to understate KT's true market power. Moreover, KT has a strong position on external backbone channels, thus having considerable power over downstream Internet service providers and other competitors.

The expansion of mobile communications has generated a more competitive telecommunications market. KT has 35% of the telecommunication markets, if all segments are considered, due to the fact that mobile communications make up 47% of the market and that KT's mobile operator, Altel, only has 11% of the mobile market. Altel was the only operator granted a 4G (LTE) licence available in 2011, allowing the operator to rapidly grow its subscriber base, but other operators obtained licences and began to deploy 4G in 2016.

Perhaps as a consequence of the composition of the market and of the importance of mobile telecommunications, fixed broadband subscription appears to be low in Kazakhstan compared to other countries (Figure 2.16). With a fixed broadband subscription of 11.3 per 100 persons, Kazakhstan's subscription rate is lower than Azerbaijan's (17), Russia's (16.6) or China's (13.6). Furthermore, the country's international bandwidth is behind the more developed economies. Norway, Canada and Germany all had an international bandwidth greater than 100 kbps/user In Kazakhstan, international internet bandwidth is 49.8kbps/user, which is comparable to that of Russia, Azerbaijan or Chile. (Figure 2.16). When all means of access are considered, 55.8% of Kazakhstanis are estimated to have access to the Internet.

Figure 2.16. **Broadband in Kazakhstan**

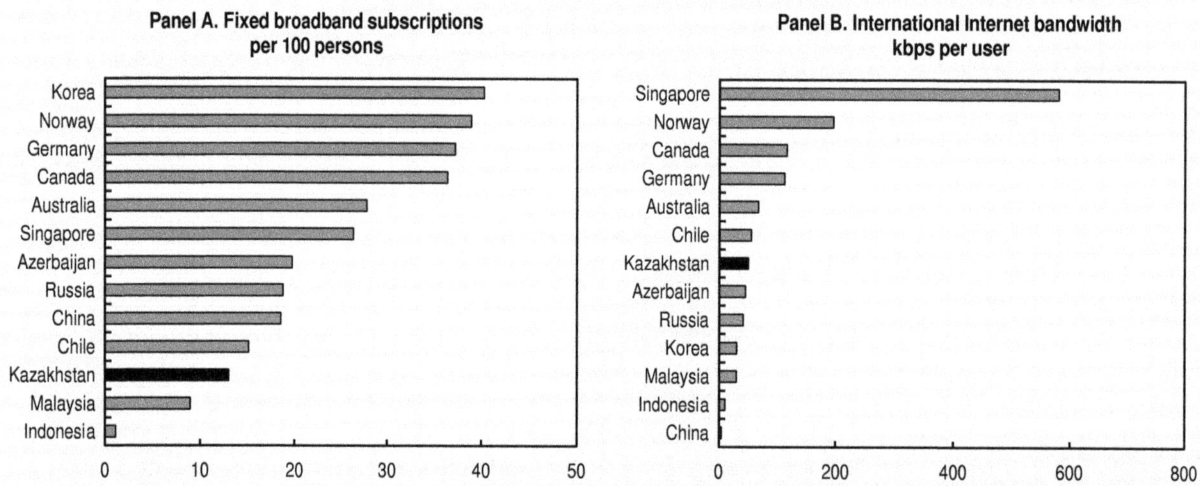

Note: Subscriptions are total fixed broadband Internet subscriptions to high-speed access to the public Internet. International bandwidth refers to the sum of the capacity of all internet exchanges offering international bandwidth measured in kilobits per second (kbps).

Source: ITU World Telecommunication/ICT Indicators Database 2014, ITU (2014).

StatLink http://dx.doi.org/10.1787/888933445479

Fixed broadband subscription and international Internet bandwidth are critical to enabling a greater variety of business services such as video conferencing and remote access. In addition, improvements in Internet bandwidth and affordability are also critical to enabling more productive technologies such as cloud computing and the Internet of things.

An important aspect in enabling higher added-value production is the use of business-related services on the part of production firms, including manufacturing firms. The ability to outsource certain functions, including labour recruitment, information technology (IT) services, marketing, market analysis or research and development (R&D) increases the productivity of firms. In Kazakhstan, business services, finance and IT services are a much smaller part of inputs to critical sectors such as agriculture, manufacturing and mining than in developed economies. Business services are virtually unused by manufacturing firms in Kazakhstan, while they constitute over 10% of inputs in Germany. Similarly, business services, finance, and IT costs constitute 8.5% of inputs in mining firms in Kazakhstan, compared to 19% and 21% in Australia and Canada respectively (OECD, 2016a).

Kazakhstan is well placed to become a regional leader in IT and business services. The development of the sector would benefit firms in Kazakhstan, both domestic and foreign. Moreover, given its stability, relatively low labour cost and generalisation of basic skills, the sector could become a major player in business services outsourcing. India remains the main player in the sector, but the importance of language compatibility would help sustain regional development of the sector (OECD, 2011). Kazakhstan has made great progress in e-government for example (see Box 2.2).

Kazakhstan is also well-placed to develop green services and technologies. The legacy of neglect of the environment has generated a very significant need for environmental services across a number of areas. Important policy steps in the adoption of the Green Economy concept and the establishment of carbon trading in 2013 mean that firms will be looking to reduce their carbon intensity (see Felipe and Rhee, 2013; and Chapter 5 in this volume).

The development of services sectors faces a number of challenges, including sector-specific challenges. An analysis of challenges to ICT and business services sectors (OECD, 2011) identified skills composition, available human capital, the lack of public-private dialogue, and ICT infrastructure as main constraints. Despite adequate Russian language skills, which provide a competitive advantage to Kazakhstani business service providers, both soft skills – in particular communication skills – and IT-specific technical skills were found to be major hurdles, as was the lack of a specific governmental strategy for the development of the sector. This latter point matches the emphasis of sector-level policy on manufacturing sectors. The gap in technical sector-specific skills is also found in other services and manufacturing sectors. Kazakhstan has since began implementation of the State programme Informational Kazakhstan 2020, which includes support measures for the development of the local ICT market as well as for the development of IT skills and for expanding the use of ICT in a number of sectors.

The development of services also has requirements in terms of other sectors, notably infrastructure. Despite progress in both the use and availability of ICT infrastructure, Kazakhstan still faces notable gaps. International experience suggests that increasing competition in the various segments of the telecommunications sector can go a long way towards increasing the affordability of telecommunications infrastructure. Singapore's introduction of an open access policy, obliging owners of physical telecommunications infrastructure to provide access to Internet service providers, led to a fall in broadband prices of almost 50%, boosting subscription rates. Such "unbundling" is one of the regulatory tools that can be used to foster competition, and which should be assessed in the light of main goals in ICT development (e.g. encouraging infrastructure investment, innovation, competition to improve service). A critical element is to ease the introduction of new platforms and technologies from incumbent or new operators.

Conclusion: Towards well-thought out and flexible industrial policy

Industrial policy in Kazakhstan has worked primarily by promoting medium-term investment in focus sectors via financial support and the attraction of FDI. The first phase of the state programme on advanced industrial-innovative development (SPAIID) had disappointing results relative to its ambitious goals, meeting two of its six headline targets[14] but contributed to halting the relative deindustrialisation process and created a series of institutions that can be leveraged to further development objectives. The design of the second phase of SPAIID has incorporated a number of important lessons from the implementation of the 2010-14 programme, including the provision of support to clusters, the greater role given to the private sector and to regions. The second phase programme has also strived to reduce fragmentation in the implementation of industrial policy and introduced a number of co-ordination mechanisms.

Setting consistent objectives and principles for industrial policy and adapting monitoring and evaluation

Clear and shared objectives would help catalyse the actions of the many actors involved in implementing industrial policy. The main objectives can be linked to sector performance as is the case in SPAIID II. Indeed, in the first phase implementation, several of the main targets set for the programme went beyond the domain of implementation. For example, there was a target for GDP level, but performance in GDP growth in Kazakhstan cannot be attributed to industrial policy given the relatively small share of GDP generated by manufacturing. Successful diversification is first and foremost the development of new activities, especially at the level of development of Kazakhstan, rather than the decline of traditional activities. Beyond the accumulation of dynamic sectors, export concentration imposes volatility and gives rise to a diversification imperative.

Fundamental principles for industrial policy should be clearly stated. This is particularly important in terms of sector selection and sector-specific support. Sector-specific or "vertical" industrial policy can help solve co-ordination issues in a given sector, by providing platforms for actors to co-ordinate or by taking on the cost of investments, the social value of which is higher than the private value. However, the basis for providing support to specific sectors should be clearly stated and transparent, especially when the sectors concerned are concentrated or dominated by SOEs.

Introduce greater flexibility in the design and implementation of policy. The ongoing revision of industrial policy programmes in the light of changes in external circumstances underlines the need for a more flexible planning and implementation framework. Especially given the exposure of Kazakhstan to external risk, the optimal composition of the economy in the future cannot be easily determined, as it will depend on the prevailing terms of trade. A programmatic and institutional framework that allows for more agile adaptation to changing circumstances would also assist actors in the various industries to adapt. Consultation platforms can help detect and correct implementation issues. However, specific instruments may be more adapted to upscaling or downscaling than others at appropriate times – as was, for example, the use of DAMU to channel credit during the 2008-10 crisis.

Move from investment programmes to policies. The sector programmes in SPAIID I were largely implemented as large investment programmes. This spirit is still, albeit to a lesser extent, at the core of the SPAIID 2015-2019. Specific support, like that provided in the context of the Map of Industrialisation, is suited to a programme approach, which signifies its time-bounded nature. However, stimulating entry in new sectors requires predictable framework conditions and business environments, including in terms of regulatory quality and access to finance. Moving to general policies for those elements can help ensure predictability for private foreign and domestic actors.

The monitoring of, and reporting on, industrial policy should be strengthened. Work for this report has highlighted the difficulty in obtaining a clear picture of activities across programmes and actors. Publicly available reports on the various actions are *ad hoc* and not consistent across implementing agencies. Given the sizeable public resources involved, monitoring should include not only investment but also other actions. And support-equivalent measures should be developed to provide valuations of the actual level of support and its budgetary cost, rather than the resulting investment or credit, so as to make different instruments and programmes comparable.

Strengthen evaluation functions and align them to policy objectives. Evaluations of SPAIID 2010-2014 by institutions such as MNE and KIDI, while informative, often stopped at remarking on the success or failure in achieving headline indicators, themselves often not designed to be attributable to the policy. Clear benchmarks for success or failure should be set at project or target level, and be regularly and transparently evaluated, ideally by an independent body. The evaluating body should not be primarily responsible for design or implementation of the programme, lest its incentives be misaligned.

Define the functions, streamline the implementation and adapt the instruments of industrial policy

Clarify the functions of the state, the SOE sector and private enterprise. The state does not need to carry out all the functions needed for industrial upgrading. In particular, state institutions may not be the best placed to generate jobs or to provide finance. On the other hand, given the size of the SOE sector in Kazakhstan and its close relations with the state, the co-ordination role is of great importance for the various levels of government.

The set of functions should be expanded beyond the traditional investment promotion and co-ordination roles of the state. Successes in economic transformation are characterised by the capacity to anticipate opportunities and changes, by the capacity to adapt to changing external conditions, by the capacity to create long-term linkages and create local value, by the capacity to create and sustain networks in production and innovation, and by the capacity to learn and upgrade. These functions (anticipation, adaptation, embeddedness, interconnectedness, learning) require action on the part of both public and private actors. Indeed private-public institutions have been instrumental in fulfilling these functions in successful countries. Future-scanning functions can also be provided as a public good by the public sector or a coalition of public and private interests.

The set of instruments of industrial policy should be consolidated and streamlined. Instruments should be matched to the functions they fulfil and the objectives they contribute to achieving. A number of programmes and instruments could be consolidated to avoid duplication and provide greater visibility to end-users.

Put greater emphasis on non-financial instruments. Currently, certain instruments of industrial policy (e.g. the Map of Industrialisation) are mainly considered in their financial role. While this role is of course important, their co-ordination role is also very important. The focus on FDI attraction and investment promotion should not deter from the importance of co-ordinating across actors and levels of government. In a fiscal consolidation environment, these should survive as co-ordination mechanisms even if and when their financial support facet is less significant.

Expand the participation of the private sector, including through expanding the use of indirect instruments. Financial support should include the participation of private sector actors, whether directly or as channels of disbursement. This not only reduces the direct cost to the public purse, but mobilises the sector-specific knowledge that private actors have, and aligns their incentives. In the current situation, SOEs may not be good substitutes for private actors, as they have different objectives and are explicitly tasked with public interest functions, including the implementation of industrial policy itself. As privatisation progresses, market-active SOEs may be better substitutes for private actors when the latter do not exist in a given sector. The direct participation of the private sector would complement their participation in consultation and co-ordination bodies, which is itself dependent on the progress of the development of private sector representative instances such as the Chamber of Entrepreneurs.

Include other sectors in the realm of industrial policy

Industrial policy is also relevant beyond manufacturing, including agriculture and services. Kazakhstan has the potential to develop a dynamic, high value-added service sector by developing business services, IT and environmental services, as well as services specific to its natural-resource industries. The development of services requires linkages to industrial sectors in particular to ensure that advanced infrastructure is in place. Conversely, the development of critical services sectors, including the financial sector, can help boost competitiveness across the economy.

Ensure progress in complementary reforms to create appropriate framework conditions

While this chapter has focused on the role of industrial policy, success in structural transformation is dependent on the availability of critical resources and the establishment of appropriate framework conditions. Crucial actions to address transversal constraints include maintaining macroeconomic stability, strengthening the financial sector, improving the quantity and quality of infrastructure, improving the quality and relevance of education and skills, creating labour and financial market institutions to allow workers to cope with increased volatility, enhancing the links between innovation and industrial policy, addressing corruption in both the public and private sectors and ensuring a level playing field through SOE reform and competition policy reform.

Sustaining productivity increases in a range of industries and sectors in the long run will require that education and innovation systems are not only well-developed but also better aligned with the needs of productive sectors. Current efforts in increasing the quality of education should be continued and complemented with further actions to ensure that education and training match the needs of the labour market. Sector-level public-private dialogue is critical in anticipating the future needs of the economy and designing appropriate curricula and training. The nascent innovation system has yet to generate results on a transformative scale. Certain provisions, such as the obligation of subsoil users to spend 1% of income on R&D, offer great promise but face implementation hurdles.

Box 2.4. **How could the scenarios affect the context of implementation of diversification policies?**

For details of the scenario storylines, please see section: Anticipating trends and preparing for future challenges: scenarios for the future of Kazakhstan in Chapter 1.

Scenario 1: "The New Commodity Super-cycle" would revive the external forces dominant during the 2000s in Kazakhstan. The improved terms of trade would lead to exchange rate appreciation and hinder the competitiveness of tradeable goods, in particular manufacturing. Diversification would therefore be difficult, with the necessity to increase productivity in non-natural resource sectors, in particular through better education and innovation policies. Concurrently, a new super-cycle would significantly improve fiscal space in Kazakhstan, which is now better equipped with key institutions to manage the macroeconomic implications via the National Fund and a floating currency. This could increase funds available for buttressing the emergence of new sectors. Changed terms of trade over the medium term would require an adjustment of the priorities of industrial policy to: i) support local linkages of extractive industries, which are stronger in mining than in oil extraction; and ii) allow the emergence of new sectors with export potential, possibly in industries with higher added value. The implementation of indirect industrial policy instruments would allow for a more agile adaptation to these new circumstances.

Scenario 2: "The Great Dissipation" would result in an enduringly depressed external environment which would oblige Kazakhstan to focus on diversifying its export markets, over and above diversifying its products. Lower exchange rates would make local manufactured and agro-industry products more competitive in both foreign and domestic markets. More constrained public finances would merit added focus of industrial policy on non-financial instruments to support public-private and private-private co-ordination, market scanning, innovation and technology adoption. Limited fiscal space would also require focus in the use of public resources to support new investment, with greater emphasis on improving the efficiency of banks' lending, and on raising returns for private investment.

Scenario 3: "The New Silk Road and Central Asia Resurgence" would entail the implementation of the Belt and Road Initiative (BRI). The increased investment in physical transport infrastructure and logistical capacity in the south of Kazakhstan and its neighbours would alleviate a key constraint on export performance and diversification in Kazakhstan. Greater value-chain integration across borders in Central Asia would offer new opportunities for Kazakhstan-based producers. It would add attractiveness for market-seeking FDI, which policy should support, even though it may not fit the priority sectors of industrial policy, as it would contribute to diversify both products and market partners for exports. However, this scenario also offers significant risks for diversification: lower transport costs will translate into greater openness, putting less competitive sectors or firms in difficulty. In this context, strengthening complementary inputs (specific infrastructure, logistics capacity, etc.) would be particularly important for Kazakhstan to become a regional hub in the provision of business services and higher-value added segments of manufacturing value chains.

Scenario 4, "New Green Technology Solutions" would see a shift in global demand patterns away from hydrocarbons would be a major challenge for Kazakhstan. However, if demand for other key exports, including agricultural goods and other natural resources, were maintained this configuration would generate incentives to diversify domestic production and exports and also reduce exposure to external risks. Among key sectors, agriculture would be a great asset for Kazakhstan in this environment. A key decision would be the choice to utilise oil and gas resources domestically, where they could lower the price of energy and replace coal, or to invest in adapting green technology to processes in Kazakhstan, which would necessitate stepping up efforts to green the economy.

Source: Authors.

Notes

1. Resource rents are measured by the difference between the value of the resource at production at world prices and total costs of production (World Bank, 2011).
2. The Kashagan offshore oilfield, discovered in 2000, is among the largest discoveries of the last 30 years. Total recoverable reserves of crude are estimated to be 13 billion barrels. However, its development has been tumultuous and beset by delays. With deep reservoirs of oil under high pressure, shallow water, and a cold climate, the difficult operating conditions of Kashagan have contributed to repeated delays and cost overruns. After briefly beginning production in September 2013, eight years behind the original planned production date of 2005, operations were halted because of the discovery of leaks in the pipes. The pipes are being replaced, with production restarting by early 2017 at the latest according to the government of Kazakhstan (Sorbello, 2015). Once complete, the project will augment Kazakhstan's existing petroleum and other liquids production with an initial expected output of 0.37 m/bpd during the first phase (EIA, 2015).
3. Natural gas re-injected into underground crude oil and gas reservoirs helps increase pressure within the reservoir, enhancing the recovery of crude oil. This is especially important in mature oil fields and those with heavier oil.
4. Natural gas can be measured in both volume (cubic metres) and energy content (joules). Volume is often used to describe natural gas reserves, while the energy that can be released in burning is often used to describe consumption levels.
5. Commodity definitions are taken from the Harmonised Commodity Description and Coding System, more commonly known as the Harmonised System (HS). The definitions used here are from the HS4 level, with trade data from the UN COMTRADE database (United Nations, 2016).
6. The Herfindahl-Hirschman Product Concentration Index is the sum of squared shares of each product in total export.
7. Total energy subsidies include coal, electricity, and gas in addition to fossil fuels.
8. Products are considered discoveries if they were exported in large and consistent values (USD 10 million over three consecutive years, in 1985 dollar terms). The time of discovery is the first year when exports of the product were above USD 1 million.
9. The IFK has recently changed strategy to focus on restructuring and management of stressed assets.
10. State programmes: "2020 Information", Countering of religious extremism and terrorism 2013-2017, development and functioning of languages of Kazakhstan 2011-2020, education development 2011-2020, modernisation of the law enforcement system for 2014-2020, Salamatty Kazakhstan (health) 2011-2015, industrial innovative development 2015-2019, development and integration of transport infrastructure system, Nurly Zhol (infrastructure development), management of water resources for 2014-2020.
11. This number is somewhat inflated by the consideration of different financing tranches of programmes as separate programmatic elements.
12. Calculated on the basis of data from gis.damu.kz, consulted mid-2016.
13. For example, the production of titanium ingots and alloys in Kazakhstan was initiated under SPAIID 2010-2014.
14. SPAIID had six headline targets setting out improvements relative to 2008 of which it met two: increasing labour productivity by 150% between 2008 and 2014 (actual increase was 157%) and diminishing energy consumption by 10% (it achieved 18.6% by 2013). It missed targets related to overall real GDP increase (31% against the target of 38%) , increase in value-added in non-extractive industrial sectors (31% against the target of 39.5%), increase in real production of the manufacturing industry (24% against the target of 43.6%) and increase in the volume of exports of manufacturing (which fell, against the target of a 30% increase).

References

Aizu, I. (2002), "A comparative study of broadband in Asia: Deployment and policy", *Research Institute of Economy, Trade & Industry Symposium, discussion paper*, 21 May 2002, Asia Network research, Tokyo, *http://www.rieti.go.jp/en/events/02042201/aizu_1.pdf* (accessed 12 February 2016).

Al-Jazeera (2014), "Kazakhstan: Poisoned legacy", *People and Power*, *http://www.aljazeera.com/programmes/peopleandpower/2014/02/kazakhstan-poisoned-legacy-2014219142030905812.html*, accessed on 12-02-16.

Antoncheva, S. (2012), "Rio Tinto to invest 100 million in Kazakh copper project", *BloombergBusiness*, *http://www.bloomberg.com/news/articles/2012-04-18/rio-tinto-to-invest-100-million-in-kazakh-copper-project-1-*, accessed on 5-11-15.

Blattman C., J. Hwang and J. G. Williamson (2007), "Winners and losers in the commodity lottery: The impact of terms of trade growth and volatility in the periphery 1870-1939", *Journal of Development Economics*, Vol 82.

BP (2015), *Statistical Review of World Energy 2015*, British Petroleum, *http://www.bp.com/en/global/corporate/energy-economics/statistical-review-of-world-energy.html*, accessed 30-10-15.

CID (2016) *The Atlas of Economic Complexity*, Center for International Development at Harvard University, *http://www*.atlas.cid.harvard.edu, accessed July 2016.

Committee on Statistics of the Republic of Kazakhstan (2016) Official statistical information published in *www.stat.gov.kz/* , accessed July 2016.

DAMU (2016) DAMU entrepreneurship development fund (database) *http://gis.damu.kz* , accessed July 2016.

Dentons (2015) "Kazakhstan's accession to the WTO: new local content requirements", *http://www.dentons.com/en/insights/alerts/*, published 17-11-2016, accessed on 07-03-2016.

EIA (2015), *Kazakhstan Country Report*, US Energy Information Administration, *http://www.eia.gov/beta/international/analysis_includes/countries_long/Kazakhstan/kazakhstan.pdf.*

EITI (2015), *The 10th National Report On Implementation of the Extractive Industry Transparency Initiative in the Republic of Kazakhstan for 2014*, Extractive Industry Transparency Initiative, *https://eiti.org/sites/default/files/documents/2014_kazakhstan_eiti_report.pdf.*

Elliott, S. (2013), "The history of the Kashagan oil field", Platts, *http://www.platts.com/news-feature/2013/oil/kashagan-oil-field/kashagan-timeline*, accessed 4-11-15.

Ernst and Young (2014), *Kazakhstan Oil and Gas Tax Guide 2014*, Ernst & Young, *http://www.ey.com/Publication/vwLUAssets/EY-2015-Global-oil-and-gas-tax-guide/%24FILE/EY-2015-Global-oil-and-gas-tax-guide.pdf.*

Farchy, Jack (2015a), "Eurasian Resources Group seeks to draw a line under scandals", *Financial Times*, 1 November 2015.

Farchy, Jack (2015b), "ERG taps China for more than USD 2.5 billion of new project financing", *Financial Times*, 2 September 2015.

Farchy, Jack (2015c), "Kazakhstan faces oil dilemma as prices plunge", *Financial Times*, published 1-11-15.

Felipe, J. and C. Hidalgo (2015), "Economic diversification: Implications for Kazakhstan", in *Development and Modern Industrial Policy in Practice: Issues and Country Experiences*, J. Felipe (ed.), Edward Elgar and Asian Development Bank, Cheltenham and Manila.

Felipe, J. and C. Rhee (2013), *Report to the Government of Kazakhstan: Policies for Industrial and Service Diversification in Asia in the 21st Century*, Asian Development Bank, October.

Forde, B. (2016), "How the blockchain will enable self-service government", *The Wired World in 2016*, 5 January 2016, accessed 9 February 2016, *www.wired.co.uk/news/archive/2016-01/05/blockchain-is-the-new-signature.*

Frankel, J.A. (2013) "Exchange rate and monetary policy for Kazakhstan in light of resource exports", mimeo, John F. Kennedy School of Government, Harvard University, Cambridge, Mass.

Frankel, J.A. (2012), "The natural resource curse: A survey of diagnoses and some prescriptions", *HKS Faculty Research Working Paper* RWP12-014, John F. Kennedy School of Government, Harvard University, Cambridge, Mass.

Government of the Republic of Kazakhstan (2014), "Program of Geological Exploration in the Republic of Kazakhstan 2015-2019".

Government of the Republic of Kazakhstan (2013), "On approval of the Concept of Industrial and Innovation Development of the Republic of Kazakhstan for 2015-2019", Resolution of the Government of the Republic of Kazakhstan dated December 31, 2013 No 1497.

Hausmann, R. and R. Rigobon (2002), "An alternative interpretation of the 'resource curse': Theory and policy implications", *National Bureau of Economic Research Working Paper* 9424, NBER, Cambridge, Mass.

Hausmann, R. et al. (2014), *The Atlas of Economic Complexity: Mapping paths to prosperity*, Harvard University and MIT.

IEA (2015a), Statistics, Kazakhstan Oil for 2013, *www.iea.org/statistics/*, accessed on 11-01-16.

IEA (2015b), IEA Energy Atlas, *http://energyatlas.iea.org/*, accessed on 11-01-16.

IEA (2015c), IEA World Energy Outlook Fuel subsidies database. *http://www.worldenergyoutlook.org/resources/energysubsidies/fossilfuelsubsidydatabase/*.

IEA (2014), "Kazakhstan energy policy review", *Eastern Europe, Caucus and Central Asia Energy Reviews*, International Energy Agency, Paris.

Imbs, J. and R. Wacziarg (2003), "Stages of diversification", *American Economic Review*, Vol 93(1).

IMF (2014), "Article IV consultation staff report", International Monetary Fund, Washington, DC, *https://www.imf.org/external/pubs/ft/scr/2014/cr14242.pdf*.

International Comparative Legal Guides (ICLG) (2015), *Oil & Gas Regulation 2015: Kazakhstan*, International Comparative Legal Guides, *www.iclg.co.uk/*.

ITU (2014), ITU World Telecommunication/ICT Indicators Database 2014, International Telecommunications Union, Geneva.

KIDI (2015a), *Steel Industry of Republic of Kazakhstan*, Kazakhstan Industry Development Institute, Astana.

KIDI (2015b), "Итоги ГПФИИР РК на 2010-2014 годы" [Conclusions on SPAIID in Republic of Kazakhstan for 2010-2014 years], "Kazakhstan Industry Development Institute" JSC, Astana, *http://kidi.gov.kz/docs/otchety/1493134.pdf* (accessed 26 October 2016).

Klinger, B. and D. Lederman (2004), "Discovery and development : An empirical exploration of 'new' products", *World Bank Policy Research Paper* No. 3450, World Bank, Washington, DC.

Lederman, D. and W. F. Maloney (2008), "In search of the missing resource curse", *Economía, Journal of the Latin American and Caribbean Economic Association*, Vol 9(1), pp. 1-57.

Lee, Dmitry (2015), "Kazakhstan considers building fourth oil refinery in Mangistau region", Astana Times, *http://astanatimes.com/2015/08/kazakhstan-considers-building-fourth-oil-refinery-in-mangistau-region/, accessed* 4-11-15

Ministry of Investment and Development of the Republic of Kazakhstan (MID) (2016), "Within realization of the second five-year industrialization 8 sectors in 5 fields will be of higher priority", posted 19 July 2016. *www.mid.gov.kz/en/news/within-realization-second-five-year-industrialization-8-sectors-5-fields-will-be-higher*.

Ministry of Investment and Development of the Republic of Kazakhstan (MID) (2015), "The company 'Rio Tinto' explores new investment opportunities in exploration projects of Kazakhstan", Ministry for Investment and Development Kazakhstan – Committee of Geology and Subsoil Use *http://geology.gov.kz/en/news/1018-kompaniya-rio-tinto-izuchaet-novye-vozmozhnosti-investirovaniya-v-geologorazvedochnye-proekty-kazakhstana*.

Ministry of National Economy of the Republic of Kazakhstan (MNE) (2015) "Справка по итогам оценки 5 лет хода реализации ГПФИИР",*[Evaluation of the implementation of 5 years of SPAIID] manuscript, a summary is available at: http://economy.gov.kz/ru/ministerstvo/detail.php?ELEMENT_ID=67612*.

Ministry of Finance of the Republic of Kazakhstan (2014), *The Report of the Minister of Finance of the Republic of Kazakhstan at the presentation of the Republic of Kazakhstan government's report on execution of the republican budget for 2014 in the Parliament of the Republic of Kazakhstan*, the Ministry of Finance of the Republic of Kazakhstan, Astana, *http://www.minfin.gov.kz/*.

Ministry of Finance of the Republic of Kazakhstan (2014), *Explanatory notes to the Report of the government of RoK on Republican budget execution for 2014*, the Ministry of Finance of the Republic of Kazakhstan, Astana, *http://www.minfin.gov.kz/*.

Ministry of Finance of the Republic of Kazakhstan (2013), *The Report of the Minister of Finance of the Republic of Kazakhstan at the presentation of the Republic of Kazakhstan government's report on execution of the republican budget for 2013 in the Parliament of the Republic of Kazakhstan*, the Ministry of Finance of the Republic of Kazakhstan, Astana, *http://www.minfin.gov.kz/*.

Ministry of Finance of the Republic of Kazakhstan (2013), *Explanatory notes to the Report of the government of RoK on Republican budget execution for 2013*, the Ministry of Finance of the Republic of Kazakhstan, Astana, *http://www.minfin.gov.kz/*.

Ministry of Finance of the Republic of Kazakhstan (MOF) (2012), Доклад министра финансов РК на презентации отчета Правительства Республики Казахстан об исполнении республиканского бюджета за 2012 год в Парламенте РК [*The report of the Minister of Finance of the Republic of Kazakhstan at the presentation of the Republic of Kazakhstan government's report on execution of the Republican budget for 2012 in the Parliament of the Republic of Kazakhstan*], the Ministry of Finance of the Republic of Kazakhstan, Astana, *http://www.minfin.gov.kz/*.

Ministry of Finance of the Republic of Kazakhstan (2012), *Explanatory notes to the report of the government of RoK on Republican budget execution for 2012*, the Ministry of Finance of the Republic of Kazakhstan, Astana, *http://www.minfin.gov.kz/*.

Nazarbayev, N. (2014), "Kazakhstan's way – 2050: common aim, common interests, common future", *Address of the President of the Republic of Kazakhstan N. Nazarbayev to the nation*, January 17, *http://www.akorda.kz/en/speeches/*.

Nurshayeva, R and M.Gordeyeva (2015), "Kazakhstan may cut 2016 oil output if prices fall further", Reuters, *http://www.reuters.com/article/2015/09/09/kazakhstan-oil-forecast-idUSL5N11F1OH20150909#63Gf7SDpPWYFUW0j.97*, accessed 5-11-15.

OECD (2016a), *Multi-dimensional Review of Kazakhstan: Volume 1, Initial assessment*, OECD Development Pathways, OECD Publishing, Paris, *http://dx.doi.org/10.1787/9789264246768-en*.

OECD (2014), *Regulatory Policy in Kazakhstan: Towards Improved Implementation*, OECD Publishing, *http://dx.doi.org/10.1787/9789264214255-en*.

OECD (2013), "Energy subsidies and climate change in Kazakhstan", Taskforce for the Implementation of the Environmental Action Program for Central and Eastern Europe, Caucasus and Central Asia, *www.oecd.org/env/outreach/Energy subsidies and climate change in Kazakhstan.pdf*.

OECD (2012), "Promoting energy efficiency in the residential sector in Kazakhstan: Designing a public investment programme", Taskforce for the Implementation of the Environmental Action Program for Central and Eastern Europe, Caucasus and Central Asia *http://www.oecd.org/env/outreach/KAZ report_programme design_ENG_web version.pdf*.

OECD (2011), *Competitiveness and Private Sector Development: Kazakhstan 2010 — Sector Competitiveness Strategy*, OECD Publishing. *http://dx.doi.org/10.1787/9789264089792-en*.

OECD (forthcoming)a, *Investment Policy Review of Kazakhstan*, OECD Publishing, Paris.

OECD (forthcoming)b, *Innovation Policy Review of Kazakhstan*, OECD Publishing, Paris.

OECD (forthcoming)c, Comparative analysis on the performance of stabilisation funds and investment options, DEV/GB(2015)15/REV1, OECD Development Centre, Paris.

OECD/IEA/NEA/ITF (2015), *Aligning Policies for a Low-Carbon Economy*, OECD Publishing, Paris. *http://www.oecd-ilibrary.org/environment/aligning-policies-for-a-low-carbon-economy_9789264233294-en*.

Oil and Gas Journal (OGJ) (2015), "Kazakhstan advances refinery modernisation program", Oil & Gas Journal, *http://www.ogj.com/articles/2015/01/kazakhstan-advances-refinery-modernization-program.html*, accessed 4-11-15.

Prisco, G. (2015), "Estonian Government Partners with Bitnation to Offer Blockchain Notarization Services to e-Residents", *Bitcoin Magazine*, 30 November 2015, accessed 9 February 2016, *https://bitcoinmagazine.com/articles/estonian-government-partners-with-bitnation-to-offer-blockchain-notarization-services-to-e-residents-1448915243*.

Reuters (2016). "Kazakhstan cuts growth, oil output forecasts in budget review", Thompson Reuters, available at: *http://www.reuters.com/article/kazakhstan-economy-idUSL3N1623NM*.

Rieländer, J. and B. Traoré (2016) "Explaining diversification in exports across higher manufacturing content: What is the role of commodities?" *Journal of International Commerce, Economics and Policy*, Vol. 7(2).

RFE (2015), "Oil exporter Kazakhstan forced to revise budget" Radio Free Europe/Radio Liberty, *http://www.rferl.org/content/kazakhstan-budget-revise-oil-production-economy/26798409.html*, accessed 29-10-15

Sondergaard, L. and M. Murthi (2012) *Skills, Not Just Diplomas: Managing Education for Results in Eastern Europe and Central Asia*, World Bank, Washington, DC.

Sorbello, Paolo (2015), "Kazakhstan: Kashagan hopes are up". *The Diplomat*, *http://thediplomat.com/2015/06/kazakhstan-kashagan-hopes-are-up/* accessed 4-11-15.

The Economist (2015), "The great chain of being sure about things", *The Economist*, 31 October 2015, accessed 9 February 2016, *http://www.economist.com/news/briefing/21677228-technology-behind-bitcoin-lets-people-who-do-not-know-or-trust-each-other-build-dependable*.

United Nations (2016), UN COMTRADE (database), *http://comtrade.un.org, accessed July 2016*.

UNCTAD (2016), "Merchandise: Concentration and diversification indices of exports and imports by country, annual, 1995-2014", *http://unctadstat.unctad.org/* , accessed on 08-04-16.

UNIDO (2015), INDSTAT4 Industrial Statistics database, 2015 edition, United Nations Industrial Development Organization, Geneva. *www.unido.org/resources/statistics/statistical-databases/indstat4-2015-edition.html.*

UNIDO (2013), *Industrial Development Report 2013: Sustaining Employment Growth : The Role of Manufacturing and Structural Change*, United Nations Industrial Development Organization, Geneva.

US Energy Information Administration EIA (2015a), International Energy Statistics, *http://www.eia.gov/beta/international/*, accessed 28-10-15.

World Bank (2015), World Bank Open Data, *http://data.worldbank.org/?display=default*, accessed 29-10-15.

World Bank (2014), "Asia - Increasing domestic procurement by the mining sector in Central Asia", World Bank Group, Washington, DC.

World Bank (2013), *Beyond Oil: Kazakhstan's Path to Greater Prosperity through Diversifying*, Kazakhstan Country Economic Memorandum, World Bank, Washington, DC, June. Available at: *https://openknowledge.worldbank.org/handle/10986/16720.*

World Bank (2011), *The Changing Wealth of Nations: Measuring Sustainable Development in the New Millennium*, World Bank, Washington, DC.

World Trade Organization (2015), "Overview of Kazakhstan's Commitments", World Trade Organization, *www.wto.org/english/news_e/news15_e/kazakhannex_e.pdf* , accessed on 07-03-16.

Multi-dimensional Review of Kazakhstan
Volume 2. In-depth Analysis and Recommendations

Chapter 3

Mobilising financing to transform Kazakhstan's economy

Kazakhstan's financial sector is unusually shallow. No comparable country achieves income levels higher than Kazakhstan with a pool of deposits and credit of such little depth. Kazakhstan's entrepreneurs cite access to finance among their major obstacles to investment, especially newer or smaller firms, while larger firms circumvent the domestic financial system by tapping international sources. Domestic securities markets are anaemic, but this is unlikely to significantly slow economic transformation. This chapter describes how the availability of domestic finance is constrained by the limited pool of domestic investable funds, which can be attributed to both transitory and structural factors that encourage capital outflows. The government's various financing programmes provided some support during the financial crisis, but without generating lasting gains in the availability of credit, either for the sectors targeted or more generally, and weaker oil revenues make them difficult to sustain. A more sustainable response would support banks' access to loanable funds, from international sources and by strengthening the institutional infrastructural surrounding the financial sector to encourage domestic savings. The shift to an inflation-targeting monetary policy regime in 2015 and the development of the Astana International Financial Centre will help achieve these objectives if domestic institutions governing the financial sector are also strengthened.

The Kazakhstani financial sector needs to expand and deepen if it is to fulfil its role of essential enabler of the country's economic transformation. Kazakhstani investors have told researchers that access to finance was an important constraint on investing and doing business, especially for smaller and newer firms (World Bank, 2013). These surveys are corroborated by various macroeconomic indicators of financial sector development and depth, and by supporting anecdotal reports. Yet the Kazakhstan state has made significant efforts to remedy this situation. The government and institutions closely connected with it have embarked on large programmes to support firms' ability to finance their investments. Meanwhile an overhang of bad loans lingering from stresses associated with the 2005-10 global financial boom and subsequent crisis was cleared from the banking system by 2016, and the central bank took important steps to strengthen and clarify the monetary policy regime in 2015. However, cyclical factors have slowed revenue growth for most firms, but these factors are likely to be temporary as Kazakhstan's terms of trade and the value of the tenge stabilise at lower equilibria. This will create new opportunities and challenges across the economy. This chapter assesses why the financial sector is holding back entrepreneurs' ability to access the financing needed to realise these opportunities, and how policy could improve the situation.

Figure 3.1. **Access to finance is an important constraint for many firms**

Share of respondents citing access to finance as an barrier for the enterprise, and ranking of the barrier among those cited, 2013 enterprise survey

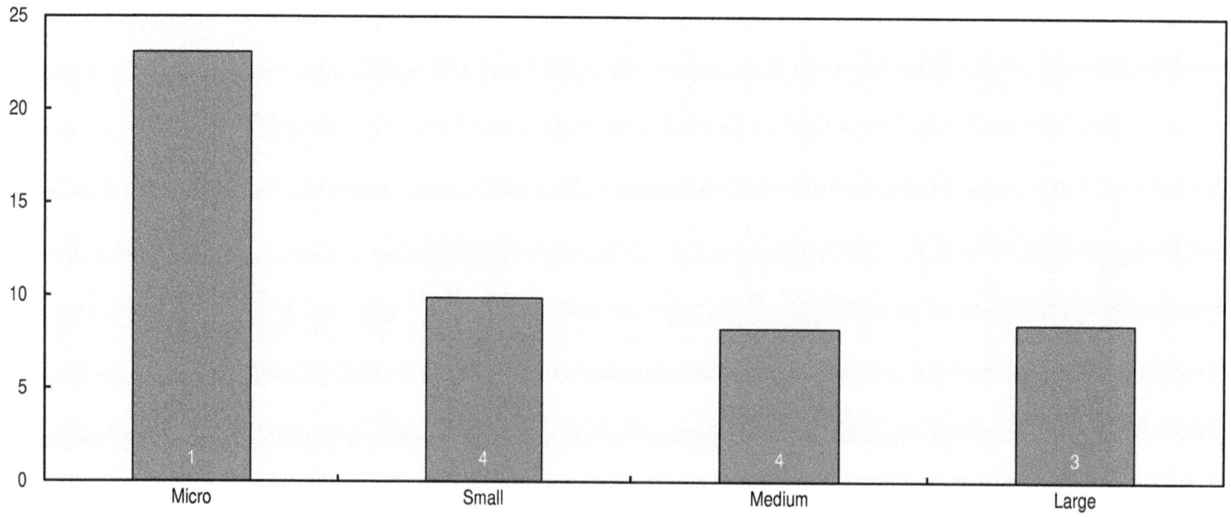

Note: "Micro" enterprises are those with fewer than five employees; "small" firms have between five and 19 employees; "medium" between 20 and 99, and "large" firms are defined as those with more than 100 employees.

Source: World Bank (2013) Enterprise Survey and authors' calculations.

StatLink http://dx.doi.org/10.1787/888933445483

A dynamic and deepening financial sector enables economic transformation

A deepening and dynamic financial sector enables faster growth and economic transformation, generates employment and government revenues, and is especially important in countries around Kazakhstan's stage of development. The important role of a deepening financial sector in enabling growth has been consistently found across nearly a quarter-century of research. Constrained access to finance slows output growth, and the effect is stronger than other frequently-cited constraints to investment, according to cross-country firm-level evidence (Paşalı, 2013). Access to finance is associated with innovation and job creation (World Bank, 2014). These effects appear to be particularly strong in lower and middle-income countries, for smaller firms that face greater constraints in accessing finance, and as an unusually undersized financial sector grows towards typical sizes. These overall macroeconomic effects of a deepening financial sector can be even stronger at the microeconomic level. For example, the entry of banks that are adapted to the needs of a specific sector or group of firms, such as agriculture firms or businesses operating informally, can significantly support the development of those firms, and hence of their employees and the larger sector. These microeconomic effects can be significant but are often not recorded by macroeconomic indicators.

A dynamic financial sector provides services that raise households' well-being. Access to savings and payments facilities improves welfare, especially for poorer households (World Bank, 2014). It allows households to maintain consumption through income shocks, such as an illness or a loss of business. It also provides products that help households manage short-term spending pressures to realise long-term investments. Social insurance and retirement savings facilities can improve the responsiveness of the labour market to evolving opportunities and its ability to absorb shocks. Having a form of guaranteed income reduces the risk for workers of shifting to new employers in expanding sectors, for example from unemployment if a start-up fails. While compulsory social insurance schemes may serve this purpose, they are often supplemented by private schemes, especially where the formal social protection system is weak or incomplete. These savings products can better mobilise households' savings for investment by firms, generating a virtuous circle. Indeed, some work suggests that financial sector development disproportionately benefits poorer households, who suffer more from information asymmetries limiting access to financing for specific projects and are less able to raise the lack the collateral required by banks, restricting the exploitation of investment opportunities (Zhuang et al., 2009).

A well-functioning financial sector is also essential to realise evolving opportunities across the economy, and can also help mitigate "Dutch disease" effects. The global commodity cycle means that countries such as Kazakhstan experience large shifts in relative returns between sectors over time. The scale and speed of these swings make it essential that the sectors offering the greatest potential returns at a given time are able to access nimble financing, while that financing offers a term structure that will outlast weaker periods. More sophisticated and better managed financial sectors can help this process, while smoothing fluctuations in the overall economy over the commodity cycle (IMF, 2015b). For example, large commodity production facilities are often self-financing (through credit secured by export contracts) or financed through foreign direct investment (FDI). These investments often surge during periods of rising commodity prices, and then come to a halt as commodity prices weaken. By contrast, the domestic non-tradeable and non-resource sectors are generally more reliant on domestic banks and financial institutions to finance investments and operations. If the domestic financial sector is not robust and operating effectively, these investments will not occur and opportunities will be lost, both to exploit high returns while resource prices are high or new-founded competitiveness in non-resource sectors when commodity prices retreat.

Conversely, a thin and poorly functioning financial sector can amplify the variations in external conditions, as Kazakhstan's has done over the past two decades. A poorly regulated and thin financial sector tends to be more sensitive to swings in commodity prices and other external factors, and amplifies their effects on the larger economy. Their operations are less efficient at transforming domestic savings into assets (loans), and are more reliant on wholesale funding that tends to be highly pro-cyclical, expanding strongly while conditions are supportive then coming to a sudden stop when conditions and perceptions deteriorate. At the same time, weaker internal management means that poorer assessments are made of the quality of loans, with the result that while credit is readily available during strong periods, much of it is allocated less efficiently, with a lower share converted to investment and that investment less efficiently generating additional production. When conditions deteriorate these loans are more likely to become distressed, generating greater losses of capital and sharper retrenchments in lending activity, including for assets (Kinda et al, 2016).

Box 3.1. **An alternative scenario – how a stronger financial sector might have helped protect Kazakhstan's entrepreneurs from the shocks of the 2000s**

During the 2000s bank lending in Kazakhstan accelerated and loan quality declined. Much of the additional lending was for construction and property investments, and many projects proved to be unsustainable when economic conditions and banks' access to international wholesale funds deteriorated with the global financial crisis. Growth in the stock of outstanding credit far outpaced new investment, and the efficiency of that investment appears to have declined, as indicated by the increase in total production relative to the volume of investment.* As the quality of their loan books and access to funding fell, banks cut their lending to private businesses in real terms over the following years. Weaker bank lending translated into more sluggish investment in the non-resource sector, slowing overall growth and diversification of the Kazakhstan economy, as compared with a scenario in which banks were able to manage a more consistent growth in lending.

An alternative scenario makes it possible to assess how the overall economy might have evolved if growth in credit to the private sector had been more consistent through the early 2000s to the mid-2010s. A plausible scenario would see the ratio of credit to the private sector grow at a constant rate sufficient to reduce the gap between Kazakhstan and the average of countries near its income level. At the same time, the ratio of the stock of outstanding credit to investment, and the transformation of investment into production, would both be expected to have declined by less than they in fact did over this period. The result would be somewhat weaker investment and activity during the boom years before the global financial crisis, but stronger lending, investment and activity during the years after, such that gross domestic product (GDP) growth would be less volatile and by 2015 GDP could be higher and more diversified than was realised.

While this scenario is highly speculative, it helps illustrates the long-term cost of a more volatile and less well-managed financial sector. Once balance sheets were stabilised after the 2008-10 crisis, Kazakhstan's commercial banks generally focused on strengthening their internal systems and capacity, through mergers and investments. Prudential regulatory capacity also strengthened.

Box 3.1. **An alternative scenario – how a stronger financial sector might have helped protect Kazakhstan's entrepreneurs from the shocks of the 2000s** *(cont.)*

Figure 3.2. **Private sector credit could have followed a smoother path**

Outstanding real private sector credit, tenge trillions

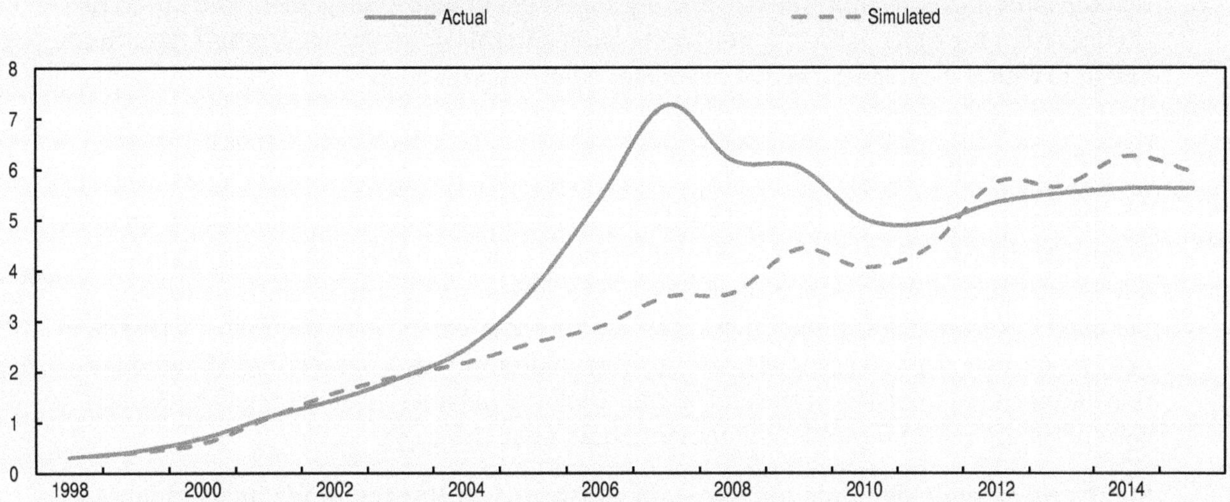

Note: 2007 real tenge, deflated by the GDP deflator.
Source: IMF International Financial Statistics, authors' calculations and simulations.

StatLink http://dx.doi.org/10.1787/888933445493

Figure 3.3. **Growth in investment would have been more sustained**

Annual real investment, tenge trillions

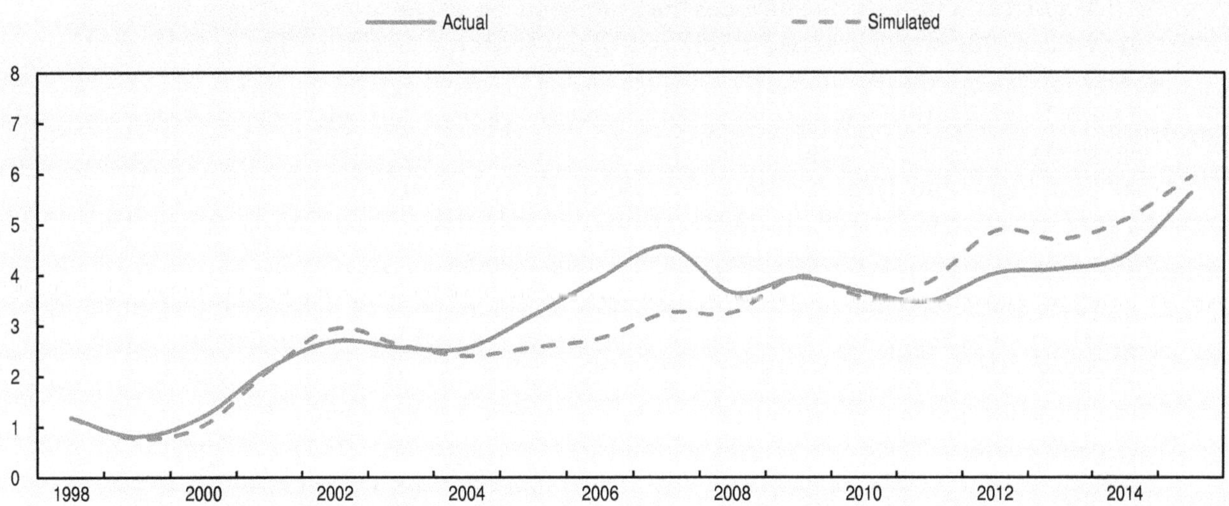

Note: 2007 real tenge, deflated by the GDP deflator.
Source: IMF International Financial Statistics, authors' calculations and simulations.

StatLink http://dx.doi.org/10.1787/888933445508

* This is the "incremental capital-output ratio" or ICOR.

The quality of the financial sector's performance is shown by whether Kazakhstan's real economy can effectively access financial services, rather than whether the financial sector is converging towards a preferred structure. There are common trends in how the structure of the financial sector evolves as economies become more sophisticated. These trends, and where Kazakhstan fits among then, can identify where improving access to finance may bring the greatest gains and highlight the obstacles to achieving these. These trends are described below. However there are also significant variations between economies around those trends. These variations reflect differences in the structure of the economy, as well as each country's history and institutions. Thus, the key indicator is how well firms across the real economy can efficiently and sustainably access credit, risk management and liquidity services from the financial sector built on healthy and robust institutions, rather than the extent to which the financial sector resembles a particular model.[1]

After strong but short-lived expansion, Kazakhstan's financial sector remains undersized and lacks resources

Banks are central to providing finance for development in Kazakhstan, as they are in other countries near and above Kazakhstan's level of economic development. Banks are the dominant source of finance for private sector enterprises, and this financing is increasingly provided in tenge. Investments in businesses dominate banks' loan portfolios. Loans to private non-financial corporations made up three-quarters of banks' assets in 2015, although this had declined from 82% at the end of 2009. Deposits in banks, in both tenge and foreign currencies, are most households' dominant liquid financial asset.

Shortages of lendable funds are the main constraint on Kazakhstan's increasingly efficient financial sector

Kazakhstan's banking sector is shallow for a country at its income levels, across a range of measures. In absolute terms, the size of Kazakhstan's financial sector is ranked mid-range at about 50th globally. But it is undersized relative to the size of Kazakhstan's economy or income levels. The broadest indicator of financial depth is liquid liabilities as a percentage of GDP, given that the measure includes the balance sheets of banks and non-bank financial institutions (NBFIs) and is scaled by the size of the economy. At 30% of GDP in 2014, only two countries have achieved higher incomes with a financial system shallower than that of Kazakhstan, and both have important oil extraction sectors (namely, Gabon and Mexico; Venezuela has a slightly larger financial sector).[2] The path of Kazakhstan's financial sector has been highly pro-cyclical, with a period of rapid and unsustained growth supported by external economic conditions being followed by a contraction that coincided with less supportive external conditions (discussed in detailed below).

Credit to the private sector from banks is limited. Credit to the private sector in Kazakhstan was 36% of GDP at the end of 2014, compared with a peak immediately before Kazakhstan's banking crisis of 57% of GDP. The current rate is one of the lowest rates among middle and higher-income countries, and reflects a range of factors, including less supportive external conditions. Again, all countries that had achieved higher incomes than Kazakhstan with smaller provision of credit had important commodity extraction sectors, with the exception of Romania. This variable is the standard indicator in analyses of the relationship between finance and growth – countries with higher levels of private credit have been shown to grow faster and experience faster rates of poverty reduction.

Other indicators confirm the undersupply of credit in Kazakhstan, despite efforts by the regulator, rather than low credit growth reflecting limited demand. The number of Kazakhstani firms reporting the need for a loan is typical (nearly half in 2013, which is at the average across countries accounting for income levels). However, fewer than 20% of firms were able to access bank loans (2013 data) for investment or working capital, although they may be better able to access other forms of credit. The only middle and high-income countries where businesses were less likely to have a bank loan were Latvia and Hungary.

Figure 3.4. **Few countries have achieved higher incomes with as shallow a financial sector as Kazakhstan**

Liquid liabilities of banks and non-bank financial institutions relative to GDP, and income per capita (log scale)

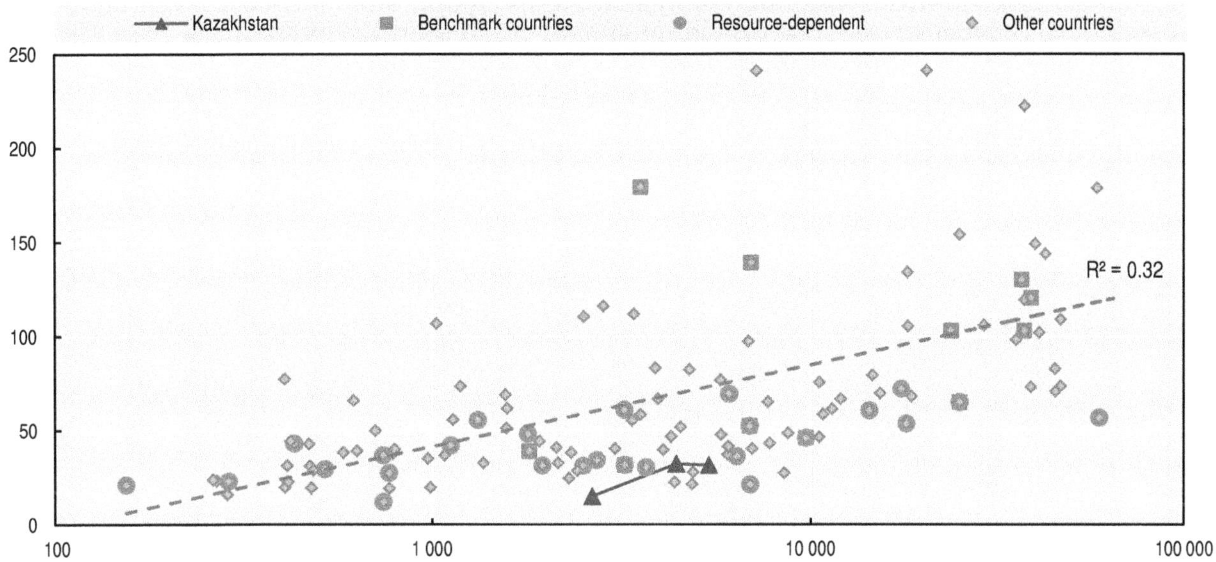

Note: Data are reported for 2013, except Kazakhstan, which is reported for 2001, 2007 and 2013. GDP per capita is in constant 2005 USD. Countries classified as "resource-dependent" are those with total natural resource rents greater than 15% of GDP in 2015.

Source: World Bank Global Financial Development database, 2015.

StatLink http://dx.doi.org/10.1787/888933445513

Bank credit is largely directed at domestically focused sectors. Loans orientated towards consumer sectors (loans to households, and to trade and selected services sectors) constituted almost three-quarters of loans outstanding in late 2015. Energy and extractives rely primarily on foreign financing, while construction and real estate sectors relied on wholesale foreign funding until it became scarce as the global financial crisis started in late 2007.

The domestic financial system suffers from limited resources. Deposits in the financial system are low relative to Kazakhstan's GDP and income levels, indicating that there are unusually limited domestic resources available for lending by banks. Sources of these deposits appear to be unusually concentrated: one-third of corporate deposits in banks are attributed to the national wealth fund, Samruk Kazyna Operations, reflecting its oversized role in the economy (IMF, 2013), while businesses hold about 60% of total deposits. Economic agents' reluctance to hold deposits in the domestic banking system may reflect negative real interest rates and expectations of a depreciation of the tenge. They occur despite moderate levels of deposit guarantees and despite the fact that depositors did not suffer losses from the 2009-10 crisis.

Banks seem to be stretching deposits as far as they can. Bank credit was 127% of bank deposits in 2013, higher than in most other countries especially among those near Kazakhstan's level of development. This ratio indicates the extent to which banks are effectively intermediating between savers and investors, and is generally positively correlated with other indicators of financial sector development. An indicator significantly above 1 suggests that resources other than deposits are funding a significant share of bank lending. These other sources can generate instability in banks' operations if they become unreliable, as banks from Kazakhstan and many other countries experienced during the global financial crisis. For Kazakhstan, this risk particularly relates to the use of offshore securities markets to finance domestic lending.

Figure 3.5. **Few countries and none of Kazakhstan's comparators have achieved higher incomes without providing greater credit than Kazakhstan**

Private credit by banks and other financial institutions to GDP, and income per capita (log scale)

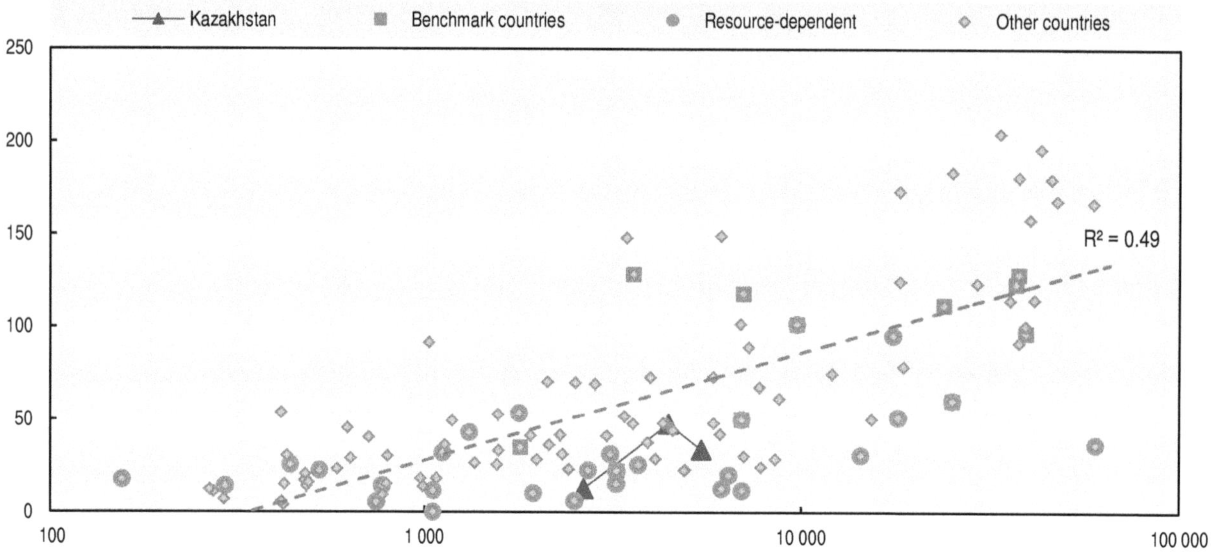

Note: Data are reported for 2013, except Kazakhstan, which is reported for 2001, 2007 and 2013. GDP per capita is in constant 2005 USD. Countries classified as "resource-dependent" are those with total natural resource rents greater than 15% of GDP in 2015.

Sources: World Bank Global Finance Development Database 2015.

StatLink http://dx.doi.org/10.1787/888933445529

Adding to banks' challenges are cyclical pressures of currency mismatching, but these are likely to abate as conditions stabilise and depositors become more willing to hold tenge. The fundamental determinants of the tenge's value weakened substantially between 2014 and 2016. These include the price of Kazakhstan's oil and other commodity exports and the inflow of foreign investment. In response, the NBK is allowing the tenge to depreciate, and is focusing instead on inflation control and economic stability (see Box 3.3). Anticipating future weakening of the tenge, depositors have sought to shift deposits from tenge into foreign currency, especially USD.[3] This currency mismatch represents an additional challenge for banks, as the foreign currency deposits represent a growing liability relative to the static value of the tenge asset. Banks approximately balanced tenge and foreign currency loans and deposits up to 2014, but as uncertainty grew around the exchange rate's peg, banks found that the balance of their deposits was in foreign currency and of their loans was in tenge. The central bank has helped banks manage this currency mismatch and risks by selling foreign currency repurchase (repo) agreements, as well as using its foreign reserves to ensure foreign currency remains liquid in the domestic market. As the tenge reaches a new equilibrium, the currency speculation advantage for depositors should abate and banks should have less difficulty in attracting and retaining tenge deposits.

Figure 3.6. **During periods of tenge depreciation, banks are challenged by growing preferences of depositors for foreign currency and borrowers for tenge loans**

Tenge millions and KZT per USD

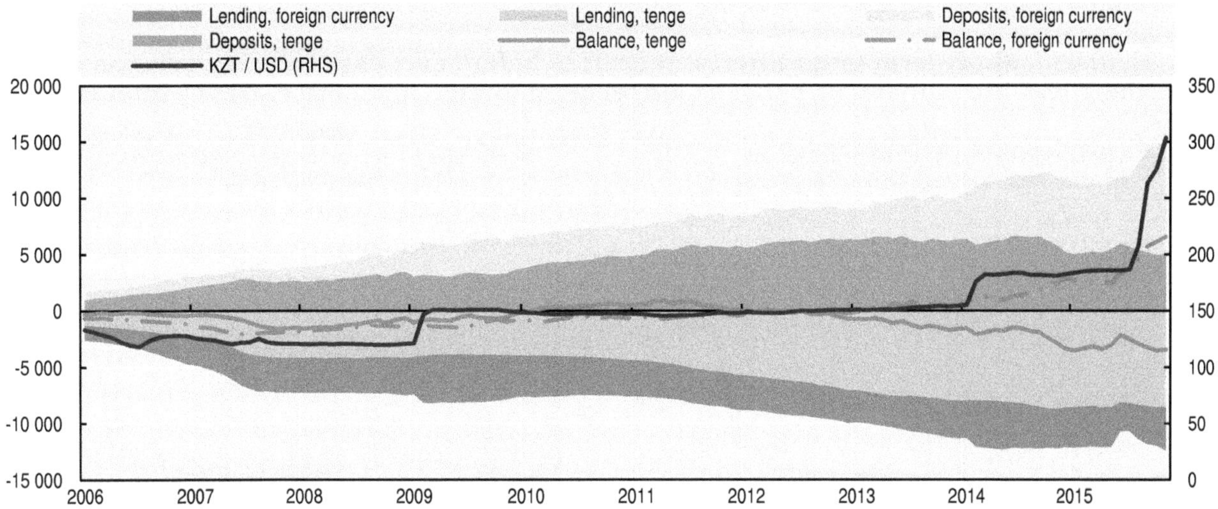

Sources: NBK Statistical Bulletin (2016); World Bank Global Economic Indicators (2016); authors' calculations.

StatLink http://dx.doi.org/10.1787/888933445534

Banks appear to be allocating scarce credit by rationing rather than adjusting the cost of funds

Lending interest rates are modest and do not appear to reflect a shortage of loanable funds, with short-term rates driven largely by exchange rate management goals. The cost of borrowing for Kazakhstani firms fell following the financial crisis and has since been modest after accounting for domestic inflation. Interest rates paid by a firm on a five-year tenge loan averaged 10.6% between 2011 and 2015, compared with average inflation of 8.1% over those years. If the firm had instead borrowed the funds in Kazakhstan but in foreign currency, it would have saved little interest, with interest rates averaging around 9.5% on convertible currency loans. This rate contrasts with exceptionally low global interest rates during this period, for example at 0.77% on one-year USD London Interbank Offered Rate (LIBOR). Short-term tenge loan rates rose when pressure for the exchange rate to depreciate was building, then retreated as the exchange rate was allowed to move towards a new equilibrium. Longer-term rates appear less responsive to these short-term pressures. Deposit and lending rates appear to be remarkably disconnected. This may reflect factors including the reliance on foreign funding to finance additional lending. Between 2009 and 2011, following the financial crisis and reduced access to international sources of funds, rates paid by banks on longer-term deposits rose while those paid by borrowers declined. Rates on demand deposits gradually declined in the years to late 2012, before moving around two percentage points higher, to between 3% and 3.5%, although this remained strongly negative in real terms.

Movements in interest rates appear to be at most of secondary importance for deposit and lending flows. Interest returns appear to not be a driving factor in determining deposit decisions, especially given that tenge deposit interest rates have consistently been well below inflation rates. However, NBK's statistical analysis does suggest that movements in deposit interest rates do statistically lead growth in deposits, despite real deposit rates being negative. Further, temporary outflows of deposits from the banking system can induce liquidity pressures for banks, leading to spikes in short-term interest rates in the inter-bank market. Nonetheless, negative long-term real yields on deposits are likely to be an ongoing constraint on attracting funds into the domestic financial system.

Figure 3.7. **Short-term tenge interest rates rose before exchange rate depreciations, while there was little difference between longer-term foreign and local currency interest rates**

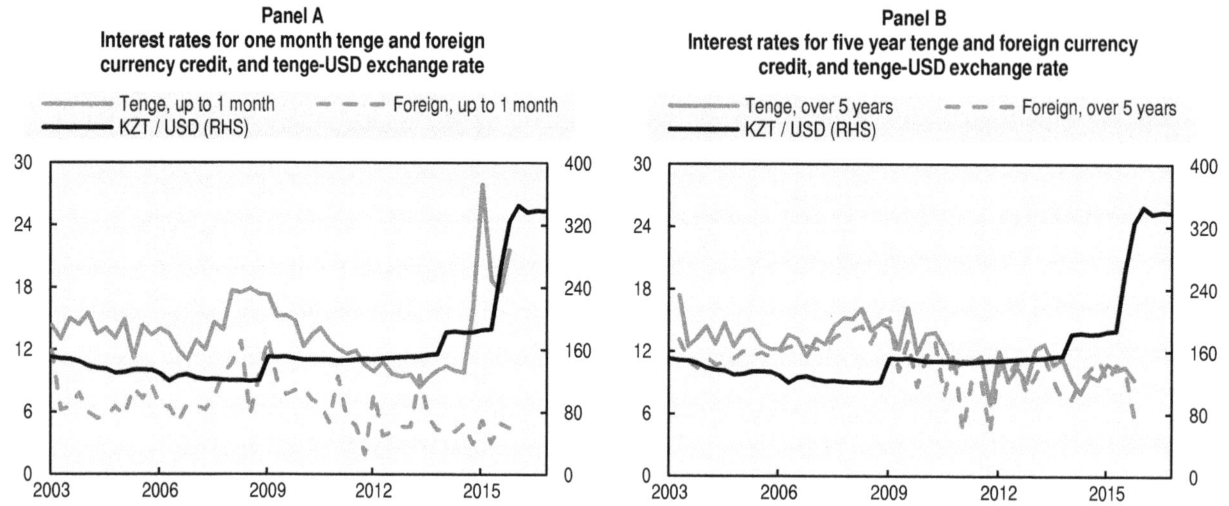

Source: NBK Statistical Bulletin (2016) and World Bank Global Economic Monitor (2016b).

StatLink http://dx.doi.org/10.1787/888933445541

Collateral requirements are not atypical, also suggesting that banks are rationing credit rather than pricing it beyond firms' capacity to pay. Another means of increasing the cost of borrowing is very high collateral requirements, which requires firms to have more capital guaranteeing the loan, and reducing the cost of non-payment for the bank. However in Kazakhstan both the share of loans requiring collateral, and the value of that collateral relative to the amount lent, are only modestly higher than global averages. Nonetheless firms' limited asset bases makes even these modest collateral requirements a challenge to meet, particularly for SMEs (OECD, 2013).

The banking system's poor performance appears not to be attributable to its structure or efficiency

The structure and reach of the banking sector appear to be typical. The apparent competition structure of Kazakhstan's banking sector is not markedly unusual. Over 30 banks operated in Kazakhstan at the end of 2015, and the sector was relatively unconcentrated. For example, in 2012 the three largest banks held less than half of the banking system's total assets – only 14 out of 124 countries had less concentrated banking systems by this metric. Other indicators also suggest that banks have a wide reach – there are more automated teller machines (ATMs) per 100 000 population than in any of the benchmark countries, while debit and credit card penetration rates were only a little below average given income levels in 2011. The NBK, as banking regulator, has sought to ensure that individual sectors of the economy do not become dominated by one or a few banks. Its main instrument for dong this has been its policy on mergers, through which it encourages banks concentrated in a particular sector to merge with banks operating in other sectors. This is intended to make the overall sector more robust by limiting the effects of a sector-specific downturn on any individual bank. However, the efficiency of this strategy is questioned by research suggesting that access to finance improves when banks have deeper knowledge of the needs and characteristics of firms operating in specific sectors, while ensuring that the market is contestable and other banks are able to enter. For example, in many countries a small number of banks specialise in agricultural lending.

The regulator adopted a counter-cyclical approach to capital requirements towards both strengthening banks' balance sheet and supporting ongoing credit availability. After raising minimum capital requirements for banks, in December 2015 the regulator responded to the economic slowdown by abolishing the earlier requirement of an increase in capital, and by including a decrease in the risk-weights on mortgage loans and loans to SMEs.[4] These amendments raised the number of banks with existing capital, so reducing pressure on banks to merge and reducing barriers to entry for new banks. Reducing pressure to merge may also allow banks' management to focus on their ongoing operations.

Banks overall do not appear to be suffering from outstanding inefficiencies, even while they undertake restructuring programmes to improve their operations. Overhead costs and interest margins tend to be correlated with economic and financial sector development. Larger and more dynamic financial sectors operate more competitively with tighter margins and lower costs. Kazakhstan's banks could operate more efficiently if their deposit and lending books were larger. For example, bank interest margins are wider and overhead costs (relative to total assets) are slightly above average for countries near Kazakhstan's income levels. But these indicators have improved over the past 15 years, with most efficiency measures moving towards typical levels. For example, overhead costs fell from over 8% of asset values in 2000 to around 3.3% in 2013, interest margins narrowed, non-interest income fell to a typical share of total income, while bank costs relative to total income fell from above to well below the average of other countries.

Figure 3.8. **Kazakhstan's banks have raised their operational efficiency to international standards, despite being undersized**

Bank overhead costs as a percent of total assets, and income per capita (log scale)

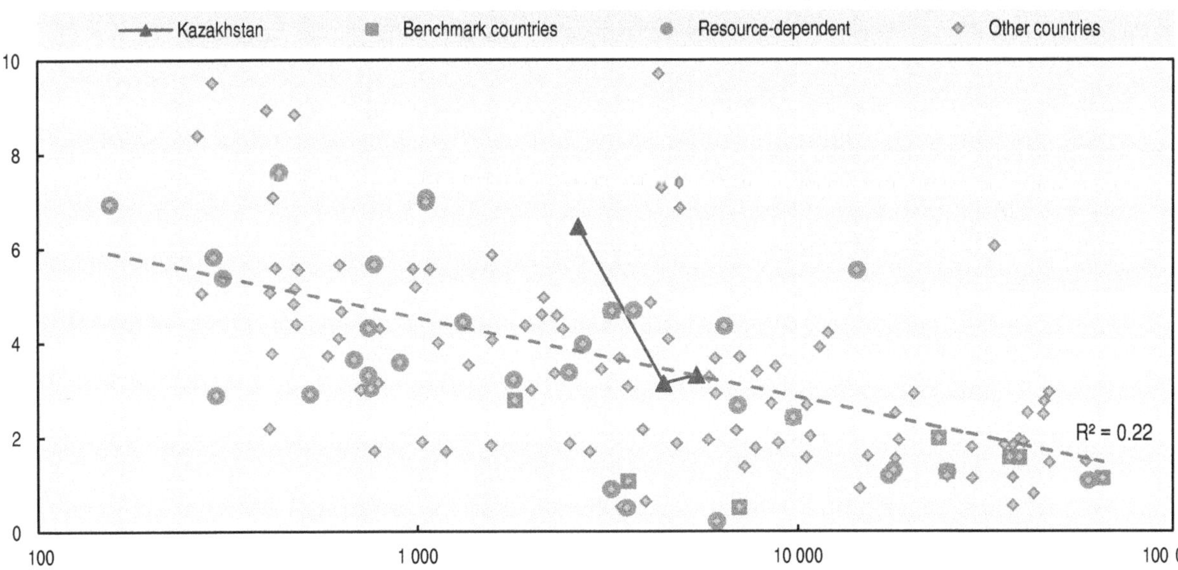

Data are reported for 2013, except Kazakhstan, which is reported for 2001, 2007 and 2013. GDP per capita is in constant 2005 USD. Countries classified as "resource-dependent" are those with total natural resource rents greater than 15% of GDP in 2015.

Source: World Bank, Global Finance Development Database, 2015.

StatLink http://dx.doi.org/10.1787/888933445551

Rapid early growth of bank lending was unsustainable, delaying the sector's development

Once Kazakhstan's economy stabilised in the late 1990s, the banking sector grew quickly, but unsustainably. Kazakhstan's banks rapidly increased lending through the 2000s. Outstanding private credit rose 30-fold from 2000 to its peak ahead of Kazakhstan's banking crisis in 2009, from KZT 280 billon, or 8.4% of GDP, to KZT 8 142 billion, or over 50% of GDP. But this growth in credit far outpaced other aspects of financial deepening. For example, total deposits in the financial system grew strongly, but not as strongly as loans, from 8.7% of GDP in 2000 to peak at 32.1% of GDP in 2009, while growth in the financial system's overall liquid liabilities was more moderate still. Other measures of the presence of the banking system grew more slowly, if at all. For example, there was some increase in the number of adults with a bank account, but the number of bank branches fell. The banking system became somewhat less concentrated over this period.

Easy access to international finance enabled the growth in credit. For example, Kazakhstani financial institutions' exposure to Bank for International Settlements (BIS)-domiciled banks rose from USD 3 billion (KZT 381 billion) at the start of 2005 to a peak of USD 25 billion (KZT 3 015 billion) by the end of 2007. At the same time, other international sources became more willing to lend to Kazakhstani non-financial entities as well as the banking system. Loans from non-resident banks rose from 2.7% of GDP in 2000 to 16.3% of GDP by 2006. In 2007 alone, Kazakhstan's banks absorbed almost USD 10 billion of net additional capital, more than 9% of GDP. These sources of finance were increasingly costly to service. Annual private debt service costs rose 11-fold from just over USD 3 billion in 2002 to almost USD 33 billion in 2008, equivalent to about 25% of GDP.

The assets underlying the banks' offshore-sourced credit became impaired during the global financial crisis, leading to a system-wide banking crisis, although depositors were spared losses. Significant proportions of banks' international borrowing were used to finance credit to highly cyclical sectors, notably property and construction and sectors reliant on oil export revenues. These sectors suffered from the slump in incomes and activity and depreciation in the tenge associated with the 2009 global financial crisis. At the same time as these loans started becoming stressed, banks had difficulty rolling over their international debt, as the surge of international financing to developing countries during previous years came to a sudden stop. The result was a banking crisis that started in 2008 and became systematic by 2010 (Laeven and Valencia, 2012). Non-performing loans rose to 20.9% of the value of outstanding loans in 2010, from 7.1% in 2007, generating total net losses of USD 19.1 billion, and three banks defaulted on their debt. An expanded public guarantee of deposits in mid-2008 stabilised deposits, and the government purchased equity or nationalised a number of banks. Depositors in two banks that collapsed before the global financial crisis did suffer losses, which were partially covered by the Kazakhstan Deposit Insurance Fund, but the fund was not tapped during the 2008-10 banking crisis.

The lingering effects of the banking crisis undermined new lending and development of the financial sector. Banks were less able and less willing to lend, as deposit growth slowed, international sources of funds were more difficult to access, and regulators and bankers became more cautious. Credit outstanding contracted after 2009, falling by as much as KZT 700 billion in nominal terms (or by KZT 4 000 billion in constant 2015 prices) and at the end of 2015 remained below its pre-crisis levels, after accounting for inflation. There was also a rebalancing of lending from construction and trade sectors towards "other" (mostly household or consumer borrowing), agriculture and industry. Liquidity in most other market-based components of the financial sector also plumbed new lows.

Banks' access to international finance was limited. By late 2015 foreign banks' exposure to the Kazakhstani financial system was between one-fifth and one-third of the pre-crisis peaks, depending on the measure. For example, BIS-reporting banks' ultimate exposure to Kazakhstani domestic banks declined from a peak of USD 25 billion in November 2007 to USD 5 billion in August 2015. Meanwhile growth in financing for banks from domestic sources slowed after the crisis. Growth in total deposits held by individuals stalled in the second half of 2008. By 2010 some confidence had been restored in the management of the banking system and growth in deposits resumed but at less than half of its pre-crisis pace (Tumenbayeva, 2013). This boom-bust path has created volatile returns on assets and equity of Kazakhstani banks. While these measures improved after the 2009 crisis, by 2013 Kazakhstan was still among the weaker fifth of countries.[5]

In the mid-2010s the banking system remained vulnerable to a deterioration in conditions. Changes in the tax treatment of non-performing loans (NPLs) impeded their clearance from banks' balance sheets until the tax arrangements were adjusted again in 2014. By late 2015 the legacy bad loans were on a path to resolution, by merging the bad loans into one financial entity and revoking its banking licence. This advanced the Kazakhstani banking system towards the Basel III prudential standards for risk-weighted capital and liquidity. However the banks remained highly exposed to a worsening in their operating environment, particularly linked to oil prices (IMF, 2015a). Dollarisation of deposits and the impact of the depreciation of the tenge on the cash flow of borrowers would generate risks of new pressures on banks' cash flows and increases in non-performing loans. The weakening of oil prices in 2014 reduced the assets of a number of banks below the regulatory minimum, and 2015 testing of the effects of plausibly lower-than-expected oil prices and growth of emerging markets, plus a significant depreciation of the exchange rate suggested that banks responsible for half of the banking system's assets would be short of minimum capital requirements, by the equivalent of 2.5% of GDP.

Figure 3.9. **Lending grew unsustainably fast up to the 2008-10 crisis, then far more gradually over the following years**

(Total credit, KZT trillions)

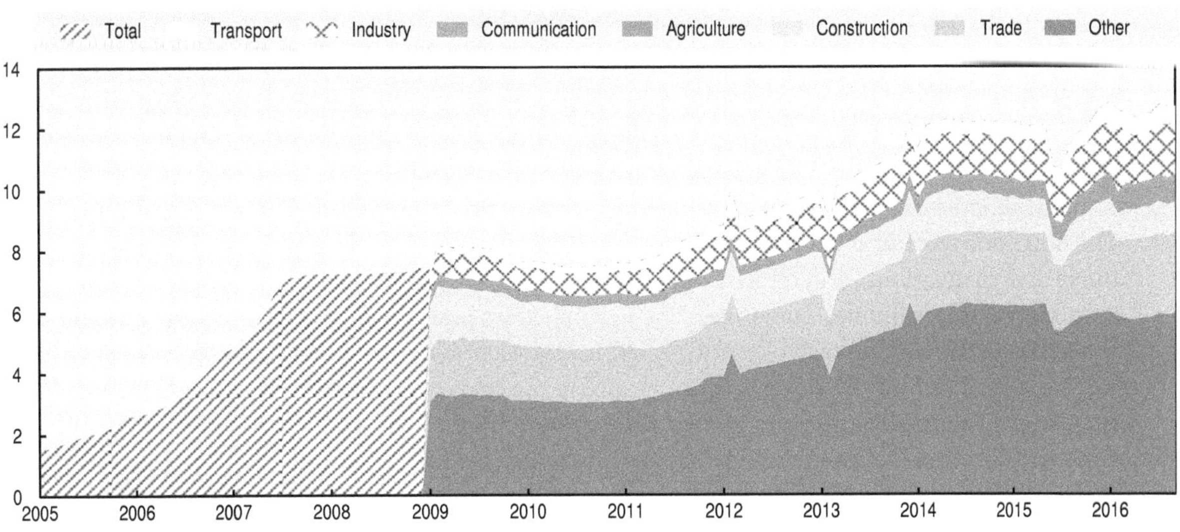

Source: NBK Statistical Bulletin (2016).

StatLink http://dx.doi.org/10.1787/888933445565

Figure 3.10. **Bank lending to small business followed similar trends, with some shifting in lending post-crisis from construction to manufacturing and trade**

Credit to small businesses, KZT billions

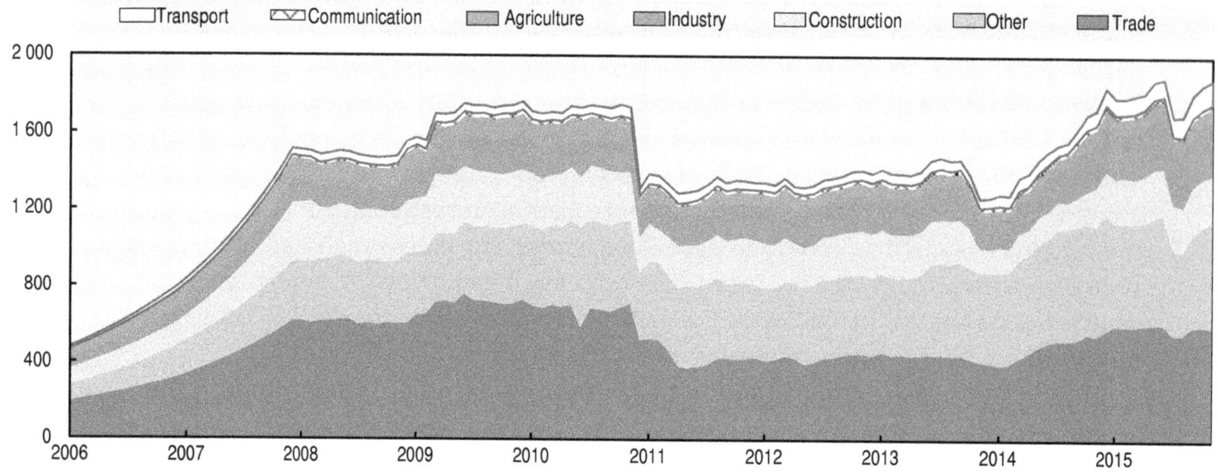

Source: NBK Statistical Bulletin (2016).

StatLink http://dx.doi.org/10.1787/888933445579

The securities markets are also underdeveloped

Kazakhstan's securities markets are illiquid and inactive, but on balance this has limited implications for medium-term economic development objectives. The securities markets are similarly characterised by inactivity, because of the consolidation of pension assets in the single accumulative pension fund and withdrawal from the market of large institutional investors managing the private accumulative pension funds. The connection between the size and turnover of the stock market and economic development is looser and more contested than that with banking credit to the private sector. Various empirical analyses suggest that inactive securities markets may not hold back broader economic development in countries near Kazakhstan's stage of development and economic structure (Demirguc-Kunt et al, 2012). Generally, it appears that stock and securities markets do little to support broader economic development in middle-income countries and those with economies smaller than around USD 500 billion (Demirguc-Kunt et al, 2012; Paşalı, 2013). As economies become larger and richer, the size of securities markets becomes a more important determinant of ongoing economic transformation. They become important financiers of development once an economy has reached the scale and complexity where further growth is enabled by more novel, longer-term investments that employ more intangible inputs, which banks tend to be less effective at financing than securities markets.

Kazakhstan's securities markets are trapped in a low-liquidity, low-activity equilibrium. The domestic stock and bond markets are undermined on both supply and demand sides: by the lack of institutional and retail investors, and by larger Kazakhstani firms' easier access to financing in international exchanges. The few investors prefer to buy and hold assets, rather than trade actively. The lack of institutional investors reduces demand for large issuances. All these factors limit liquidity, further reducing the attractiveness of the markets for new issuances or for purchases, and increase the cost of funds. The bond market receives some support from time to time through issuance by public entities. However, the position of the pension fund as the principal purchaser of securities and its current management by the central bank, which is also seeking to establish a conventional monetary policy framework, generates tensions that may limit the market's effectiveness. The planned shift in the pension fund's management to independent bodies, and the creation of competing fund managers, are likely to improve the functioning of the bond market.

Kazakhstan's securities markets have not been able effectively to mobilise capital for investment. Kazakhstan's stock market was established very early in the country's reform process after independence, and the number of companies listed and the value of their market capitalisation (15% of GDP in 2013) is only a little lower than would be expected for an economy the size of Kazakhstan's. Similarly to the banking system, over the past 15 years the development of Kazakhstan's capital markets has essentially followed an inverted U. Market capitalisation and turnover rose strongly in the early 2000s, peaking around 2007-08, and then declined sharply, and by more than in other countries including other middle-income countries. Today trading in the markets is minimal apart from foreign exchange. Primary issuances are few, while turnover in the secondary market is extremely low – during the first nine months of 2015, each day on average USD 25.6 million was traded across 156 deals.

The domestic bond market is also modestly sized and is just as illiquid as the stock market. During the first nine months of 2015, on average each day USD 23.4 million of bonds were traded and USD 11.8 million of government securities, through seven and one transactions respectively. The development of the domestic private bond market does appear to be weakly positively correlated with economic development, at least from higher middle-income levels. Meanwhile, the strong asset net financial position of the Kazakhstan state means that it has little need to access domestic or international securities markets – in contrast to most among countries around Kazakhstan's income levels. The Kazakhstan state readily tapped international markets for USD 6.5 billion of ten and 30-year bonds in late 2014 and mid-2015.

The insurance sector, often an important pool of investable funds, is also unusually small, although it is growing rapidly (Box 3.2). The assets of both life and other insurances are small (relative to GDP), although there are a large number of insurers operating in Kazakhstan. These insurers have limited access to reinsurance, making the sector highly exposed to events such as an earthquake near Almaty, which could exhaust the sector's resources. As is the case with other components of the finance sector, the only countries with smaller insurance sectors and with income levels near or above Kazakhstan's have large oil sectors (i.e Libya, Saudi Arabia and Kuwait). The importance of both life and risk insurance tends to increase with economic development. Insurance is a service that helps purchasers to manage risks better and make more productive use of their resources. Accumulated insurance premiums are also a pool of patient savings that can finance long-term investments, especially when the insurance risks are diversified through international reinsurance.

Pension savings do not play their typical long-term investment role

Kazakhstan's sole pension fund is the one significant pool of resources, but its management arrangements have affected the ability of this financing to support economic transformation. Kazakhstan's pension fund assets approached 12% of GDP by mid-2015. In 2014 the government merged the assets of 11 second-tier funds into one nationalised fund managed by a special unit of the NBK. The goal of this merger was to strengthen the management of the savings, so raising their returns. The management arrangement is not conducive to the implementation of monetary policies as the NBK controls both the supply and the vast number of means of acquiring long-term domestic securities. In addition, there is a risk of conflict of interest between the government and the NBK, because of pressure to apply the pension fund assets to finance the state budget or activities, rather than to obtain the maximum long-term investment income. Since December 2015, under the President's instructions, the government with the NBK are working to transfer the pension fund assets into the management of private Kazakhstani or foreign entities, and to remove the single accumulative pension fund from the control of the NBK.

Figure 3.11. **Kazakhstan's equity market stands out for its low capitalisation and minimal turnover**

Percent of GDP and income per capita (log scale)

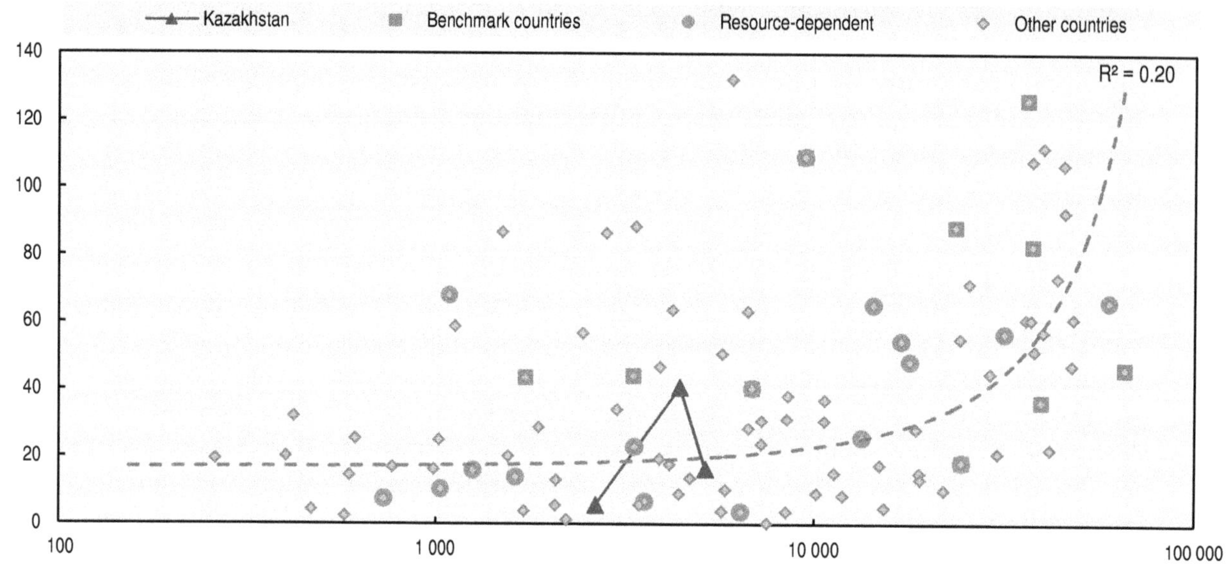

StatLink http://dx.doi.org/10.1787/888933445588

Stock market turnover, percent of GDP and income per capita (log scale)

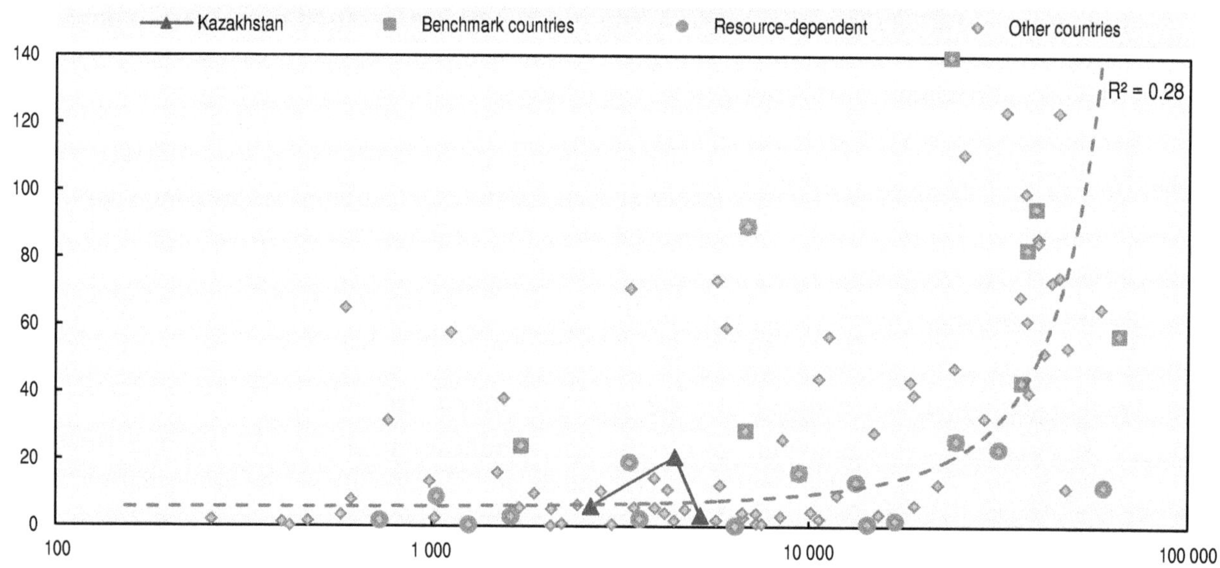

Note: Data are reported for 2012, except Kazakhstan, which is reported for 2001, 2007 and 2012. GDP per capita is in constant 2005 USD. Countries classified as "resource-dependent" are those with total natural resource rents greater than 15% of GDP in 2015. Exponential trend lines are fitted.

Source: World Bank, Global Finance Development Database, 2015.

StatLink http://dx.doi.org/10.1787/888933445592

Box 3.2. **The potential of Kazakhstan's insurance sector as a new pool of investable funds**

Kazakhstan's insurance sector has consolidated with growing assets over recent years. At the end of 2015, 33 insurers (26 general insurers, seven in life insurance) and 15 insurance brokers operated in Kazakhstan, compared with 35 general insurers, five life insurers and 12 insurance brokers operating a decade earlier. Assets under management have increased sevenfold and capital quadrupled over the same period. However the sector remains small relative to GDP, at around 2%.

Compulsory insurance requirements should support the deepening of the insurance sector. In Kazakhstan nine types of insurance are mandatory, and regulated by specific laws. Civil liability for vehicle owners is the most common type of compulsory insurance. At the end of 2015 compulsory insurance made up 25% of total insurance premiums, voluntary property insurance made up 46%, and voluntary personal insurance made up 29%. Insurance is largely sold through second-tier banks and agency networks.

Life insurance also generates long-term savings and can support social development by providing self-funded protection from income loss, but is a particularly underdeveloped part of Kazakhstan's insurance market. Life insurance made up 8% of insurance premiums in 2015, despite its potential role in offsetting weaknesses in the social protection system. Explanations for the limited development of life insurance include the limited demand from the population, lack of confidence in the integrity of long-term savings, the lack of investment instruments, and the lack of tax incentives for insuring.

The development of the insurance market is constrained by undercapitalisation and by limited scale. Low capitalisation of the Kazakhstan insurers limits their ability to retain premiums and develop their asset base. To manage this, insurers transfer premiums and risk to reinsurers outside Kazakhstan. A total of 31% of insurance contracts were transferred to reinsurers in 2015, 84% of which were held by non-residents, with the reinsurers retaining 9% of the original premiums. Development is also slowed by the relatively high cost of insurance, as a result of the lack of data for actuarial calculations, or weak demand and the small scale of individual insurance companies, as well as limited appreciation of the value of insurance.

Kazakhstan's development and rising incomes, and its deeper integration into the global economy, generate evolving objectives and opportunities for the national insurance sector. To support the insurance market's development, and so expand financial markets in Kazakhstan, the NBK is planning to:

- Introduce in phases an assessment of the adequacy of standards of equity of insurance and reinsurance companies, in accordance with Solvency II. This will increase the capitalisation of the insurance companies and the adequacy of insurance reserves.
- Introduce the electronic sale of insurance policies, which will require the transformation of business models and the development of the system of electronic insurance services.
- Improve the regulatory framework for reinsurance in order to ensure capitalisation and capacity of the insurance market, and to enhance the competitiveness of insurance companies.
- Revise the existing scheme of interaction among insurance intermediaries;
- Introduce tax incentives for life insurance products.
- Expand investment opportunities for insurance companies.

Sources : NBK and authors.

The fund's management structure means that the pension fund's resources are readily directed to investments other than those likely to generate the maximum returns or that offer agreed minimum levels of security. For example, the pension fund provides financing for the "Business Roadmap 2020" prioritised sectors, as well as purchasing short-term public financing instruments. The management structure means that the pension fund's resources are readily directed to investments in the state programme for accelerated industrial innovative development (SPAIID) prioritised sectors, including in some cases into assets that are conventionally assessed as being below "investment" grade, rather than the investments likely to generate the maximum returns or that offer agreed minimum levels of security.

A pension fund structure focused on long-term investments could contribute significantly to deepening Kazakhstan's financial sector and mobilising finance for transformational investments. Efficient pension fund systems tend to be characterised by multiple funds, where transparent competition ensures that investment strategies are efficient, seek maximum long-term returns while offering security. These systems are subject to clear and effectively enforced prudential regulation and supervision. A number of benchmark countries have developed such systems as a pool of long-term investable funds that support national investment and economic development, while ensuring retirement incomes for ageing populations. The OECD has established a number of guidelines around the governance, regulation and management of pension funds.[6]

International sources of finance play an unusually large role

Kazakhstani entities make an unusually large use of international finance, with the aim of circumventing thin domestic finance, although this use has unwound following the 2009-10 crisis. As economies develop, the use of offshore banks and financial markets for deposits tends to decline and that for financing investments expands. Savers in lower-income countries, where institutions are weaker, make greater use of offshore deposit-taking banks, although in most countries this use has declined since the 1990s. Conversely, enterprises in higher-income countries make greater use of offshore borrowing. This may reflect both more demand and greater willingness by lenders to lend into those countries. Kazakhstan's private entities raise as much finance from international sources (relative to GDP) as those in countries at several times Kazakhstan's income level, although this too followed an inverted U-shape between the start of the 2000s and the mid-2010s. In the mid-2000s Kazakhstani entities raised significant amounts of finance from offshore banks, and external facilities remained important locations of loans and deposits in 2015. Liabilities to offshore banks relative to GDP peaked at above 25% in 2009, and then net new issuance lagged behind the expansion of the overall economy. Even so, the next country with this level of outstanding private debt securities relative to GDP had an income level over three times that of Kazakhstan. In contrast, the public sector has a large net positive international investment position, reflecting the transformation of Kazakhstan's petroleum wealth into offshore financial holdings in its national oil fund, even as the government resumed issuing Eurobonds in 2014.

Figure 3.12. **Private Kazakhstan entities make unusually large use of offshore financing, even if net new issuance slowed after the 2008-10 crisis**

International private debt securities as % of GDP, and income per capita (log scale)

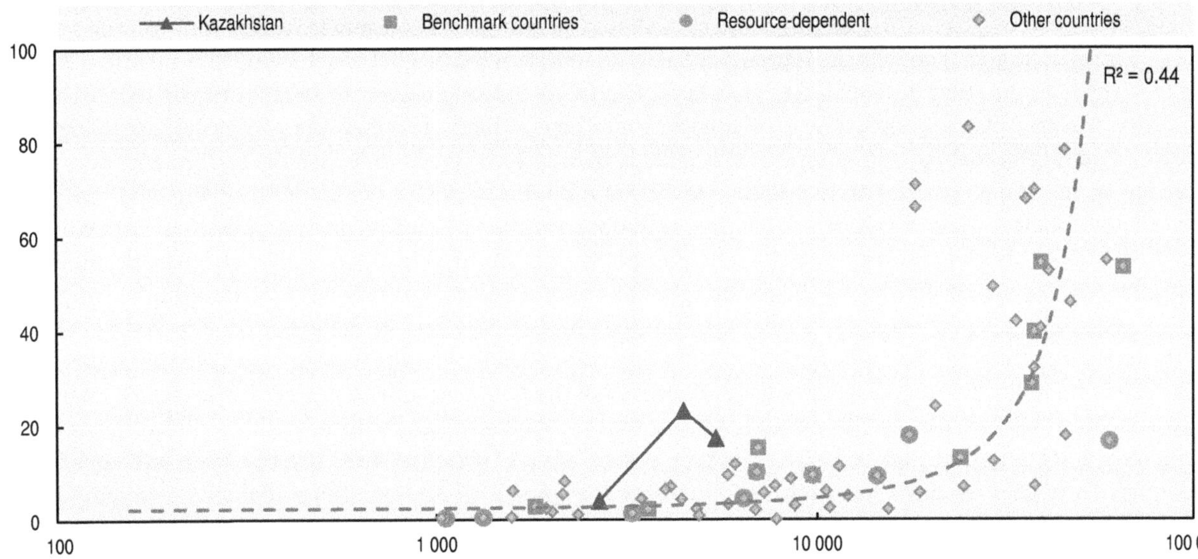

Note: Data are reported for 2012, except Kazakhstan, which is reported for 2001, 2007 and 2012. GDP per capita is in constant 2005 USD. Countries classified as "resource-dependent" are those with total natural resource rents greater than 15% of GDP in 2015. Graph truncated at 100%. Exponential trend line fitted.

Source: World Bank Global Finance Development Database, 2015.

StatLink http://dx.doi.org/10.1787/888933445604

Box 3.3. **Strengthening monetary and exchange rate policy to deepen tenge financing**

After the 2008-10 crisis, Kazakhstan's monetary policy tool was a stable exchange rate to achieve the objective of price stability, but this approach proved to be sustainable only while external conditions were supportive. After the 2008-10 financial crisis the NBK's monetary policy regime focused on stabilising prices and the economy by maintaining a stable exchange rate relative to the USD. This was sustainable while external shocks were positive and while the domestic financial system was rebuilding its balance sheets and so credit growth was slow. The strong real exchange rate and moderate growth in domestic demand reduced inflationary pressures. As external conditions became less supportive, efforts to maintain the tenge's value detracted from the government's economic stabilisation and diversification goals. Declining terms of trade as the prices of oil and Kazakhstan's other commodity prices fell, brought lower export receipts and reduced investment inflows. At the same time, the USD appreciated against most currencies, meaning the tenge appreciated against important trading partners and competitors which had allowed their currencies to depreciate (e.g., the Russian rouble).

Economic actors switched from tenge to foreign currency for deposits and transactions, increasing demand for foreign currency and undermining the NBK's efforts to slow and smooth the exchange rate's depreciation. This created short-term liquidity pressures for banks, leading to spikes in short-term interest rates. The NBK attempted to maintain the tenge's stability against the USD through both public statements and its regular auctioning of foreign exchange, as well as providing instruments such as long-term currency and interest rate swaps with banks. While these measures reduced instability, they also offered banks opportunities to make greater profits than through conventional financial intermediation. Despite these efforts, economic agents continued to move away from tenge, anticipating the exchange rate's eventual depreciation and the pass-through into domestic inflation. These developments also undermined long-term goals of developing the financial sector and diversifying the economy, by reducing the money supply and diverting increasingly scarce loanable funds towards financial instruments, while also reducing the competitiveness of Kazakhstan's exporters.

Box 3.3. **Strengthening monetary and exchange rate policy to deepen tenge financing** *(cont.)*

NBK's shift to using a policy base rate as the policy instrument to achieve price stability breaks this dynamic, by allowing movements in the exchange rate to cushion the domestic economy from external volatility and helps domestic financial deepen. In September 2015 NBK announced its goal of achieving annual inflation of 3% to 4% by 2020, and that the exchange rate would float freely, although interventions continued to maintain liquidity and dampen overshooting. This inflation rate goal is likely to allow the economy's structure to evolve, without the costs of higher inflation. It is likely to take some years to realise the full benefits of these policies. In the short term, credible inflation-targeting monetary policy risks working against the goals of sustained economic growth and diversification. Initially, controlling inflation during a period of substantial negative supply shocks and associated exchange rate depreciation will mean higher short-term interest rates, to slow capital outflows and the exchange rate's depreciation, and reduce the risk of higher import prices becoming entrenched in expectations of ongoing higher inflation. In the months following the shift in its policy instrument, NBK raised its new policy base rate by five percentage points, to 17%. As conditions stabilised and inflation progressed as expected, over 2016 the NBK was able to progressively reduce its base rate, reaching 12.5% by October. Estimates suggest that a 10% depreciation of the exchange rate raises the consumer price inflation rate by two percentage points after 12 months, and that the scale and speed of this pass-through may have risen with the increased openness of Kazakhstan's economy following the implementation of the Eurasian Economic Union. This import price inflation is likely to spike following the tenge's 50% depreciation against the USD over 2015, adding to the challenge of building confidence in monetary authorities' inflation-management capacity.

Reconciling competing monetary policy objectives will be a challenge in the near-term, and a simple, clear goal is likely to be the most effective approach. Monetary authorities are seeking to reduce inflation while other factors are unsupportive. The decline in the international prices of Kazakhstan's exports effectively constitutes a negative supply shock, reducing the value of Kazakhstan's production and national income. This can be partly absorbed by allowing the exchange rate to depreciate, with the associated pass-through into higher prices of imported items relative to domestic goods and services. At the same time, the government has longer-term goals of developing the availability of finance to support economic diversification. When it shifted the objective of monetary policy to inflation targeting, the central bank increased the costs of funds and so slowed lending. Lending slowed with the reduction in credit demand associated with the weakening in economic conditions. The availability of funds also retreated, given the decline in the availability of tenge funds in anticipation of the exchange rate's depreciation. The NBK's research finds a positive relationship between the growth of lending to the economy and economic activity (for example, the discussion in NBK 2013), although IMF analysis suggests that the relationship varies considerably between different economic sectors (IMF 2015a).

In the longer term, conditions are likely to stabilise if many of the challenges of the mid-2010s pass, and the benefits of a floating exchange rate and inflation targeting monetary regime are realised. Commodity prices and Kazakhstan's terms of trade are likely to stabilise, albeit at lower levels, along with the exchange rates of Kazakhstan's trade partners and competitors. As the real exchange rate reaches a new equilibrium, market participants will no longer expect further exchange rate depreciation or intervention by the NBK, thus reducing the incentive to shift funds out of tenge. The central bank can build its credibility by remaining committed to reducing inflation while ensuring its interventions in forex markets are directed at maintaining market liquidity rather than holding the exchange rate away from its medium-term equilibrium. Given that perceptions about exchange rate movements can be self-fulfilling in the short term, changed perceptions and stronger clarity and credibility of the central bank around its goals can help entrench stability, allowing it to rebuild its buffers of foreign reserves. In turn this stability would reduce inflationary expectations and ongoing pressures and the cost on the economy of reducing those pressures, allowing the central bank to lower its benchmark interest rate. In turn this would help rebuild tenge liquidity, supporting lending by banks, and the long-term goals of developing and diversifying the domestic economy.

Sources: Authors and Frankel, 2013.

Unlocking finance for development

The government has introduced various schemes to improve firms' access to finance

The Kazakhstan government has offered subsidised credit through a complex array of mechanisms mostly targeted at firms investing in priority sectors (Box 3.4). In the years following the 2009-10 crisis the government developed at least 23 programmes intended to improve firms' ability to finance investments and operations. The various programmes provided stabilisation and stimulatory functions, although there is significant heterogeneity among the programmes, with some having dominant social purposes. In addition, Kazakhstan's development partners implemented other programmes to support access to finance. The stabilisation programmes included programmes for housing finance, programmes targeted towards female entrepreneurs and to supporting SMEs and a programme for agriculture development (Table 3.1). In 2014 this cornucopia was consolidated into a coherent programme targeted at firms operating in the national priority sectors, focused largely on industry and manufacturing (Chapter 2), although firms in other sectors may be able to access some of these programmes. Support for SMEs was combined into the "Business Road Map 2020", and that for agro-industry was consolidated into the "Agribusiness 2020", and individual budget programmes of the Ministry of Agriculture. However the launch of the SPAIID II programme also introduced additional government programmes to support access to finance through banks.

Box 3.4. **The schemes supporting SMEs' access to finance**

The Kazakhstan State supports the provision of finance for private sector investments and business operations through a number of mechanisms. While each scheme is intended to target the needs of different groups of investors, the schemes do overlap.

Damu

Damu is the principle mechanism supporting SMEs' access to credit. It works through a mix of developing SME businesses' capacity, and by subsidising the cost of credit that SMEs can obtain from second-tier banks through interest subsidies or collateral guarantees. Between 2010 and 2014, Damu subsidised KZT 626 billion of credit through its 17 individual programmes – equivalent to one-third of outstanding credit to SMEs in 2014. The interest rates paid by borrowers ranged between 8.1% and 15.5%. Damu operates through the second-tier banking system. The commercial banks provide the interface with borrowers, screening loan applications, facilitating the application to Damu for the subsidy, and managing the loan provision and repayment process. The Damu programme is funded partly through transfers from the Samruk-Kazyna, with special programmes funded by Kazakhstan's development partners such as the Asian Development Bank.

Damu focuses its subsidised credit on the government's prioritised sectors, especially processing industries, rather than those with greatest demand for credit or where the most SMEs operate. For example, in each year from 2010 to 2014, between 27% and 31% of total subsidised credit was allocated to processing industry firms, which make up around 2% to 3% of SMEs. In contrast, between 33% and 46% of total subsidised credit was allocated to firms in trading, which is the principal activity of between 41% and 46% of SMEs. This reflects the goal of reducing the role of extractive sectors in the economy (Figure 3.13).

From the start of 2008 to late 2014, Damu supported 66 419 different loans to 13 134 borrowers, with an average loan value of KZT 63.68 million. The average loan duration was 32.74 months, and the weighted average interest rate was 11.95%, substantially lower than the typical commercial rates. Damu reported that the loans enabled the recipients to create 33 651 new jobs. While it is complicated to calculate, the subsidised interest rate and the risk guarantee overall are estimated to be worth about KZT 31 million per loan. One example of the effectiveness of the subsidy was a KZT 1.75 billion loan provided through JSC Sberbank that is likely to have made a beverage bottling plant in Arkalyk viable.

Box 3.4. The schemes supporting SMEs' access to finance *(cont.)*

However there is little evidence that greater access to Damu credit has led to greater access to finance overall. The largest effects of the programme appear to have been in lending to industry, where greater lending benefiting from the Damu programmes appears to lead to faster growth in overall credit. But the relationship is weak and does not appear to lead to a sustained growth in credit. No relationship between Damu activity and overall lending could be found for SMEs in other sectors.

Over 2015 to 2020 Damu plans to continue its existing programmes. The Business Road Map 2020 programme projects that Damu will provide SME's with KZT 310.4 billion of support between 2015 and 2020. The programme will be supported by the allocation additional funds from the National Fund, which will reduce to 6% the interest rate that second-tier banks charge to SME borrowers. The first tranche was totally disbursed in 2014 (most of the credit was provided to SMEs in the food production and chemistry sectors). The second tranche of KZT 50 billion was allocated and fully dispersed in 2015, with almost half dispersed into the metallurgical and engineering sectors. The third tranche of KZT 50 billion is to be dispersed in 2016. In addition, KZT 155 billion will be allocated from the Asian Development Bank (ADB), the European Bank for Reconstruction and Development (EBRD) and the World Bank for SMEs support through Damu between 2015 and 2017. Together these programmes bring Damu's total financial support to SMEs between 2014 and 2020 at KZT 675 billion.

Development Bank of Kazakhstan (DBK)

The DBK is intended to be the lead national institution financing the modernisation and development of non-resource and infrastructure sectors of the Kazakhstan economy. These tend to be larger investment projects. It forms part of the Baiterek Holding structure, and at the end of 2013 received KZT 125 billion from the National Fund to support projects that contribute to the second five-year plan of industrialisation and the New Economic Policy, "Nurly Zhol". The DBK prioritises projects that generate chains of technologically connected production with high added value, and projects that support Kazakhstan producers' entry into global markets. The DBK includes a leasing arm, that provides lease financing for investment projects by medium and large-scale businesses in processing industries, production and transportation infrastructure. DBK is subject to a particular regulatory regime.

Sources: Damu (2016) and authors.

Table 3.1. Examples of programmes supporting access to finance

	Stabilisation programme			Stimulus programmes			
Public support programmes	Joint Action Plan of the Government, NBK, and the agency for financial sector supervision, to stabilise the economy and financial system, 2008-11	Special plan for business development in Zhanaozen, 2012-14	Programme of refinancing mortgage housing loans	Support programmes for SPAIID	Agribusiness Support Programme	SME Support Programme	Mortgage and housing programmes
Programme operators	National Welfare Fund Samruk-Kazyna; NMH "KazAgro"	JSC EDF "Damu"	JSC "Non-Performant Loans Fund"	JSC "DBK"	JSC "NMH" KazAgro"	JSC "Damu"	JSC "KMC", JSC "Kazakhstan ZHSSBK"
Specific purpose	Strengthen business & agribusiness entities post-crisis	Financial support for entrepreneurs in Zhanaozen	Refinance mortgage-loans / mortgages	Support for projects in non-primary sectors of economy	Improve the competitiveness of agribusiness entities	Support national and regional SME projects in the priority sectors	Improve the living conditions of the population
Operational	No	Yes	Yes	Yes	Yes	Yes	Yes

Sources: Statistical Bulletin (2016) and Damu Fund (*http://www.damu.kz/*).

Figure 3.13. **Lending through the Damu programmes focuses on the government's priority sectors**

Sector share of total credit, percent

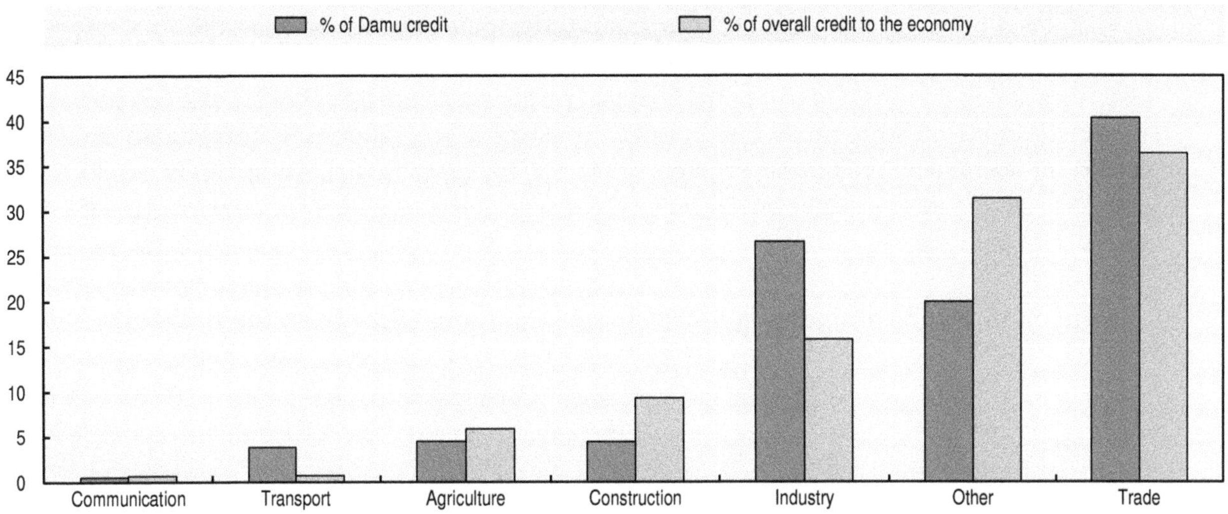

Sources: NBK Statistical Bulletin (2016), Damu Fund and authors' calculations.

StatLink http://dx.doi.org/10.1787/888933445618

The programmes target funding new investments, ahead of providing working capital or refinancing. They use a range of methods, all implemented and managed by private second-tier banks: providing the funds themselves for lending to targeted sectors, subsidising interest rates, or providing risk guarantees on the loans provided by commercial institutions. The funds for the programmes are placed by the state programme operators with the banks for on-lending, in the form of deposits for up to 20 years, depending on the state support programme. These subsidised credit programmes are complemented by others intended to address other deficits that limit firms' ability to raise and manage financing, for example by providing training in business management, preparing business plans, and financial reporting.

The Kazakhstan finance subsidy schemes are designed to avoid common weaknesses of such programmes, especially to limit distortions to the banking system. Importantly, second-tier commercial banks identify and assess loan applicants, and provide the finance and manage the loan. Eligibility for the subsidy is assessed by the quasi-government agency responsible for implementation (Damu). The lead involvement of the second-tier banks increases the role of commercial viability in allocating and managing credit. By contrast, many countries have relied on state-owned "development banks" to implement subsidised finance schemes. While these can provide some short-term and counter-cyclical support to lending, badly designed facilities are undermined by governance-related issues. These lead, for example, to pressure to provide non-commercial loans to select borrowers or not to pursue certain bad debts which can mean that credit is not allocated to where its returns are highest or it best supports broader economic growth, but to politically connected borrowers (World Bank, 2012). This misallocates scarce credit, and shifts the cost of the loan on to the public budget. These programmes can also suffer from a lack of additionality in generating lendable funding.

These programmes enable smaller firms to access offshore funds via the National Fund, and so help address the shortage of tenge liquidity. The programmes source their financing through various disbursement mechanisms from a mix of the National Fund, as well as the national Republican and local budgets (Figure 3.14). A total of KZT 1 trillion (USD 2.86 billion) was shifted from the National Fund's offshore holdings to various firms via subsidised loan programmes between 2010 and 2014, and an additional KZT 750 billion is programmed to be disbursed between 2015 and 2019 for the programmes supporting access to finance. Given that the National Fund's investments are split between liquid, low-risk government securities and higher- risk international financial assets, these programmes act as a conduit to transfer some offshore funds into physical investment programmes in Kazakhstan via credit. The sustainability of these transfers or their effectiveness at achieving the economic stabilisation and inter-generational savings objectives of the NFRK is beyond the scope of the current analysis.

Figure 3.14. **Funds supporting SMEs' access to finance flow from the national wealth fund**

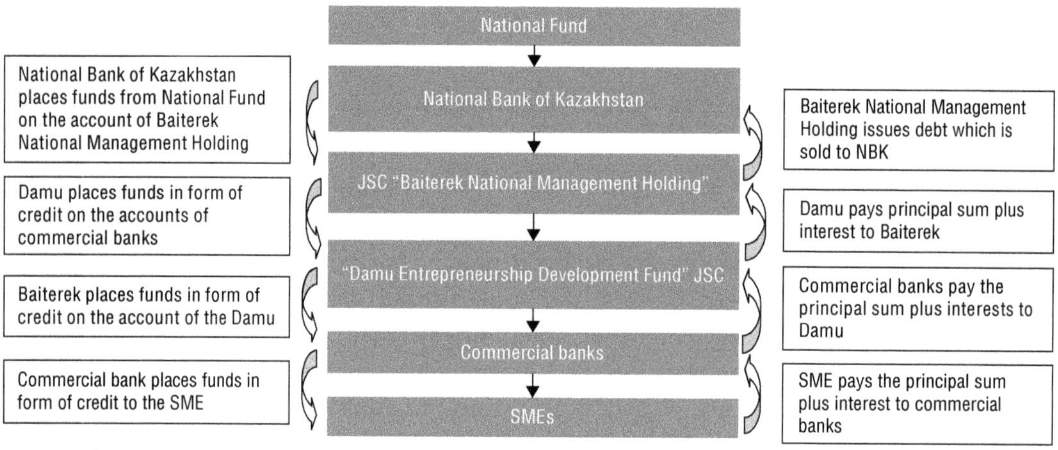

Source: Authors.

Targeted lending subsidies can be effective responses to a crisis but offer limited long-term benefits

The various schemes supported access to credit during the financial crisis, but their effects became limited as conditions stabilised. An analysis of Damu-linked lending shows that the main stimulus to credit for SMEs was during the depths of the financial crisis, from mid-2008 to the end of 2009. During this period the "Damu Regions" programme and the programme supporting financing from the second tier banks were the main actors. The programmes provided as much as three-quarters of credit to SME during the peak of the crisis. However this support made a far more modest contribution to SME financing once conditions stabilised and banks resumed lending. Including the post-crisis period, the Damu-administered programmes provided only 3.6% of total credit to the economy. Further, these schemes targeted SMEs in prioritised sectors, reducing their benefits for the larger economy (Figure 3.15).

The credit provided through Damu's programmes largely offset lower credit from banks, rather than accelerating the availability of credit overall for SMEs. An econometric analysis for the period between December 2007 and November 2014 finds that the change in new lending to SMEs is very weakly influenced by additional financing support of the type provided by the Damu programmes. Credit benefiting from the Damu programmes statistically significantly contributed to overall credit during periods when overall lending was volatile. Once credit conditions stabilised, overall lending was not significantly influenced by increased availability of funds through the Damu programmes. Across the full period, the estimates suggest that an increase of credit provided by the Damu programmes of KZT 1 million would increase growth in overall credit to SMEs by 0.0034%. Such a relation suggests that the KZT 836 billion invested through the programmes during the observed period generated KZT 224 million of additional credit. These results, plus specific analyses by periods and industries suggest that the credit support was mostly effective at offsetting banks' unwillingness to lend during the crisis, rather than a sustained expansion in access to finance. Agriculture is the only sector where credit provided through the programme could be found econometrically to have generated additional lending.

Figure 3.15. **The financing support programmes maintained access to finance during the crisis, but have since become minor players**

New loans to SMEs and loans benefiting from the Damu programme, monthly (billions of KZT)

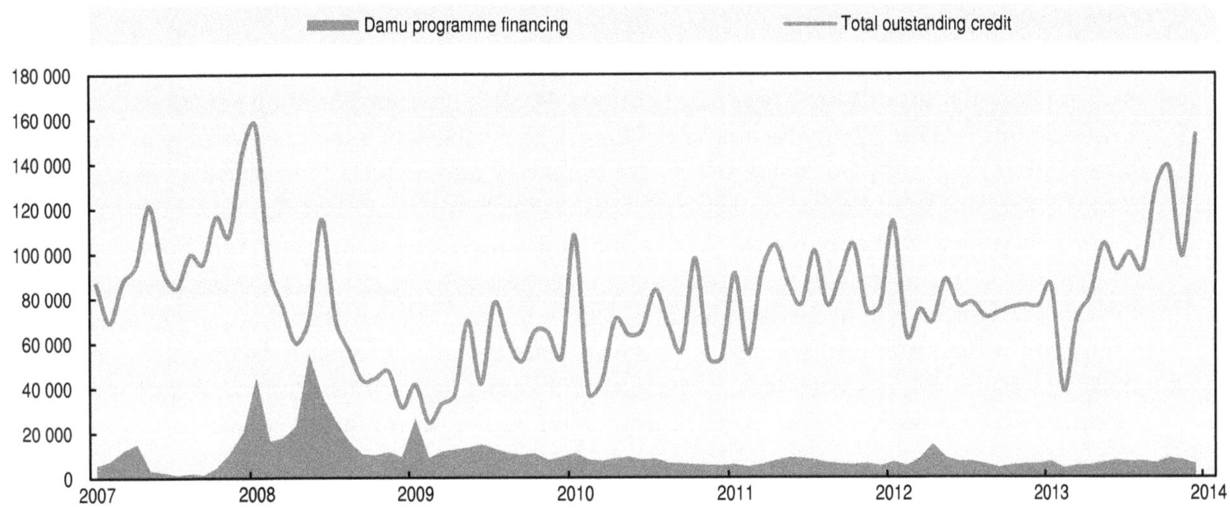

Sources: NBK Statistics Bulletin (2015), Damu Fund *http://gis.damu.kz/bvu/bvuanalysis2.aspx?programmID=5&lang=en* and authors' calculations.

StatLink *http://dx.doi.org/10.1787/888933445629*

Beyond their effectiveness in responding to the crisis, the programmes can be challenged in the control of their financing, ensuring disbursement meets targets, and generating lasting gains in credit availability or investment. The amount of subsidy relative to the amount lent or share of total lending that benefits from the programmes is uncorrelated with the growth of lending overall for a sector. This suggests that while the programmes may be subsidising individual firms' operations and making some investments viable, but that these effects are not sufficient to affect aggregate outcomes.

Larger, highly directed programmes managed by the Development Bank of Kazakhstan (DBK) and JSC Samruk-Kazyna do reduce shortages of funding in Kazakhstan. The DBK has disbursed KZT 24.8 billion in loans to finance priority large investment projects between 2010 and 2014, of which 83.8% was provided in tenge. These funds, sourced from the NFRK, are likely to have materially contributed to reducing the demand for tenge liquidity in Kazakhstan. However the highly directed nature of the lending though sectoral programmes, largely focused on priority oil and gas projects (around 52% of flows), raises the question of whether these investments represent the most efficient use of these scarce funds (discussed further in Chapter 2).

Programmes designed to stabilise financing following banking crises need sunset clauses. Measures to ensure the ongoing availability of finance during a banking crisis can undermine the sector's competitiveness and sustainability if they are allowed to continue operating once conditions normalise. Interventions including expanded guarantees, liquidity support and recapitalisations or nationalisations can be effective immediate responses to bank distress. But if they are allowed to continue beyond the immediate crisis they can have the effect of subsidising unsustainable components of the financial system and can push competitive pressures too far, resulting in unsustainable margins and low profitability and greater risk of instability in the face of future shocks. Most pertinent in Kazakhstan, banks rendered bankrupt by bad loans need to be able to make an expeditious and orderly exit from the banking system, rather than being allowed to continue to operate and compete with healthy banks despite their impaired balance sheets. Similarly, an effective regulatory environment is one that offers certainty to participants and over the regulatory environment requires that regulatory measures are applied consistently across different financial institutions (Kane, 2000; Beck et al, 2010).

Public interventions can help jump-start financing in particular sectors or during periods when private institutions are atypically cautious. Publicly financed lending schemes can provide an immediate fillip to the amount of financing available in a sector especially in the wake of a banking crisis, but these effects are transitory and do little to improve access to finance in the long term. These interventions can be effective at ensuring firms have ongoing access to finance while banks recover from a shock. But these effects are only transitory and last at most as long as it takes for banks to stabilise their balance sheets. The effectiveness of these interventions, and lasting gains in access to finance, rely on deeper improvements in the institutional environment. The environment needs better to ensure that private and public providers of finance are able to operate efficiently and with certainty around the regulatory environment, and that environment reduces the risk of future crises.[7]

Conclusion: Generating sustained gains in access to finance by expanding banks' access to loanable funds and strengthening the institutional environment

Banks secure funds to lend from a range of sources, some of which can be expanded in the short term while others require more patient efforts. Banks lend funds from their deposits, from funds they have borrowed in wholesale markets at shorter and longer-term maturities and with and without collateralisation. Their capital base, interacting with prudential requirements, determines the amount of funds that can be lent and the risk attached to those loans, given the deposit base or the amount and type of wholesale financing raised. All of these are influenced by the quality of banks' internal management, the supervisory regime, and the quality of broader macroeconomic management. Access to wholesale funds and the capital base can be influenced in the short-term. The other determinants take a more patient process of strengthening institutions and of building market participants' understanding and confidence in those systems.

The immediate need of Kazakhstan's financial sector is expanded access to wholesale funds

Helping banks gain better access to international wholesale finance may be the fastest way to improve financing for firms. The most effective immediate means of expanding the availability of finance is by reducing the constraints around accessing funds, immediately through international sources and in the longer term by improving the institutional environment for domestic savers and investors. Expanding access to longer-term international funds can be achieved through joint ventures with international financial institutions, and through greater access of wholesale funding markets. Collateralisation of wholesale funding can improve access but can also be subject to more volatility in the availability of funds. The collateralisation involves linking the funds borrowed on wholesale markets with the assets securing the final loans. Strategically, Asian wholesale financial markets may offer significant potential, especially via intermediation in Japan and via Hong Kong, given the low interest rates and availability of capital in the region – indeed the Astana International Financial Centre (AIFC) is negotiating a partnership with the Hong Kong Stock Exchange. The AIFC will help ease the availability of funds by providing an international centre for financial intermediation next to the domestic financial system, although it will take some time for the centre to become established and for these benefits to emerge. It will create various legal and regulatory institutions and a new exchange, and develop human capital in financial services and technology.

Domestically sourced funding for banks will be inadequate for the foreseeable future, and Kazakhstan is likely to remain a net importer of funds as long as domestic investment generates strong returns. The domestic savings pool is weakened on both the demand and supply side. A pool of domestic investable funds will take some years to form. The emergence of a mass retail investor market based on a sizeable middle class with significant investable assets is curtailed by modest incomes and a limited choice of savings instruments. As discussed above, the Single Accumulative Pension fund is managed by the NBK, with the policy to shift management to independent and possibly competing agencies. Its management objectives appear to be focused on ensuring that the funds maintain their value and support the government's broader economic development and financing objectives. Meanwhile inflows of direct and portfolio investment are likely to remain available at relatively moderate costs as long as monetary policy in high income countries continues to be targeted at expanding liquidity and while Kazakhstan can offer investment opportunities with strong returns at little risk, especially in the longer term and for direct investment. At the same time, the AIFC capital market can supplement the banking system and may better mobilise financial resources within the country and the region to support the needs of the domestic national economy.

Using external finance to realise domestic investment opportunities follows the practice of several benchmark economies that are rich in resources and investment opportunities but short of capital. These economies have managed the volatility in international capital flows through flexible exchange rates supported by strong, well-managed macroeconomic, monetary and supervisory institutions and high-quality institutional environments.

Partnerships between Kazakhstani banks and international wholesale finance may also help improve access. International banks and other financial institutions have long-established and reliable means of accessing wholesale finance. Partnering with these institutions would improve Kazakhstani financial institutions' ability to access these same sources. One model for these partnerships would be for international banks to make significant equity investments in Kazakhstani financial institutions (i.e. at least 10% shareholdings). This would increase the Kazakhstani institutions' capital, immediately expanding their lending capacity. The equity ownership would also allow for stronger involvement by the international firm in management, which would improve the operations of the Kazakhstani entity and provide greater transparency to support its ability to tap lower-cost international funding.

Kazakhstan will need to strengthen the quality of its operating environment if it is to compete in an increasingly challenging landscape for international financial institutions. Both domestic and international developments create significant challenges for the strategy of using a greater role for international financial institutions in Kazakhstan to expand the availability of finance. Since the global financial crisis, prudential regimes have been become stricter, requiring banks to hold more capital and to take greater account of the riskiness of their investments. This has made it more difficult to invest in markets such as Kazakhstan. This is especially the case after the downgrading of Kazakhstan's sovereign debt rating by international credit ratings agencies to just within investment grade, in the light of the deterioration in Kazakhstan's terms of trade and the rapid draw-down of its national fund. The ratings downgrades reduce the risk-adjusted value of investments in Kazakhstan entities by international banks. To limit further ratings-driven mark-downs it will be important to ensure that Kazakhstan's use of offshore financial resource is sustainable and does not create a growing risk of default. Meanwhile, the management of distressed banks following the 2008-10 crisis undermined confidence in the operating environment. Three foreign banks exited the Kazakhstan market in the early 2010s, amidst declining certainty around governance and the non-transparent financial transactions including the sale of the nationalised banks.

Significant pools of Kazakhstani funds are held and invested offshore, but these are unlikely to support domestic financing in the short term. Wealthier Kazakhstani investors prefer to hold their funds in foreign currency and in vehicles offshore, with varying degrees of transparency and traceability. This preference may reflect investment diversification goals, the origins of those funds, and concerns around security of property rights and the transparency and consistency of the enforcement regime. Official records suggest that Kazakhstani financial institutions held USD 18 billion in offshore investments in late 2015, while the various government and social security funds held USD 65 billion in portfolio investments. But the official statistics capture only a fraction of flows, with as much as USD 160 billion estimated to be held offshore through various vehicles by Kazakhstani entities. Some of these funds return to Kazakhstan through direct and portfolio investments; for example in international bond placements and even deposits in Kazakhstani financial institutions by offshore entities. In the medium term, the AIFC is intended to attract some of these funds, and greater security in the domestic institutional environmental may also attract additional repatriation.

In the long-term, a more proactive regulatory approach towards enabling a dynamic wealth management sector would help deepen the pool of investable funds within Kazakhstan. Kazakhstan needs to develop a competitive wealth management sector that offer robust financial products at moderate cost to a large numbers of investors with moderate investable wealth. These products would generate the pool of long-term investable funds that can finance development of smaller enterprises as well as larger, privatised SOEs and public private partnerships (PPPs). In recent years a number of countries have worked to improve the regulatory and competitive environments for the financial savings product industry, notably through the *Future of Financial Advice* (FOFA) review in Australia and the *Financial Advisory Industry Review* (FAIR) in Singapore. The sector is active in most countries that have grown beyond middle income and will become increasingly important as incomes in Kazakhstan grow. Developing the sector will also help repatriate funds held offshore or in foreign currency into the tenge market. As households' wealth grows, international experience suggests that funds flow from basic deposit accounts into more sophisticated investment products, and if these are not available within the domestic market households will seek offshore products, highlighting the shallowness of the domestic financial system. Investor education programmes should also be developed to complement the sector's development, to help investors self-protect and to encourage a competitive and dynamic market.

Better long-term access to finance requires a more robust institutional environment for the financial sector

As domestic banks have greater access to funding, constraints around the quality of the institutional environment for the financial sector will increasingly act as a drag on SME lending. These constraints include the quality of information about firms' finances, and investor protection and the efficiency and transparency of bankruptcy procedures. As the economy develops into the longer term, access to more sophisticated financial services for more complex transactions will become important. Lenders report that a secondary constraint on providing finance is weaknesses and uncertainty in the enforcement of the investor protection regime and in the reliability of other aspects of the business operating environment, and that legislative changes in 2014 worsened the situation. Financers cite slow and costly mechanisms for protecting investors' interests and amendments to those systems to favour borrowers as important constraints on their willingness to lend. International surveys also suggest that protection of investors in Kazakhstan is weaker than in many benchmark countries, although Kazakhstan's ranking has risen significantly in recent years. All of these issues raise the cost of lending to SMEs relative to other potential uses of scarce financing, and reduce banks' willingness to lend, especially for new businesses or clients whom they do not know well. These issues reflect weaknesses in both the law and the court system. The creation of a system of commercial courts helps address the latter. The independent judicial system and adoption of English commercial law at the AIFC may help with the former, if the domestic legal system is able to incorporate relevant principles and practices from the English system (Box 3.5).

Box 3.5. **The potential of the Astana International Financial Centres (AIFC) better to finance Kazakhstan's economic development**

The Astana International Financial Centre (AIFC) is intended to act as an offshore financial centre located in, but institutionally independent from, Kazakhstan's capital. The financial centre is expected to start full operations in 2018 after two years of development, with the goal of leapfrogging to be one of the top ten financial centres in Asia and one of the top 30 financial centres in the world by 2020. It follows the efforts to create the Almaty Regional Financial Centre which was initiated just before the global financial crisis with the intention of developing the Kazakhstan financial sector.

An independent, well-recognised legal regime is an essential element for developing a financial centre in an emerging market. The Astana Financial Centre builds on the experience of the Almaty Regional Centre by establishing an independent institutional framework, featuring an independent court system, overseen by foreign judges, operating in English and implementing English law (practical details were still being developed at the time of writing). This follows the model of other international financial centres in emerging contexts, such as the financial centres in Dubai, Qatar or Singapore. Further, the AIFC may form a "strategic partnership" with a leading stock exchange that would enable the sharing of expertise and technology, with talks being held with the management of the Hong Kong Stock Exchange. This partnership will lead to the dissemination of technology to support the full cycle for trading in securities, commodities and derivatives. The AIFC will be a platform for subsoil developers by enabling the raising of capital to finance projects.

Box 3.5. **The potential of the Astana International Financial Centres (AIFC) better to finance Kazakhstan's economic development** *(cont.)*

Significant tax and other incentives are intended to make the AIFC a hub for an international financial services workforce. Participating companies and their employees will be exempt from income, property and land taxes for 50 years. There will be a 30-day visa-free regime for citizens of OECD countries, the UAE, Malaysia and Singapore, as well as a special five-year visa regime for employees of participants. Participants will be connected by direct flights to "leading international financial centres". The NBK and the domestic stock exchange will remain in Almaty.

The AIFC is intended to have narrow linkages with the domestic financial system, to insulate the domestic real economy from volatility in international financial markets. The AIFC will not directly finance investments within Kazakhstan or in tenge. Indeed, the domestic private financial sector is to remain in Almaty, one thousand kilometres from the AIFC. In its initial form, the connections between the AIFC and the domestic financial sector and real economy will be largely limited to two mechanisms. First, as a centre for private banking and investment management it is hoped that the AIFC will attract as much as USD 80 billion of the estimated USD 160 billion of funds held offshore by Kazakhstani nationals. These funds would re-enter Kazakhstan via the securities exchanges, which would relocate to the AIFC, and via national second-tier banks selling debt securities through the AIFC. Second, and relatedly, it will be a securities market where major Kazakhstani state-owned enterprises can be listed for foreign and domestic investment. This would focus on Kazakhstan's largest state-owned companies, such as KazMunaiGas, in oil and gas, Kazakhtelecom, the main telecoms operator, Kazakhstan Temir Zholy, the national railway, Kazatomprom, the nuclear holding company, and Samruk Energy. On a smaller scale the AIFC can help develop and diversify the economy of the Almaty region away from public administration towards other service activities, although the tax waivers provided to the centre reduce this benefit. These limited linkages reduce both the benefits and the risks to the domestic economy and financial system from the presence of the AIFC and its exposure to volatility in international financial markets and capital flows.

The measures intended to ensure the success of the AIFC mitigate its benefits for the larger Kazakhstan economy. Special economic and legal zones most benefit their host country when they encourage deepening linkages with the national economy, and when they provide sound models for institutional development that the rest of the country may adopt. They most benefit diversification of economic activity and public finances when they draw on other sectors for inputs and when they make meaningful contributions to public revenues. But significant tax concessions can encourage transfer pricing and other aggressive tax minimisation techniques that curtail both the financial centre's direct contribution to the economy and the broader domestic revenue base. Independence from national legal institutions and national supply can be essential to achieve the international interest and scale, but can lead the financial centre to exist disconnected from the national economy, without spill-overs into larger economic capacity and productivity. Thus there is a trade-off between the various goals. As a result, maximising the success of the AIFC in the longer-term will also require developing links to Kazakhstan's broader economy and institutions.

Sources: Authors; Bekmukhanbetova and Masters (2015).

The state and its bodies should support development of the institutional infrastructure surrounding private sector lending. The public sector can play an important role in supporting provision of credit by the private sector to SMEs by fulfilling fundamental public sector functions of providing public goods and solving collective action problems; for example, by ensuring through regulation that a system is in place efficiently to provide credit scores, the public sector can help reduce the cost of lending for private firms. Credit scores have been shown to improve the provision of credit to SMEs even in jurisdictions where SME credit is well supported by other institutions, such as the United States or in Europe through the European DataWarehouse initiative comprising mandatory loan level reporting for underlying loans of securitisation issued in Europe (Nassr and Wehinger, 2015a). This system can be developed and managed by a public or a private agency, such as a co-operative among financial institutions, and potentially in partnership with successful systems operating in other countries. Similarly, Kazakhstan's collateral registry could be readily strengthened by allowing for easier registration of collateral, and for greater online access to details of the registered collateral. Again, these systems could be developed in partnership with agencies elsewhere.

The most effective institutions supporting lending provide readily available, reliable and transparent information about the finances of creditors. Uncertainty about the quality of credit proposals and viability of a business undermines banks' willingness to lend, accentuating the challenges of the scarcity of funds (OECD, 2015). Collecting this information adds to the costs of lending to SMEs relative to other uses of banks' funds. Being able to rely on firms' financial accounts is fundamental for credit markets to function well and asymmetries of information, particularly prominent in small business financing, inhibit the provision of financing to SMEs not only through bank credit but also through capital market financing (Nassr and Wehinger, 2015b). Larger Kazakhstani firms have accounts that are prepared and audited by large international accounting firms and are assessed as being reliable. They have also developed track records with their financiers and through their use of international wholesale financial markets. Smaller, domestic enterprises lack the resources to purchase this level of advice, and are less known among financiers. They instead rely on domestic accounting and audit firms to help prepare and verify their accounts. Bankers question the reliability and authenticity of these accounts and audit opinions, which reduces their usefulness as a signal of credit quality. Some banks have worked around this by conducting their own audits of financial accounts, but this is expensive and makes borrowers dependent on the one bank, so reducing competition between banks in addition to adding to the cost of lending. This approach is not unique to Kazakhstan, with banks in many countries where financial data are of poor quality following similar practices. However, in benchmark jurisdictions dishonesty or misleadingly prepared certified accounts or audit reports bring penalties ranging from fines and loss of the accountant's practising certificate through to liability for the damages generated by the misleading or false statements and even criminal penalties. More confidence in financial statements would reduce the cost of lending to smaller firms. It can be achieved by introducing such penalties, accompanied by efforts to raise the capacity of accountants and auditors.

Where regulators ensure providers of finance compete with each other and encourage new entrants, credit is less expensive and more readily available. Regulators and competition authorities can ensure that different actors continue to compete across the financial system, and that new actors can readily enter the financial sector. Conversely, effective regulation also ensures that failing financial institutions are allowed – or encouraged – to exit with minimum distortions and loss of funds for the larger financial system. Effective competition also requires strong consumer protection and competition institutions, which reduce the risk of market practices that are anti-competitive or that exploit information asymmetries or other market failures.

Efforts to expand the availability of financing, for SMEs in particular, should extend beyond the banking sector and allow for the provision of financing through different channels and by different actors, including long-term institutional investors. In particular, capital market financing, whether direct (small bonds, mini-bonds, public equity listing) or indirect (securitisation and covered bonds issued by banks), has the potential to fill the gap left by the banking sector, complement bank credit availability and alleviate financing constraints facing SMEs (OECD, 2015). That said, the fixed-cost nature of loan origination, as well as infrastructure requirements related to sourcing, monitoring, credit analysis and local relationship building with small companies render local banks the dominant players in SME financing (Nassr and Wehinger, 2015a).

The latest Financial System Stability Assessment (FSSA) provided a detailed roadmap of immediate tasks to strengthen Kazakhstan's financial sector, which the authorities are progressively implementing. The 2014 IMF FSSA focused on measures to strengthen the banking supervisor and its capacity to monitor banks' health, to improve the resolution of bad loans and insolvent institutions, and regulatory measures to improve liquidity. The assessment also made immediate recommendations to improve the robustness of the insurance sector and operations of the pension fund, which are likely to improve the sector's operating efficiency and stability, and so help deepen its funding. However, the assessment did not develop longer-term recommendations to improve the sectors' structures or the development of the larger funds management industry.

Investments in prudential supervision and the monetary policy regime take some time to translate into easier access to finance for firms. Priority improvements in prudential supervision include investing in the capacity of supervisory staff to assess banks' balance sheets and the risks surrounding their assets, and to improve co-ordination with foreign supervisory counterparts where Kazakhstan banks operate. Weaknesses in the management of probity checks of banks' clients add to their risks. These measures require investments in the regulatory regime, the structure of institutions and in the capacity of the experts who staff them. The lags between such investments and their effects on actors' behaviour can be long. These lags make it imperative to form and consistently implement a programme for strengthening institutions. Where there is a long-term need to build trust in institutions, the confidence-building process may be accelerated by taking actions that show a re-setting of institutional practices, such as re-writing the supervisory institution's constitution, introducing a stronger, clearer mandate, or even changing management. For such "re-setting" to be effective, it must be seen as extraordinary and it must be left in place once it occurs, otherwise the new arrangements will lack credibility and the investments in reform will not bring the intended benefits.

Box 3.6. **How could the scenarios affect the context of implementation of financial development policies?**

For details of the scenario storylines, please see section: Anticipating trends and preparing for future challenges: scenarios for the future of Kazakhstan in Chapter 1.

Scenario 1: "The New Commodity Super Cycle" would generate a new surge of current account surpluses and foreign direct investment for Kazakhstan. This would generate new pressures on the exchange rate and inflation control, while the appreciation of the tenge relative to other currencies would accelerate a repatriation of Kazakhstanis' offshore savings. With such rapid progress in deepening the pool of funds within the domestic financial systems, institutional challenges would quickly become the constraint on further financial development, and progress in these efforts would become imperative. The government's various programmes to encourage investment in priority sectors may continue to be effective in encouraging sectors that are likely to be uncompetitive in the short term relative to resource extraction, and are sustainable given the surge in revenues associated with the strength of commodity prices; however they remain a short-term fillip rather than a longer-term solution.

Box 3.6. **How could the scenarios affect the context of implementation of financial development policies?** *(cont.)*

Scenario 2: "The Great Dissipation" presents the opposite challenge, of limited external funds investing in Kazakhstan, and ongoing weakness in Kazakhstan's income, slowing accumulation of savings. This scenario is likely to see the ongoing shift of funds from the National Oil Fund play a greater role in Kazakhstan's financial deepening, although weak oil prices create dangers around the sustainability of these transfers. In this scenario, given the likely difficulty in expanding the pool of loanable funds, efforts to develop the financial sector's institutional environment should take priority, with the aim of ensuring the available funds are used with maximum efficiency. Subsidised credit programmes are not sustainable given the reduced fiscal space and do not adequately address the underlying issues to justify their continuation.

Scenario 3: "New Silk road and Central Asia Resurgence" is likely to see greater demand for finance for investment and working capital, possibly outpacing gains in the availability of funds. The scenario sees new opportunities in the non-resource tradeable and non-tradeable sectors that would be particularly reliant on bank financing. At the same time, the increased opportunities are likely to attract more direct and portfolio investment to Kazakhstan, and repatriation of savings held offshore, deepening the financial sector. As the non-extractive economy would be the lead driver of growth, fiscal space is likely to grow less rapidly and the funds available to support targeted lending programmes will be scarcer, suggesting that the government's focus should be on strengthening the institutional environment for the financial sector and lending, rather than supporting lending to priority sectors.

Scenario 4: "New Technology Solution" presents the most challenging scenario for the development of the financial sector. It suggests a protracted period of reduced revenues for Kazakhstan from its resource wealth, reducing ready financing for Kazakhstan through oil revenues and foreign investment, given that the economy is likely to be weaker relative to those of other countries. This would make attracting foreign portfolio and other investment, and repatriation of offshore savings, more challenging, and also means that funds would be scarcer to continue the subsidised lending programmes. This would again prioritise efforts to improve the institutional framework towards longer-term financial deepening.

Source: Authors.

Notes

1. The discussion in this chapter focuses on finance for firms' investment and working capital. Other more specialised types of finance are important for firms' ongoing operations, for example trade finance. Developments in these products generally mirror those in the mainstream types of financial products, and are further supported by specific government programmes.
2. Liquid liabilities are also known as broad money, or M3, and includes the sum of currency and deposits in the central bank (M0), plus transferable deposits and electronic currency (M1), plus time and savings deposits, foreign currency transferable deposits, certificates of deposit, and securities repurchase agreements (M2), plus travellers checks, foreign currency time deposits, commercial paper, and shares of mutual funds or market funds held by residents. This is presented as a ratio to nominal local currency GDP, which is deflated using the following deflation method: {(0.5)*[Ft/P_et + Ft-1/P_et-1]}/[GDPt/P_at] where F is liquid liabilities, P_e is end-of period CPI, and P_a is average annual CPI. Data are taken from the electronic version of the IMF's International Financial Statistics.
3. NBK data present foreign currency deposits in terms of tenge (KZT), and so by construction the reported value of foreign currency deposits will reflect movements in the exchange rate. The rise in foreign currency deposits is still apparent when controlling for the exchange rate movements, for example by converting the KZT value of foreign currency deposits to USD or EUR using current or long-term average exchange rates.
4. The amendment was introduced by the Resolution of the Board of National Bank of the Republic of Kazakhstan, 19 December 2015 No. 222 "On amendments and additions to some legal acts of the Republic of Kazakhstan on regulation of banking activity".

5. This assessment is based on the so-called "z-score" summary indicator. It is the returns on assets plus the ratio of capital to assets, to the ratio of the standard deviation of return on assets. The z-score should show the inverse of the probability of insolvency, assuming that profitability follows a normal distribution. The z-score indicates the number of standard deviations that a bank's return on assets has to fall below its expected value before the bank's equity is depleted and the bank is insolvent.
6. The various guidelines are accessible at: *www.oecd.org/daf/pensions/guidelines*.
7. Various studies that have reached this finding and are summarised in World Bank (2012).

References

Asian Development Bank (2012), *Country Partnership Strategy: Kazakhstan 2012-2016*, Manila, *http://www.adb.org/sites/default/files/institutional-document/33638/files/cps-kaz-2012-2016.pdf*.

Beck, T et al. (2010), *Bailing Out the Banks: Reconciling Stability and Competition*, Centre for Economic Policy Research, London.

Bekmukhanbetova, G. and C Masters (2015), "Kazakhstan's new international financial center", *Baker & McKenzie Legal Alert*, 22 May. *http://www.bakermckenzie.com/en/insight/publications/2015/05/kazakhstans-new-international-financial-center*.

DAMU (2016), *http://gis.damu.kz/bvu/bvuanalysis2.aspx?programmID=5&lang=en*; *http://egov.kz/wps/portal/Content?contentPath=/egovcontent/support/article/road_business_map&lang=en* ; Doing Business in Kazakhstan (*http://doingbusiness.gov.kz/en/investment-policy/*).

Demirguc-Kunt A, E. Feyen and R. Levine (2012), "The evolving importance of banks and securities markets", *NBER Working Paper* No. 18004. National Bureau of Economic Research.

Frankel, J (2013), "Exchange rate and monetary policy for Kazakhstan in light of resource exports", Harvard Kennedy School of Government, mimeo.

International Monetary Fund (2015a), *2015 Article IV Consultation: Staff Report For The Republic Of Kazakhstan*, IMF Country Report No. 15/241, Washington, DC.

International Monetary Fund. (2015b), *World Economic Outlook: Adjusting to Lower Commodity Prices*, Washington, DC.

International Monetary Fund (2013), *2013 Article IV Consultation: Republic of Kazakhstan*, Country Report No 13/290, Washington, DC.

Kane, E (2000). "Designing financial safety nets to fit country circumstances," *Policy Research Working Paper* 2453, World Bank, Washington, DC.

Kinda, T, M. Mlachila, and R. Ouedraogo (2016), "Commodity price shocks and financial sector fragility", *IMF Working Paper*, WP/16/12.

Laeven L. and F. Valencia (2012), "Systemic banking crises database: An update", *IMF Working Paper* WP/12/163.

Nassr, I.K. and G. Wehinger (2015a), "Unlocking SME finance through market-based debt: Securitisation, private placements and bonds", *OECD Journal: Financial Market Trends* Vol.2014/2. DOI: *http://dx.doi.org/10.1787/fmt-2014-5js3bg1g53ln*.

Nassr, I.K. and G.Wehinger (2015b), "Opportunities and limitations of public equity markets for SMEs", *OECD Journal: Financial Market Trends* Vol. 2015 pp. 49-84 , *http://dx.doi.org/10.1787/fmt-2015-5jrs051fvnjk*.

National Bank of Kazakhstan (2016), *Statistical Bulletin*, No. 7 (260) July, *http://www.nationalbank.kz/cont/Binder134.pdf*.

National Bank of Kazakhstan (2013), *Annual Report of the National Bank of the Republic of Kazakhstan For the Year 2012*, Almaty.

OECD (2015), "Opportunities and constraints of market-based financing for SMEs", *OECD's Report to G20 Finance Ministers and Central Bank Governors*, September 2015, available at *www.oecd.org/g20/meetings/antalya/Opportunities-and-Constraints-of-Market-based-Financing-for-SMEs.pdf*.

OECD (2013), *Improving Access to Finance in Kazakhstan's Agribusiness Sector*, OECD Publishing, Paris. *https://www.oecd.org/countries/kazakhstan/Improving Access to Finance in Kazakhstan's Agribusiness Sector.pdf*.

Paşalı, S. (2013), "Where is the cheese? Synthesizing a giant literature on causes and consequences of financial sector development", *Policy Research Working Paper* No.6655, World Bank, Washington, DC.

Tumenbayeva, O (2013), "Bank crisis and restructuring: Evidence from Kazakhstan", *World Applied Sciences Journal*, 27: pp.410-13.

World Bank (2016), *World Development Indicators Database*, World Bank, Washington, DC, *http://data.worldbank.org/data-catalog/world-development-indicators*.

World Bank (2015), *Global Financial Development Database*, September, World Bank, Washington, DC, *http://data.worldbank.org/data-catalog/global-financial-development*.

World Bank (2014) *Global Financial Development Report 2014: Financial Inclusion*, World Bank, Washington, DC, *doi:10.1596/978-0-8213-9985-9*.

World Bank (2013) *Enterprise Survey of Kazakhstan 2013*, Washington, DC, *http://www.enterprisesurveys.org/data/exploreeconomies/2013/kazakhstan*, accessed 10-12-15.

World Bank (2012), *Global Financial Development Report 2013: Rethinking the Role of the State in Finance*, World Bank, Washington, DC.

Zhuang, J. et al. (2009), "Financial sector development, economic growth, and poverty reduction: A literature review", *ADB Economics Working Paper Series* No. 173. *https://www.adb.org/publications/financial-sector-development-economic-growth-and-poverty-reduction-literature-review*.

Multi-dimensional Review of Kazakhstan
Volume 2. In-depth Analysis and Recommendations

Chapter 4

Privatisation and the role of the state in the economy of Kazakhstan

Kazakhstan is in transition from an economy dominated by state-owned enterprises (SOEs) to a full market economy. Since independence from the Soviet Union in 1991 Kazakhstan has made efforts to reduce, through privatisation programmes, the share of the state in the economy. The current goal is 15% by 2020. Most important industries are organised into large groups of companies owned and managed by independent national managing holdings, with politically powerful people on their boards and in top management. Yet the government has published no ownership policy to manage and reduce the number of SOEs currently under dispersed governance by several ministries. This chapter presents the national managing holdings system of state ownership; their legal framework and governance structure; generic OECD recommendations regarding state ownership and measurement methodology; the privatisation programme under way; and recommendations to meet the set state ownership goal and to strengthen the policies of Kazakhstan in governing its state-owned entities.

Introduction

There is overwhelming support for the idea that privatisation brings about a significant increase in the profitability, real output and efficiency of privatised companies (OECD, 2003). The Kazakhstan government has set a target of reducing the state's share in the economy to 15% by the year 2020. In Kazakhstan, the government dominates the economy via a complex system of holding companies. Groups of companies with full or partial state ownership are managed by holding companies, which represent, through a high level of political involvement, the interests of the government in their management.

The organisation, administration and governance of state ownership in Kazakhstan do not meet internationally agreed good practices in many respects. The *OECD Guidelines on Corporate Governance of State-Owned Enterprises* (referred hereafter as the "OECD Guidelines") (OECD, 2015b) have been used as benchmarks for the reform of state ownership by a number of nations since their introduction in 2004. One reason behind their recent revision was to ensure their relevance to non-member countries, too, and to provide guidance to countries in different economic circumstances, particularly those in transition to a market economy.

This chapter presents the extent and structure of the state's involvement in the Kazakhstan economy, and how that can be adjusted better to realise the entities' economic potential. The first half of this chapter examines the state's dominance in the economy with an analysis of the main national managing holding companies, including legal frameworks, governance structures and alignment with good practices for state ownership. The second half presents the privatisation programme under way and makes recommendations for state ownership reform towards Kazakhstan's privatisation goal.

Through their legacy Kazakhstan's state-owned enterprises still dominate its economy

The economy of Kazakhstan is dominated by state-owned enterprises (SOEs) and large, private industrial and banking conglomerates. Kazakhstan's industries were established under Soviet rule and economic planning. The new constitution recognised the right to private ownership for the first time in 1991.

A process to privatise virtually all SOEs started soon after independence. Initially, 21 000 SOEs employed 87% of the nation's workforce. Small companies were privatised through cash sales; medium-sized companies through Russian-style voucher programmes; and large companies through direct trade sales. There was widespread criticism by business people and citizens of various perceived irregularities in these processes.

Attracting foreign capital to the under-invested and deeply indebted oil and gas industry was a central motive in the first privatisation effort. The government originally intended to allocate 10% of shares to each company's workforce, sell controlling stakes to foreign strategic investors, and, over time, sell the remainder in smaller stakes on the stock exchange at increasing prices, while at the same time stimulating the stock exchange and the local capital market.

The privatisation programme met several difficulties. These difficulties resulted partly from lack of experience and skill on the part of the government officials in charge of implementation, as well as a continuation of corrupt, Soviet-era business practices. Foreign investors were interested in the oil and gas reserves but did not want to buy shares in companies with potential liabilities, including non-transparent debts, obligations to local communities and non-remediated environmental damage.

Privatisation in the 1990s gave influential business people an avenue to create industrial groupings under holding company structures, particularly in extractive industries and banking. Development of the small and medium-sized enterprises (SMEs) sector as a consequence of privatisation was much weaker. The government disposed of thousands of SOEs, but the revenue transferred to the state budget was relatively modest. The total proceeds from privatisation over the first 15 years were approximately KZT 350 billion (OECD, 2012a). After this privatisation process, SOEs still accounted for between 30% and 40% of Kazakhstan's gross domestic product (GDP) (OECD, 2014a).

Measuring the role of the state in the economy

The OECD has developed various metrics to provide complementary perspectives on the economic role of the state. Each metric seeks to reduce a complex, multi-faceted concept to a limited number of indicators. The Product Market Regulation (PMR) State Control Index is designed to assess this control by summarising results from a detailed questionnaire covering a range of key sectors and aspects of state influence in the provision of goods and services. It allows for the assessment of the extent of state control between sectors, across countries and over time (Box 4.1).

Box 4.1. **PMR State Control Index**

The OECD developed the Product Market Regulation (PMR) Indicators to assess the extent and design of regulation in product markets. They provide economy-wide indicators of regulations affecting the operating environment for product market firms across seven network sectors (electricity, gas, rail transport, road transport, air transport, postal services and telecommunications) and five services sectors (legal services, accounting services, engineering services, architecture services and retail distribution).

The PMR Index is constructed as a pyramid based on responses to a detailed questionnaire, which are then aggregated into various levels of indicators (Figure 4.1.). Responses to a questionnaire covering 18 low-level indicators form the base of the pyramid. Qualitative responses are converted into categorical measures (0-6), which are then aggregated into 16 topics. The summary indicators for these topics are weighted and aggregated into seven groups of constraints on competition, which in turn are further weighted and aggregated into three high-level indicators: state control, barriers to entrepreneurship and barriers to trade and investment. This chapter concerns the state control indicator.

The state control indicator summarises the various dimensions of the state's presence in the observed sectors according to whether a SOE is active in the sector, as well as what proportion of the most important enterprises in each sector is owned by the state. State control measures the nature of the relationship between the state and SOEs by observing the form of regulation applied, constraints on the sale of the firms, governance of the firms, degree to which they are insulated from market discipline, and political interference in the management.

Box 4.1. **PMR State Control Index** *(cont.)*

The indicator is computed using six low-level indicators:

- Scope of SOEs: the pervasiveness of state ownership across business sectors, measured as the share of sectors in which the state controls at least one firm;
- Government involvement in network sectors: the government's stake in the largest firms in six network sectors (electricity, gas, rail transport, air transport, postal services and telecommunications);
- Direct control over enterprises: special voting rights of the government in privately owned firms and constraints to the sale of the government's stake in publicly controlled firms (based on studied sectors);
- Governance of SOEs: degree of insulation of SOEs from market discipline and degree of political interference in their management;
- Price controls: extent and type of price controls in eight sectors (air transport, road freight transport, retail distribution, telecommunications, electricity, gas, water and professional services); and,
- Command and control regulation: extent to which the government uses coercive (as opposed to incentive-based) regulation.

The first four indicators measure the scale of public ownership in the economy. The last two measure the state's involvement in business operations. These two measures are then computed into the high-level state control indicator.

Figure 4.1. **Structure of the PMR Index**

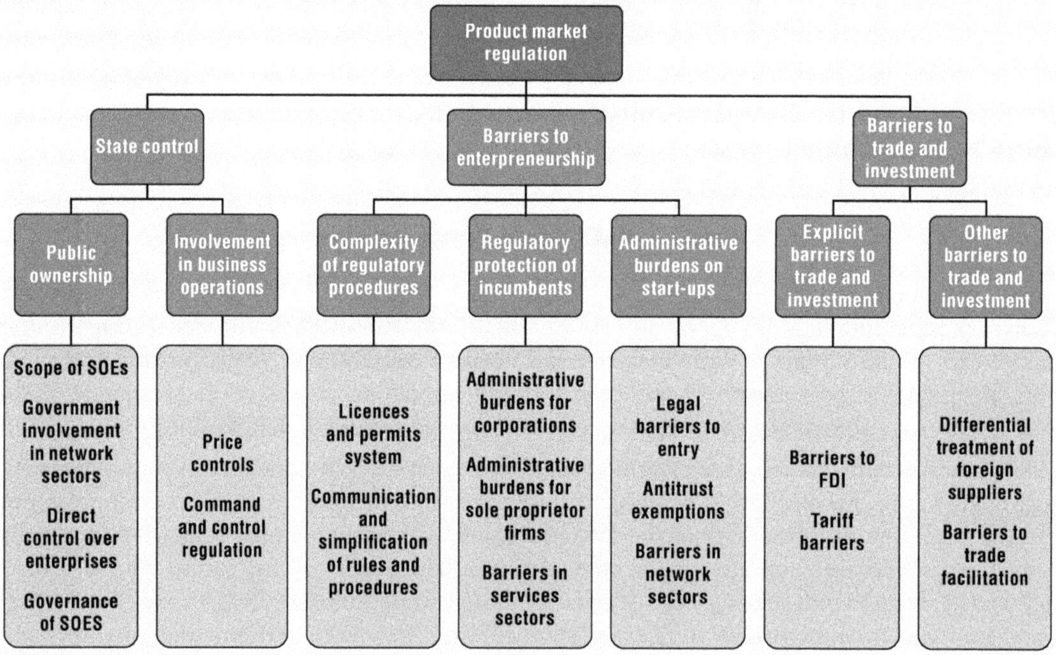

Source: Koske et al. (2015).

The SOEs are the dominant form of state control in Kazakhstan's economy. Their presence is in addition to the weight of the other parts of the state, including non-incorporated government entities at the central and sub-national levels. These entities generate considerable economic activity related to the provision of, for example, hospitals and health care, schools and education and security, as well as holding significant financial and real estate assets.

State control in the economy

The scale of Kazakhstan state involvement in the economy stands out among benchmark and OECD economies, according to preliminary PMR data. All indicators of state control, apart from the governance of SOEs, are above average for OECD economies. The summary indicator for state control is above those for all OECD countries, except Turkey, and is slightly below the values for the neighbouring economies of Russia and China. This assessment reflects the heavy involvement of government in network sectors, the preference for coercive regulation rather than encouraging desired action through incentives and price controls, and the pervasiveness of state ownership across sectors.

The strong state control of the economy is led by the government's heavy involvement in network sectors. The state controls 100% of shares in the largest firms in all branches of the gas sector, transport sector (except air passenger transport), postal sector, mobile services, and electricity distribution, supply and generation. The government holds over half the equity of firms in remaining branches of the network sectors. This is a significantly larger government holding than in OECD economies.

Figure 4.2. **The Kazakhstan state has a high level of control of the economy**

Product Market Regulation State Control Index, latest available

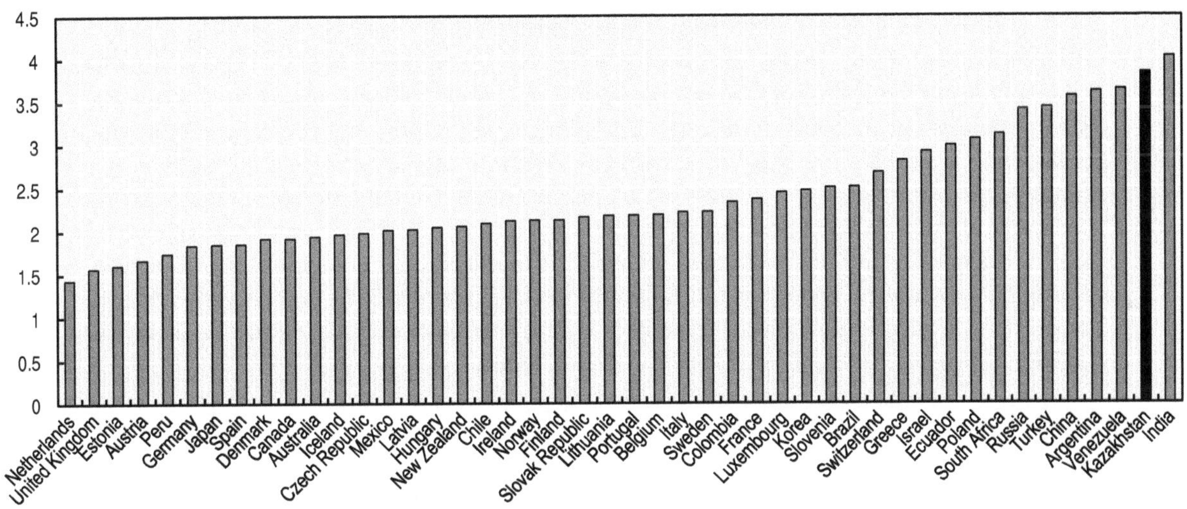

Source: Authors' calculations and OECD Product Market Regulation Indicators (database) available at *http://stats.oecd.org/Index.aspx?datasetcode=PMR.*

StatLink http://dx.doi.org/10.1787/888933445639

The state owns firms across most sectors of the economy covered by the State Control Index, although the measure is not significantly higher than in some OECD economies. The state is particularly present in energy sectors, controlling at least one firm in all branches of the electricity supply industry at either the national or regional level, with the exception of electricity imports. All branches of the gas sector (production, import transmission, distribution and supply) include state-controlled firms, as is the case for the telecommunications, postal and transport sectors. The state controls firms that refine petroleum; manufacture basic and fabricated metals; manufacture railway vehicles; transport freight by road; provide financial services, insurance, reinsurance and pension funding; and deliver health care. Overall, this presence is not significantly higher than in those OECD member countries where the state plays the largest role. It is also consistent with other former Soviet Union countries where, while generally reduced, state ownership of firms across the economy remains significant.

The state, therefore, has an important influence over resource use within and between sectors. These allocations potentially offer lower economic returns than market-based allocations. In addition, concentrated ownership means that the dominance of state control of the most important enterprises in various sectors undermines competitive pressures and efficiency (Hess, Gunasekerage and Hovey, 2008). More diversified ownership could raise the efficiency of management in firms and lead to more complex, value-added products and a competition-friendly marketplace environment.

Box 4.2. **What makes an enterprise state owned?**

The term state-owned enterprise (SOE), as applied by the OECD, denotes "any autonomous public entity i) involved in commercial activities; and ii) controlled, directly or via other government-controlled institutional units, by the central or federal level of government" (OECD, 2015a). According to the System of National Accounts, a public corporation must be i) controlled by another public unit; and ii) a market producer. Control is defined as the "ability to determine the general policy or program of an institutional unit". Being defined as a market producer depends on a separate assessment of whether or not the institutional unit charges "economically significant prices" (European Commission et al, 2008).

The definition of state in the context of SOEs also varies between nations. The question is whether only commercial enterprises owned and controlled by the central government and the subsidiaries of such enterprises should be calculated or whether the corporate assets of regional or local administrations should be taken into account to give a full picture. For example, in Germany, the states *(Länder)* are significant owners of enterprises. Likewise, in Switzerland, most SOEs are owned by the cantons and not by the federal government. In view of the relative autonomy of the *oblasts* and the municipalities in Kazakhstan, it appears appropriate to limit, following the OECD definition, the concept of SOEs to the entities owned by the central government, either directly or through the various holding companies with different rankings, and to all subsidiaries of such entities.

Treatment of fully state-owned entities is clear, but there are different practices regarding partial ownership by the state. Certain nations recognise only majority ownerships, leaving minority shares out of reporting. The OECD defines enterprises with state ownership of between 10% and 50% as partially state-owned enterprises (PSOEs). However, minority ownerships in large listed enterprises may be very valuable, and companies with an otherwise dispersed ownership could effectively be controlled by the state with, for example, 30% of the votes at the annual general meeting. In addition, some nations use the total value or output of a PSOE; others use the portion calculated on share of ownership.

State SOEs are often incorporated into joint stock companies (JSCs) or limited liability partnerships (LLPs), the same forms of incorporation available for privately owned companies. Many countries have additional, special statutory forms of incorporation reserved for governmental purposes. Taking statutory companies into consideration when assessing the state share in the economy is problematic, since they typically do not report their financial data under the same rules as JSCs or other privately owned companies. The true value of a statutory company is difficult to assess, since it cannot be sold to other owners, and the asset value on the balance sheet might be unreliable for many reasons, ranging from accounting and pricing challenges through to misaligned incentives. A similar problem arises in the evaluation of monopoly companies and enterprises with specific societal tasks.

Price control is much stronger in Kazakhstan than in any OECD member or enhanced engagement country. Preliminary assessment suggests that price control is predominant across the Kazakhstan economy. It is applied in most of the surveyed economic sectors, including domestic airfares and road freight services and to many retail products, such as petrol, tobacco, alcohol, cellular communications, Internet services, certain staples, water and energy.

The government plans to deregulate prices in Kazakhstan substantially and instead use antitrust measures to manage monopolistic industries. The Committee on Regulation of Natural Monopolies and Protection of Competition has announced plans to abolish price regulation from 1 January 2017. Antitrust tools will replace price regulation, bringing Kazakhstan into line with the conventional OECD approach and potentially allowing for the far more effective role of price signals in driving economic behaviour. This may, for example, reduce barriers to entry in the regulated market, thereby attracting additional resources and supply in industries that offer significant returns.

Regulation in Kazakhstan stands out for taking a coercive rather than incentivising approach. Regulators are also not required to assess alternative regulatory approaches before adopting new regulations. This can hamper innovation and economic efficiency. On the other hand, opening hours of shops are not regulated, and there are no restrictions on the advertising and marketing of professional services, including accountancy; legal, sole proprietorship; engineering and architecture. Command and control regulation offers no incentive to improve quality beyond the standard set by a particular law. Once the regulation is satisfied, actors have no incentive to do better, reflecting the rigidity of regulations that are unable to adapt to the cost and operating structures of individual actors.

Assessing the SOE share in the economy

The impact of the SOE sector on GDP is a meaningful metric to assess the state share in the economy. It is also practical, since all nations calculate their GDP using the same basic methodology, and international organisations ensure that these calculations are consistent across countries. Thus, the GDP provides a reliable and uniform basis for comparison. A 2011 OECD working paper (Christiansen, 2011) documented the share of SOEs in OECD member countries in terms of number, employment and the economic value of the enterprises. It compared the relative "weight" of SOEs across economies by measuring the valuation of the SOE sectors relative to GDP, although noting that measuring asset valuation relative to a flow variable such as the GDP makes only limited economic sense.

The paper found that "the average for all reporting countries is around 15% of the GDP". However, only 27 out of the 34 member countries provided their data, and several countries with substantial SOE sectors did not supply theirs. In addition, values of companies with minority state shareholdings were not included, even though they are significant in some countries. Reporting countries also had different ways of assessing the value of non-listed companies, particularly statutory companies, which were ignored altogether by some respondents.

The most economically meaningful indicator would be the assessment of the share of the SOE sector in the GDP. Since the GDP measures value added, the relevant data should be collected from SOEs entity by entity, which would be a laborious exercise. Simply reflecting aggregate output, such as turnover or gross sales relative to GDP, would introduce systematic bias since value added in the aggregate output varies greatly across sectors.

A more recent OECD report notes that "the absolute size of national SOE sectors is notoriously difficult to compare". It proposes that the share of employment by SOEs of the total non-agricultural dependent employment would be a useful measure of the weight of the SOE sector in the domestic economy (OECD, 2014b). This measure is based on relatively easily available data, it would preclude differences in valuation or accounting issues, and comparable data could be collected from most countries, allowing comprehensive benchmarking. According to data collected by the end of 2012, Norway has the largest SOE sector, employing close to 10% of the dependent workforce. When listed partially owned SOEs were included, Norway jumped to over 12%, and France, Slovenia and Finland exceeded 10%. However, the share of SOE employment of the total workforce illustrates the economic weight of the SOE sector only if the productivity of labour is at the same level in the SOE sector as in the private sector. There is ample evidence that this is often not the case. Especially in transition economies, there is a clear gap between the productivity of the workforce in the respective sectors.

Present condition of state ownership

There were 27 283 registered state-owned legal entities in Kazakhstan as of 25 August 2016. This figure includes all types of legal entities available to the state for different purposes: state institutions and state enterprises, which are financed within the budget economy, as well as JSCs and LLPs, which are established and operate under the same laws as privately held enterprises. *State institutions* are primarily intended to provide for administrative, social, cultural or other functions of a non-commercial nature. For *state enterprises*, the Law on State Property lists a large number of specific tasks, typical for state or municipal administration, such as supply of power, water, gas or heat, health care, primary schooling, etc. According to the Department on the Policy of Managing State Assets the total number of SOEs in Kazakhstan is 6 948, including 679 JSC's and LLP's, the remainder being state enterprises under the right of economic management (1 258 entities) or operational management (5 011 entities).

The majority of the registered legal entities are small. Only 1 002 entities are classified as large, i.e. with more than 250 employees. SOEs are active in all sectors of business and industry, particularly in oil and gas, energy, mining, transportation, and information and communication but with a notably thin presence in manufacturing, banking and insurance activities (Committee on Statistics, 2015). According to data supplied by the Ministry of National Economy, the gross value added by the SOE sector was 7.85% of GDP in 2014.

Legal framework

SOEs doing business or otherwise involved with economic activity are incorporated as either JSCs or LLPs.[1] Both the law on JSCs and that on LLPs are intended, in the first place, to regulate privately owned businesses, including those with foreign, non-Kazakhstani participation. Consequently, with certain exceptions, they apply international business standards and practices to state ownership equally.

Small or medium SOEs with participation by non-state parties are often incorporated as LLPs. The law on LLPs provides a simpler corporate structure, a lighter capital requirement and a less burdensome administration. A more widespread use of this corporate form for the state's small-scale businesses should be considered as an economic alternative.

Stipulations concerning state institutions and state enterprises are included in the Law on State Property 413/2011. This is a large piece of legislation covering all aspects of state ownership: corporate, real estate, machinery, public space, museums, collections, etc. The law defines state institutions and state enterprises, the two corporate forms reserved for state ownership, and regulates their governance and management at both state and municipal levels. The Law on State Property completes the laws on LLPs and JSCs by regulating in detail the governance and management of companies 100% owned, majority owned and minority owned by the state. There are stipulations on the powers of the authorised state body to act as the shareholder, on the composition and powers of the boards of directors, as well as activity planning, including ten-year development strategies and five-year development plans.

The Law on State Property also regulates the privatisation of state-owned assets. It describes in detail the procedures applied in the privatisation of various kinds of property, particularly shares in JSCs and stakes in LLPs, preparations for privatisation, use of funds received and subsequent control over execution.

Other pieces of legislation also regulate SOEs. These include the Law on Natural Monopolies and Regulated Markets and the Law on Sovereign Wealth Fund. It is of concern that the Law on Public Procurement does not apply to SOEs. The Law on Competition has been replaced by the Entrepreneurial Code of October 2015. The general laws on taxation, accounting and audit apply to SOEs and privately owned entities alike.

The state as an owner: OECD Guidelines and measurement methodology

The *OECD Guidelines on Corporate Governance of State-Owned Enterprises* provide recommendations on ownership and governance practices. The Guidelines (Box 4.3) are an OECD legal instrument, implementation of which is overseen by the OECD Working Party on State Ownership and Privatisation Practices (in which Kazakhstan takes part as a Participant). Assessing whether the Guidelines have been fully implemented thus goes beyond the scope of the present chapter. The chapter describes the Kazakhstani reality vis-a-vis an "OECD consensus" which encompasses the Guidelines as well as a number of publications issued by the OECD offering additional guidance on good practices for SOE ownership and governance.

Box 4.3. **OECD Guidelines**

The OECD Guidelines on Corporate Governance of State-Owned Enterprises were first adopted by the OECD Council in 2005 and revised in 2015. They are consistent with the likewise recently revised OECD Principles of Corporate Governance and set the complementary guidance for state-owned enterprises. The Guidelines provide a set of good practices on the legal and regulatory framework of the state ownership function and the corporate governance arrangements of the enterprises. Their purpose is to help policy makers evaluate and improve the legal, regulatory and institutional framework for the governance of the enterprises that they control. This is achieved by providing the shareholders, board members and executives with the right incentives to perform their roles within a framework of checks and balances.

Source: OECD (2015a, 2015b).

Kazakhstan lacks a general ownership policy

The OECD consensus implies that the government develop an ownership policy, which should be disclosed to the public. The policy should define the overall rationales of state ownership, the role of the state in the governance of companies and the roles and responsibilities of government offices involved in the implementation of the policy (Guideline I:B-D). The annotations to the Guidelines note that the absence of an ownership policy may lead either to a passive conduct of ownership functions or the state's excessive intervention in matters of the enterprises.

The government of Kazakhstan has yet to develop or publish any comprehensive statement to this effect. In legislation, particularly in the chapters of the Law on State Property concerning state ownership and management of SOEs, there are stipulations on the roles, powers and responsibilities of the relevant state authorities. The Law on Sovereign Wealth Fund simply states that "the purpose of the Fund shall be to increase the national wealth of the republic of Kazakhstan". Kazakhstani authorities argue that the Law on State Property and the recent Entrepreneurial Code constitute an ownership policy but in the spirit of the Guidelines an ownership policy should be a political statement, from time to time reviewed by the government, and not a legal norm. The Guidelines further specify a number of elements which are not to be read in the Law on State Property. The declarations by the president in 2015 and 2016 on fundamental economic reform programmes – particularly the Kazakhstan 2050 Strategy (Nazarbayev, 2012), the Five Institutional Reforms and the 100 Concrete Steps for implementing the reforms (Nazarbayev, 2015) – make only a few references to state ownership and privatisation.

The marketplace playing field is not level

The legal and regulatory framework for SOEs should ensure a level playing field and fair competition in the marketplace with privately owned companies (OECD, 2012b). A very large number of SOEs are active and operating in most network sectors in Kazakhstan. Enterprises with foreign ownership report that state-owned companies often enjoy better access to resources, markets, credit and licences than private enterprises. There have also been concerns about the tendency of officials to challenge the contractual rights and interfere in the operations of private companies, particularly regarding procurement decisions (U.S. DoS, 2015). As discussed in this chapter, the power of industrial conglomerates led by national managing holdings on the one hand, and the apparent under-development of privately held SMEs on the other, generates an economy that is strongly dominated by the state sector and weakens the competitive position of the private sector (OECD, 2014a).

Equal opportunity for privately held and publicly owned enterprises requires separation of ownership and regulation in the organisation of the government. The Guidelines (III: A) recommend that "there should be a clear separation between the state's ownership function and other state functions that may influence the conditions..." This is not how the government of Kazakhstan is organised. Ministries charged with ownership functions are also regulators of their respective sectors, and ministers maintain influential positions on the boards of directors of national managing holding companies which they are charged with regulating.

SOEs in Kazakhstan are subject to general laws, but these may not be applied consistently. In addition, there is a tendency of courts to favour the government, which has created obstacles in business for privately held enterprises (U.S. DoS, 2015). However, SOEs do carry the same tax burden as privately held enterprises except those which operate in the social sphere providing medical services, education, innovation etc. as specified in the Tax Code.

The Entrepreneurial Code (375/2015) limits state involvement in the market economy. Article 192 requires prior permission from the competition authority, the Committee on Regulation of Natural Monopolies and Protection of Competition under the Ministry of National Economy, before public bodies are allowed to establish new undertakings. The competition authority inspects the relevant market and bases its decision on the development of competition.

The Entrepreneurial Code provides for when the state may participate in economic activity. It describes several cases and circumstances which justify the participation of the state in entrepreneurial activity such as the absence of any other possibility of national security protection, national defence capability or protection of interests of society; the use of state-owned strategic objectives; the existence of a state monopoly; and the absence of private businesses in production of the goods or services intended.

The code also prohibits a number of anti-competitive actions by SOEs that could lead to restriction or elimination of competition or infringe upon consumer rights. The list is not exhaustive but does include failures to act, such as failures to respond to licensing requests by private entrepreneurs.

A state monopoly can only be granted to entities organised as state enterprises established by a governmental decree. The creation of monopolies is possible in cases where competition would have negative effects on the constitutional order, national security, public order, human rights and freedoms, and public health. There are currently about 20 state monopolies in Kazakhstan. Some of them operate in traditionally public services areas, such as assessment of patent applications or veterinary control. Some monopolies have been granted in sectors with environmental or social sensitivities, such as wildlife protection and security-related services (OECD, 2016b).

State-owned companies enjoy readier access to finance than their private sector counterparts, despite efforts by the government to provide additional finance for SMEs. Inadequate supply of finance is one part of the issue. Insufficient access to financing, both for investment and for working capital, is a serious problem for privately held enterprises in Kazakhstan. This is particularly relevant to SMEs, which are not in a position to approach foreign sources of financing, and are constrained by the shallowness of the Kazakhstan banking sector (Chapter 3). Local banks have difficulties mobilising wholesale financing, while also being challenged by the uncertainties in the regulatory and legal landscape, and limited expertise to assess and evaluate the risks in financing SMEs (OECD, 2012a).

The government has attempted to use its structure of SOEs to provide additional finance for private firms. It has drawn on the National Oil Fund to inject financing for private SMEs via the banks, but this has at best balanced the situation. JSC Baiterek National Managing Holding is a holding of state-owned financial institutions that provides financing through public and private firms. The practice is that funding approved by commercial banks is partly provided by Baiterek. Privately owned SMEs receive financing and development support from the Damu Entrepreneurship Development Fund JSC, a subsidiary of Baiterek. Damu channels financing through local banks and operates several programmes subsidising interest rates, guaranteeing loans and providing training to improve the competencies of private entrepreneurs (Baiterek National Managing Holding JSC, 2014).

SOEs are able to draw on the government's financial reserves. Large state-owned conglomerates have wide access to internal financing arrangements not available to private industries. For example, the Law on Sovereign Wealth Fund includes specific provisions on credits to be provided between companies belonging to the Samruk-Kazyna group on the basis of internal credit policies and a common policy on management of funds implemented by Samruk-Kazyna itself. The recent purchase by the National Bank of Kazakhstan (NBK) of 10% of the shares of the national energy company KazMunaiGas from Samruk-Kazyna was noteworthy with regard to NBK's basic regulatory role, given that it also manages both the National Fund and the National Pension Fund (Lillis, 2015). Even companies that are partly privatised enjoy privileged access to finance, as private lenders infer a state guarantee in assessing the risk of the loan.

Responsible authorities for state ownership

In Kazakhstan the organisation of the state's ownership is very dispersed. The primary ministries responsible for state ownership are the Ministry of National Economy and the Ministry of Finance. In the hierarchy of the Kazakhstan government, departments have strategic and regulatory functions, whereas committees have functions regarding implementation and control (OECD, 2014a). The Department of State Assets Management Policy in the Ministry of National Economy is the central policy-making authority for state ownership. It is responsible for the development of all regulation but is not operative in governance or the privatisation of state assets.

The OECD consensus implies that the exercise of the government's ownership rights should be centralised in a single ownership entity or at least be carried out by a co-ordinating body. The Committee of State Property in the Ministry of Finance is the authorised owner of state assets on behalf of the government. Since the Committee of State Property is the legal owner also of entities where the ownership rights have been delegated by the government to other sector ministries, it could be regarded as the centralised co-ordinating body. Legislation often references "the authorised body that has been transferred the rights of ownership". In cases of "republican" assets directly owned by the state and not by a holding company, this reference means the Committee of State Property. It represents the state's shareholding at annual general shareholders' meetings, nominates appointees to boards of directors, monitors the financial performance of companies and has an active and central role in privatisation operations. However, there are a number of responsible sector ministries which have been vested with shareholders' rights and also a number of legally independent holding companies on top of large groups of subsidiaries, resulting in a very dispersed ownership organisation.

No emphasis has been placed on the separation of ownership and regulation. Both the Ministry of National Economy and the Ministry of Finance are responsible for the regulation of several sectors that affect the operations of SOEs, including taxation, general industrial policy, competition policy, public procurements, etc. The same applies to sector ministries endowed with ownership rights, such as the Ministry of Agriculture. The organisation of large and important groups of companies under national managing holdings provides a certain distance that might be formally regarded as wide enough to break, *de jure*, the contact between regulation and ownership. However, the presence of the relevant ministers, such as the minister of finance and the minister of national economy, as members on boards of the most important national managing holdings connects, *de facto*, the decision making in practice.

Accountability is enhanced where the ownership entity develops consistent reporting on the SOEs and publishes an annual aggregate report. According to the OECD consensus such a report should be the key vehicle of disclosure to the general public, the legislature and the media. There is no aggregate public reporting on the financial and operational performance of SOEs by, for example, the Committee of State Property. The Register of State Enterprises and Agencies and the Depository of Financial Reporting publish data on the performance of SOEs on their websites. The national managing holdings and the largest companies, some of them listed on the stock exchange or having issued bonds, publish comprehensive and detailed annual reports fulfilling international standards.

The supreme audit institution of Kazakhstan is the Accounts Committee, the purpose of which is to control the execution of the republican budget. The Accounts Committee is subordinated to the president but also reports annually to the parliament on the execution of the budget. The primary role of the Accounts Committee and regional audit commissions is to ensure compliance with legislation related to the implementation of the budget. In this respect, they are also authorised to execute external audits of all types of SOEs and their subsidiaries. The OECD 2014 survey of the Kazakhstan central administration (OECD, 2014a) is very critical of state financial control and calls for building capacity and professionalism in the Accounts Committee and subordinated state audit bodies. In November 2015 Kazakhstan adopted the Law on State Audit and Financial Control restructuring and completing the system of state financial control and internal audit.

National managing holding companies and state ownership

The state's full or partial ownership of a very large number of enterprises has been organised through holding companies. A *national company* is a JSC operating in fundamental industries or facilitating regional economic development, and controlled, through majority ownership or otherwise, directly or through a national managing holding company, by the state. A *national holding company* is likewise a government-created entity which holds shares in national companies. A *national managing holding company* manages the interests of the government in national holding companies, national companies, development institutes and other entities.

Samruk-Kazyna

The most important national managing holding company is the sovereign wealth fund Samruk-Kazyna JSC, officially the National Welfare Fund. It is organised as a JSC under the relevant laws but is also covered by the special, dedicated Law on Sovereign Wealth Fund 550/2012. Samruk-Kazyna's purpose is "to increase the national wealth of the republic of Kazakhstan by increasing the long-term value of the organisations included into the group of Samruk-Kazyna and by effective management of assets belonging to the group of the Fund" (Law on Sovereign Wealth Fund, Article 4.1). Samruk-Kazyna owns and manages close to 600 companies in fundamental commodity, infrastructure and service areas. Samruk-Kazyna is the owner of important subsidiaries such as KazMunaiGas, representing state interests in oil and gas; the national atomic company, Kazatomprom; the railway company, Kazakhstan Temir Zholy; the national airline, Air Astana; and the owner and systems operator of the national power grid, the Kazakhstan Electricity Grid Operating Company (KEGOC). These companies are, in turn, mother companies of vast groups of subsidiaries. The group employs more than 320 000 people and its consolidated revenue was equivalent to 13.3% of national GDP in 2014 (Samruk-Kazyna JSC, 2015).

The Law on Sovereign Wealth Fund includes specific provisions regarding the activity of Samruk-Kazyna. In addition to the purpose, the law defines the tasks and principles of activity of Samruk-Kazyna. It extends and complements the laws on JSCs and on LLPs by explaining in detail the powers and tasks of the sole shareholder, the board of directors and the management board.

As with other national managing holdings, there is a substantial degree of active, high-level political participation in the governance of Samruk-Kazyna. The chairman and the members of the board of directors are elected by the shareholder, although the law also confirms the prime minister as chairman. Currently, the other state representative members of the board are the minister of national economy, the minister of finance and the assistant to the president of the Republic. The CEO of Samruk-Kazyna, a former first deputy prime minister, is also a member of the board. Three independent directors are very experienced, high-profile foreign businessmen. The Law on Sovereign Wealth Fund requires that no fewer than two-fifths or 40% of the board be independent. Three out of eight falls short of this requirement.

One might assume a corporate board with such high-level membership would have a formal role and hold few meetings. However, in 2014, the board of Samruk-Kazyna held 13 meetings considering 120 issues, taking 180 decisions and giving 45 instructions. The attendance of the majority of members was 100%. The board has nominated three committees: the Audit Committee, consisting of the three independent directors, the Nomination and Remuneration Committee and the "Specialised Committee".

The executive body of Samruk-Kazyna is the management board, headed by the CEO, with members appointed by the board of directors. All members are Samruk-Kazyna employees in top managerial positions. The law lists in detail the issues belonging to the exclusive competence of the management board. The management board acts as the shareholder of the portfolio companies.

The state representatives on the boards of Samruk-Kazyna subsidiaries generally hold high positions in their respective ministries. Samruk-Kazyna is also represented on the boards of subsidiaries.

Samruk-Kazyna is presently audited by Ernst & Young. Its financial reporting follows the International Financial Reporting Standards (IFRS), and annual reporting is transparent and comprehensive, with the exception of remuneration to directors.

Specific provisions in the Law on Sovereign Wealth Fund inform the special role of the Samruk-Kazyna fund in the economy:

- The basic rule is that neither the government nor other state bodies should interfere with the operations of Samruk-Kazyna or the group companies, unless otherwise stated.
- A representative of the Accounts Committee is a permanent member of the "Specialised Committee" of Samruk-Kazyna, with powers to start an external audit of any company of the group. There is a centralised internal audit service within the group.
- Samruk-Kazyna and all group companies are required to have ten-year development strategies complemented by five-year development plans.
- In the interests of national welfare, Samruk-Kazyna has priority rights to acquire strategic objects, shares of banks and rights to subsoil use.
- The main principles of interaction between the government and Samruk-Kazyna are included in an agreement on co-operation.

According to the Law on Sovereign Wealth Fund, Samruk-Kazyna and the group companies may be required to participate in the realisation of “socially significant and innovative industrial projects”. According to the 2014 annual report, Samruk-Kazyna participated in financing the construction of, for example, a multifunctional ice palace, the Choreography Theatre, schools in the Kyrgyz Republic and an exhibition centre in Moscow.

The existence and organisation of Samruk-Kazyna and the other national managing holdings imply that a major part of the wealth of the nation, both assets and cash flow, has been separated from budgetary control through incorporation into independent JSCs. These companies are financed by the state, which provides equity and loans, and they pay dividends and taxes to the state. However, this immense wealth remains under the control and management of, albeit political, boards of directors and not parliament, which otherwise has powers over the budget of the nation.

Other important holding companies: National management holdings Baiterek and KazAgro

JSC Baiterek National Management Holding is a government organisation aimed at promoting the sustainable development and diversification of the economy. Through its subsidiaries, it offers financial and investment support to the non-oil and gas sector, particularly to SMEs. (Baiterek National Managing Holding JSC, 2014.) Baiterek has 11 subsidiaries: development institutions, such as the Development Bank of Kazakhstan, that provide financing, investment and export support to large projects and enterprises; institutions, such as Damu Entrepreneurship Development Fund, that provide support to innovative activity and SMEs; and financial organisations, such as the Housing Constructions Savings Bank, that participate in the implementation of real estate and housing projects. The Baiterek group employs a relatively modest 2 400 staff but in 2014, it made a profit of KZT 41.6 billion, and its assets grew to over KZT 2.3 trillion, equivalent to 6% of GDP.

As with Samruk-Kazyna, Baiterek’s board of directors includes very high-level politicians. The prime minister is the chairman, and the other state representatives are the first deputy prime minister, the minister of industry and new technologies, the minister of finance, the minister of national economy, and an assistant to the president of the republic. The three independent directors are experienced foreign professionals. The CEO is likewise a member of the board. The members of the executive board are professionals employed by the company in top managerial positions. Baiterek is audited by KPMG, and it reports annually following the IFRS. Baiterek applies its own corporate governance code.

JSC National Management Holding KazAgro owns and leads the group of agribusiness companies of Kazakhstan. Its purpose is to increase the availability of financing and sales markets, corporate management efficiency and the development of human capital in agribusiness entities (KazAgroFinance JSC, 2015). The group includes 53 companies. Food Contract Corporation JSC is the agent for the management of state resources of grain. It was formerly active as the national regulator of grain prices, but since Kazakhstan entered the World Trade Organization, the company has operated solely as a trader of grain and cotton. Kazagrofinance and AAC Agrarian Credit Corporation provide financing to investment projects and the purchase of agricultural machinery on leasing terms. Kazagromarketing supports agricultural producers in various ways to find markets for their products.

Ownership rights of KazAgro shares have been delegated by the government to the Ministry of Agriculture. The chairman of the board is the first deputy prime minister and the present members are the minister of agriculture, the chairman of the Kazakhstan

Development Bank and the vice-minister of national economy. There are three independent directors: one Kazakhstani, two foreign. The CEO is not a member of the board. KazAgro has applied its own corporate governance code since 2010. The company has been audited by Ernst & Young, and the financial reporting follows the IFRS.

Governance of companies

Law on JSCs

Kazakh legislation tends to be very detailed and comprehensive on paper, giving rise to differing interpretations. It also frequently includes positive lists – of everything that is allowed, for example, or a complete list of the duties of an administrative body – leading to the interpretation that anything not included is forbidden.

The Law on JSCs provides a rigid base for the corporate structure of JSCs. The administration of a Kazakh JSC is one-tier, with no supervisory board. The law allows only two series of shares: ordinary and preferred. Specific provisions apply for golden shares – shares that give power over and above the share of capital they represent (e.g. veto power on some decisions) – which are, however, forbidden in public (listed) companies. The general meeting is the supreme body of the company. The board is appointed by the annual general meeting, and the chairman is elected by the board. The board appoints the executive management, including the chief executive officer (CEO), as well as the auditors, following the instructions of the general meeting.

There are only a few specific stipulations concerning state ownership in the Law on JSCs. An overdue tax liability of a JSC with state ownership may be covered by the issuance of additional shares to the state.

The state representative at shareholder meetings is the agency to whom the powers of the state as shareholder have been assigned. This is the Committee of State Property or, following a specific government decision, the relevant sector ministry, such as the Ministry of Agriculture. The Committee of State Property is authorised to take decisions independently on issues to be dealt with at shareholder meetings. The sector ministry is required to consult and to agree with the committee on certain central issues, such as approval of annual finances and issues of composition of the board of directors.

The board of directors has a central role and wide powers, performing the overall management of the company, with the exception of issues that are reserved to the competence of the shareholder meeting by law or the company's charter. The members of the board are appointed and dismissed by the general shareholder meeting. They are elected for a specific term set by the shareholder meeting, but there is no limit to the length of the term or the number of re-elections. The minimum number of board members is three. No fewer than 30% of the members must be independent.

The Law on State Property requires that the Ministry of National Economy, the Committee of State Property and the relevant sector ministry be represented on the boards of national managing holdings and national holdings. There are no requirements regarding the representation of both genders on the boards of directors. Almost all board members in state-owned companies are male, even though there are a number of women in high positions in the ministries, as well as in top managerial positions in the companies. Employee representation at the level of boards is not a practice in Kazakhstan. Board membership is strictly personal. The laws do not recognise deputy members and there is no practice of ministers or high officials sending assistants to meetings as personal representatives, as might be found in other countries.

The boards facilitate their work by establishing committees to consider important issues and to make recommendations to the board. Examples of such issues include strategic planning, nominations and remuneration, internal audit and social issues. Other experts than board members may also be appointed as committee members. The committees are to be chaired by independent directors. The fiduciary duty of care and loyalty of all officials of JSCs, including board members, towards the company and its shareholders is clearly stipulated in the Law on JSCs. The boards are required to have their performance evaluated annually.

The remuneration of members of a board is determined by the shareholder meeting. Companies are very discreet in reporting the benefits of board members, the CEO and the top management. In some companies, the independent directors are reported to receive an annual remuneration and a separate fee for each meeting attended. The Law on State Property orders that board members who are public servants do not receive remuneration for board membership.

Corporate governance codes

Kazakhstan has a general policy of striving for better corporate governance in both the public and private sectors. However, this has led to a certain overregulation, with very comprehensive corporate governance codes regulating the daily administration and operations of firms in detail.

Samruk-Kazyna recently issued a corporate governance code to be applied, in addition to Samruk-Kazyna itself, in all companies of the group where state ownership exceeds 50%. The code has been drafted with assistance from the OECD Working Party on State Ownership and Privatisation Practices. It applies the same composition as the OECD Principles and Guidelines, separating brief "Principles of Corporate Governance" and explanatory "Annotations", although the code is very detailed, comprehensive and explains Samruk-Kazyna's corporate policies even in internal administrative and operational issues. Whereas the recent version of the OECD Guidelines has 40 typewritten pages, the Samruk-Kazyna code has over 100.

There are several corporate governance codes in the state sector, and companies listed on the stock exchange have to abide by specific transparency rules linked to disclosure requirements. Each of the national managing holdings has a corporate governance code, as well as KEGOC, which has been listed on the stock exchange since 2014. Samruk-Kazyna has put much effort into drafting its new code and has proposed that it be the basis of a unified code for SOEs. A working group, co-ordinated by the Ministry of National Economy and with participation from, e.g., the NBK, is working towards a unified code for all JSCs with state participation, following the OECD Guidelines as well as the *G20/OECD Principles of Corporate Governance* (OECD 2015b).

Corporate reporting and audit

Financial reporting following the IFRS is widespread, since all corporate groups owned and managed by the three national managing holdings follow that practice. Annual reports are very comprehensive, including chapters, for example, on corporate governance, corporate social responsibility and related party transactions. The annual reporting of the large companies conforms to high international standards. Quarterly reports are published by the national managing holdings, as well as those companies with state participation that are listed on the stock exchange or have issued bonds. The Committee of State Property receives performance reports from all companies on a quarterly basis.

The external auditors are usually appointed by the sole shareholder or by the shareholder meeting. However, in national managing holdings and national holdings, including Samruk-Kazyna, this authority is by the Law on State Property delegated to the board of directors. This is exceptional, since external auditors are normally seen as agents of the shareholders auditing the performance and actions of the board as well. However, the corporate governance codes of Samruk-Kazyna, Bayterek and KazAgro give this right also to the sole shareholder, in addition to the board. Large SOEs are usually audited by the international "Big Four" companies, while smaller SOEs employ local audit firms. Procurement legislation for these contracts requires companies to run annual tendering processes, a costly system, since auditors are commonly appointed on three-year contracts. There is obligatory rotation after five years. In the audit of state-owned entities other than JSCs, the external auditors are obliged by law to report on discovered violations of legislation concerning use of public funds, state assets, guarantees, etc.

Privatisation

Legal framework, relevant authorities and decision making

The essential norms regarding privatisation of assets owned by the state are included in the Law on State Property. Enacted in 2011, it replaced the 1995 privatisation law, as well as the earlier Law on State Enterprises. The relevant authorities are the government of Kazakhstan, the Committee of State Property and the boards of directors of the holding companies owning the shares not owned directly by the state. The Law on State Property was amended in a number of details by the end of 2015 to provide regulation to the ongoing privatisation programme.

The central decision-making authority is the Committee of State Property, which holds the powers of the shareholder pursuant to state-owned shares, unless otherwise regulated. Sales of companies classified as strategic objects require a decision by the government. The boards of holding companies are authorised to decide upon sales of shares up to 25% of the total assets of the holding. According to the Law on Sovereign Wealth Fund (article 7.7), the disposal of shares owned by Samruk-Kazyna in strategic companies included on a list defined by the sole shareholder also requires a decision by the government as the sole shareholder of Samruk-Kazyna.

The two most important actors for privatisation in Kazakhstan are the Committee of State Property and Samruk-Kazyna. They are both expected, under normal circumstances, to have sufficient resources to do the job: the preparation and execution of various sorts of transactions, including professional evaluation of the assets to be offered for sale. Assistance by external advisors, as well as international investment banks, is sought particularly in connection with the privatisation of assets belonging to the group "Top 65" (a list of large state-owned assets due for privatisation starting in 2017) or to the ownership of Samruk-Kazyna. The selection and appointment of external advisors is usually done through competitive bidding.

The OECD Guidelines do not include any recommendations in terms of privatisation. The OECD has not issued any recommendations or other legal instrument bearing on privatisation processes. However, the Working Party has published a stocktaking of recent privatisation and tentative conclusions on good practices (OECD, 2010). These will be referred to in the following as the "OECD consensus".

Restrictions on privatisation

The Law on Natural Monopolies includes a list of activities that are regarded as natural monopolies, and thus are generally not to be privatised. These activities include oil and gas transport through trunk pipelines, electric and thermal power transmission and distribution, trunk railway and highway networks, ports and airports, etc. The Civil Code includes a corresponding list of assets that have strategic significance to the welfare or defence of the nation and its people. Such assets and the entities owning such assets should, as a rule, stay in the possession of the state and not be subject to privatisation. The sale and, thus, the privatisation of such assets are, however, not totally excluded, but require a specific decision by the government.

Methods of disposal

The Law on State Property regulates all processes of privatisation in detail. A number of stipulations were amended with a Law "On amendments and additions to some legislative acts of the Republic of Kazakhstan on public procurement" of 4 December 2015, effective 1 January 2016. The changes were introduced in view of the vast, ongoing privatisation programme.

The vendor of an asset is obliged to be prepared for the sale in advance by executing a vendor's due diligence process. The vendor must ascertain by evaluation the market value of the asset to be sold; finding all information on possible indebtedness, burdens or encumbrances affecting the value of the asset; defining the method and conditions of the sale; and securing the safety of the asset.

The price of an asset to be sold shall be its market price. The Law on State Property specifically notes that the market price may be lower than the book value. Assets with a book value exceeding 2 500 000 times the monthly calculation index (KZT 2 121 as of 1 January 2016) i.e. KTZ 5.3 billion, are to be evaluated by independent consultants following international evaluation standards. Assets with a lesser book value are to be valued according to Kazakhstan regulations. The law also regulates in detail the conditions of payment. The proceeds of the sales are to be directed to the state or municipal budget.

Amendments to the law have made the price decisive in determining the purchaser of an asset, with or without conditions. The law previously differentiated between an open auction, where the highest bid wins, and a tender in written procedure, where the winner offers the best overall terms. After the recent amendments an auction may be held in three steps – first, by rising bids. If the asset is not sold, a second auction is held at decreasing bids with a minimum price. If needed, a third auction is held with no minimum. Entities not sold after a third auction are liquidated. In a tendering process in writing, additional conditions may be imposed on the purchaser, including preservation of the business profile of the entity for a certain period.

The law regulates in detail the well-known method of a structured auction process. The vendor appoints, through competitive bidding, a financial advisor who assesses the market value of the asset to be sold. First the vendor and the advisor agree on a "long list" of potential purchasers to whom the advisor delivers the asset information, together with a request to place a preliminary bid. Simultaneously, the vendor makes a public announcement of the auction in newspapers. Based on the preliminary bids and negotiations between the bidders and the vendor, assisted by the advisor, a "short list" of at least two bidders is drawn up. The bidder who offers the best conditions in the second and final bid wins the sale. The process must be documented in protocols signed by the vendor, the advisor and all bidders after each phase. This method is also widely used outside Kazakhstan, since it is relatively transparent and it offers a fair possibility of attaining the best conditions for sale at a true market price. The presence and activity of the external advisor guarantees the fairness and transparency of the process.

Direct targeted sales of state assets to "strategic investors" are allowed, following the amendments to the law. A strategic investor must have experience in the relevant field of industry or business, must acquire a substantial portion of the ownership in the asset, must participate in the management of the company and must be able to transfer new technologies, as well as attract highly qualified professionals.

The purchaser in a direct targeted sale must make a number of commitments and undertakings. These may concern capital inputs; the level of output and the range of products and services; environmental protection; and job preservation and creation, maintaining a workforce with at least two-thirds Kazakhstani nationals. At the same time, the business profile of the entity should be maintained and the industrial and social infrastructure preserved. Accounts payable should be settled in a timely manner, along with salaries in arrears, if any. The resale of the purchased asset will be restricted.

All direct targeted sales must be carried out by independent external advisors. This imposes on the advisor the responsibility of ascertaining and safeguarding the integrity of the sales process, and maintaining the maximal openness and transparency and the exclusion of any corrupt practices.

The law also recognises the sale of state-owned securities, including derivatives, through the stock exchange – the Kazakhstan Stock Exchange (KASE) as well as foreign exchanges. This includes initial public offerings (IPOs) for previously non-listed shares. In secondary offerings of already listed shares, the method of accelerated book building would offer a fast and precise way to set the market price. Incentives, such as price reductions or bonus shares, are sometimes offered to domestic retail investors to boost demand in this particular group. The trade-off is that such incentives are ultimately transfers from all taxpayers to investors. Such practices may also set precedents for future privatisations (OECD, 2003).

State enterprises may be sold through asset sales as a property complex and then liquidated as an empty shell. Another possibility is to convert the state enterprise into a JSC or an LLP before the privatisation.

The securities market

The KASE is illiquid, has limited turnover and limited capitalisation. It was established in 1993 as a currency exchange and started trading in securities in 1995. It is organised as a JSC and located in Almaty. The KASE is controlled by the NBK through its 50.1% shareholding majority, reinforced by a golden share. Trading volumes are small and tending to decline. The number of listed companies dropped to 138 at the end of 2015, compared with 354 at the start of 2012. The aggregate capitalisation of the equity market is less than USD 40 billion. The average daily volume traded is less than USD 1 million. The most liquid shares are those of KazTransOil JSC, a subsidiary of KazMunayGas belonging to the Samruk-Kazyna group, and KEGOC JSC, a directly owned subsidiary of Samruk-Kazyna. Both companies were listed on the KASE through the People's IPOs in 2012 and 2014 respectively. (KASE, 2016)

Kazakhstan's strongest financial institution appears to be the NBK. As the central banking institution of the state, it manages the foreign exchange reserves of the nation and oversees the financial system as regulator. In addition, the NBK owns a majority stake in the KASE, and manages the assets of the National Oil Fund and of the National Pension Fund, where all private pension funds were consolidated in 2013, although the government plans to move pension fund management to private entities.[2] Thus, the NBK has both regulator and investor roles. It reports that internal Chinese Walls have been erected to protect against conflicts of interest.

Recent and ongoing privatisation programmes

Privatisation Programme 2014-16

Following a review of state assets in 2014, a programme was prepared for the privatisation of almost 782 entities and the reorganisation or liquidation of close to 800 entities. The programme was to be completed by January 2016 but it was cancelled by the end of 2015 with the introduction of the new "Comprehensive Privatisation Plan 2016-2020". It included all classes of entities, from state institutions and municipal enterprises to JSCs. Of these assets, 106 belonged to Samruk-Kazyna (Samruk-Kazyna, 2016). The programme was launched "for the purpose of consolidating the foundations of the market economy. The main idea of this programme was to give a momentum to further development of the private sector in Kazakhstan" (Samruk-Kazyna, 2016). It emphasised that the availability of modern technology provides more openness and transparency to the sales process and facilitates the participation of a wide range of potential purchasers in the acquisition of state-owned stakes and shares. All assets to be sold were to be evaluated in advance by external, independent appraisers.

Assets included in this privatisation programme were selected on the basis of discrepancy with the owner's core operations; market presence of private companies engaged in similar operations; lack of strategic importance; and lack of public importance (Samruk-Kazyna, 2016).

The largest number of assets were sold electronically through the web portal of the Kazakhstan State Property Registry under the Ministry of Finance. Electronic auction was used if the price was the sole decisive aspect. Electronic tender, likely the most-used method, allowed the inclusion of conditions that the successful bidder must fulfil after the change of ownership. There was also the option of a two-stage tendering process reserved for the sale of strategic assets to prequalified participants.

In addition, Samruk-Kazyna planned to introduce five companies to the stock exchange through People's IPOs in 2011. This group included KEGOC, which was listed in 2014. Partial privatisation was possible for companies that were strategic or did not compete with private industries, in which case Samruk-Kazyna would retain the majority ownership. In strategic entities, it was possible for foreign buyers to purchase a minority share only with the permission of the Government Commission of Strategic Objects. Samruk-Kazyna offered purchasers a virtual data room to facilitate their due diligence process.

Box 4.4. Listing of KEGOC

By mid-2016, minority stakes had been sold in only two companies under the People's IPOs programme launched in 2011: KazTransOil in 2012 and KEGOC in 2014. At the offering, KEGOC issued 26 million new shares minus one share at an initial subscription price of KZT 505. The issue was oversubscribed, and KEGOC was given more than 40 000 new shareholders. Now Samruk-Kazyna controls 90% plus one share, and the minority shareholders control 10% minus one share of the total number of KEGOC's shares.

The share price of KEGOC went down after the IPO, reaching a low of KZT 320, but the price has recovered since; the share was trading at prices above KZT 900 during most of the first half of 2016. KEGOC's dividend policy is to pay out not less than 40% of the net income. The dividend proposal on 2014 profits was KZT 8.6 billion, i.e. KZT 33 per share. For the initial subscribers, participating in the IPO of KEGOC has been a fairly sound investment.

From the point of view of the company, the listing does not provide access to an additional source of equity financing as long as Samruk-Kazyna holds on to its majority exceeding 90%. Merely as a consequence of the increased transparency required from a listed company, KEGOC will increase its efficiency through improved governance and added board independence. There are no politicians on the present board of KEGOC. It consists of two representatives of Samruk-Kazyna, three independent directors and the CEO of the company. None of the board members owns shares in the company. On the other hand, the company has to bear all the effort and additional cost of a listed company communicating with tens of thousands of small shareholders.

The People's IPOs programme was launched with the purpose of giving citizens the opportunity to profit from the development of successful companies, contribute to the development of the stock exchange and provide funds for the companies to invest. With the KEGOC IPO, the government and Samruk-Kazyna have provided the general public with a small slice of the dividends plus the possibility of capital gain but absolutely no power in decision making. The small shareholders may raise their voice at annual general meetings and express their possible discontent by voting with their feet: disposing of their shares.

The two IPOs gave the stock exchange a real and much needed boost: KazTransOil and KEGOC are by far the two most traded shares on the KASE.

Source: KEGOC, 2014.

By the end of 2015, a total of 239 assets had been sold. Fifteen assets were sold from the state portfolio, 50 from national holdings and companies, and the rest from municipalities and other organisations. The total sales proceeds were KZT 79 billion, of which KZT 5.5 billion were directed to the state budget and KZT 67.3 billion to the national holdings and companies. The latter figure has been reported as including the KZT 13.1 billion revenue of the Samruk-Kazyna group from the listing of KEGOC shares.[3] The Privatisation Programme 2014-2016 was annulled by the Resolution by the government 1141 "On Certain Issues of Privatization in 2016-2020" on 30 December 2015 setting forth the new programme "Comprehensive Privatization Plan 2016-2020".

Comprehensive Privatisation Plan 2016-2020 – Top 65

The Kazakhstan government has set a target of reducing the SOE share of economic activity to 15% by 2020, from approximately 30% to 40% at the end of 2015. This programme is in parallel with the current economic and societal development programmes, the Kazakhstan 2050 and the Five Institutional Reforms, although these do not make direct reference to state ownership or to privatisation. The "100 Concrete Steps To Implement The Five Institutional

Reforms" (Nazarbayev, 2015) invites international strategy partners as anchor investors to establish joint ventures with the state in priority sectors of the economy. These joint venture companies would later be introduced to the stock exchange by floating the state shares. Additionally, this declaration invites strategic investors to develop industries, such as energy saving, dairy production and meat processing, where the presence of the state is, for the time being, not substantial.

The privatisation target is very ambitious. A large number of factors affecting the success of the privatisation programme are beyond the vendor's control. It will require primarily foreign investors, given the thinness of the financial market and the low gross savings rate of the country's citizens. The timeline is very demanding, given the scale and complexity of the assets that the plan proposes to privatise within less than five years, and given the need for management of entities to be sold in whole or in part to reorganise the companies to attract investors. Current global circumstances add to the challenge of implementing the programme, given the effects on Kazakhstan of the sustained fall in oil prices, and the effects of United States and EU sanctions on Russia through Kazakhstan's membership of the Eurasian Economic Union. Kazakhstan was downgraded by all major credit rating companies in the first part of 2016, while the tenge depreciated significantly against major currencies.

The SOEs to be sold have been selected for their potential for privatisation to develop competition and private capital and to reduce the share of economic activity under state ownership. On 22 September 2015, First Deputy Prime Minister Bakytzhan Sagintayev declared that a list of the Top 60 would include 38 companies owned by Samruk-Kazyna, four owned by Baiterek, four owned by KazAgro and 14 companies directly owned by the state. The Top 60 grew into the Top 65, and the programme was given more detail when the government issued the Comprehensive Privatisation Plan 2016-2020 as the Resolution of the Government No. 1141 on 30 December 2015. The programme was first presented by the then Minister of National Economy, Yerbolat Dossayev. He remarked that large-scale privatisation is the government's top priority for 2016. The minister specifically noted that the fair market values of the assets may be far lower than their book values.[4] First Deputy Prime Minister Sagintayev was entrusted with implementing the privatisation resolution (Government of Kazakhstan, 2015).

The privatisation programme comprises 783 entities, which are divided into groups, firstly on the basis of size and secondly on the basis of ownership. The Top 65 comprise the large enterprises, which are the priority for privatisation. These are enterprises with a book value exceeding KZT 5.3 billion. The enterprises are presently owned directly by the state (e.g. Astana International Airport JSC) and by the national managing holdings and national companies Samruk-Kazyna, KazMunayGas, Kazakhstan Temir Zholy, Kazatomprom, Samruk-Energo, Baiterek and KazAgro. Seven companies presently owned by Samruk-Kazyna are marked to be listed on the stock exchange through IPOs: Kazakhstan Temir Zholy, KazMunayGas, Kazatomprom, Samruk-Energo, Tau-Ken Samruk National Mining Company, Kazpost and Air Astana. The remaining 718 entities, each with an asset value of less than KZT 5.3 billion, are a very mixed group, with companies owned by the state, the national holdings and national companies, as well as the municipalities. The Resolution No. 1141 has been written with due respect to corporate governance: in respect of assets directly owned by the state the government resolves to approve the list of enterprises to be privatised, whereas in respect of assets owned by Samruk-Kazyna or other holding companies, the government resolves to recommend, that the companies approve the respective lists of enterprises to be privatised.

The assets to be listed will be sold to strategic investors by placing shares on the stock exchange. Dual listings in both KASE and more liquid foreign exchanges would be considered. There is no single co-ordinating body but several special project offices called Delivery Units will be established for the co-ordination of the programme, with representation from the Ministry of Finance, the Ministry of National Economy, Samruk-Kazyna, Baiterek and KazAgro. They will seek assistance from international consultants to support the execution and to ensure the transparency of the process.[5] The recommendations of the delivery units on types and terms of sale, requirements of buyers and use of external consultants will be considered by the State Commission on Economy Modernisation.[6]

The OECD consensus strongly suggests that large privatisation programmes be organised under a single co-ordinating actor. This should be the unit responsible for state ownership or, in the absence of such a state shareholder, a specialised privatisation agency (OECD, 2010). Since there will be several (at least four) delivery units instead of one project office as originally planned, the authority is likely to remain with the actual owners of the assets, particularly the Committee of State Property and the national managing holdings.

The execution of the ongoing privatisation programme relies to a large extent on the employment and assistance of external independent advisors and consultants. Advisors with experience in privatisation often have access to networks of high-quality investors (OECD, 2003). Such advisors are responsible, for example, for the pre-sale evaluation of all but the smallest assets, assisting the vendor in structured auction processes and ascertaining the integrity of direct trade sales to strategic investors. Advisors with such responsibilities must be appointed in competitive processes with maximal integrity and transparency. The earlier findings of the OECD suggest that advisors with a mandate to evaluate assets and give strategic advice, such as regarding when, what and how to privatise, should not be given a mandate to advise on the actual sale of those assets to avoid conflict of interest (OECD, 2010).

The authorities have not given much information or detail on precisely how the privatisation will proceed. Except for the seven companies that are to be listed, the actual methods of sale, such as auction, tendering or structured two-stage tendering, will be decided on a company-by-company basis by the present owners and the delivery units. Also undisclosed is how much of each entity is going to be privatised and whether present owners are expected to abandon ownership completely, or are intending to retain some participation. The People's IPO policy consisted of selling 10% minus one share of the entities.

The requirement of maximal transparency and accountability in all aspects of the privatisation process is essential. Political interventions will undermine credibility for investors and ultimately reduce privatisation revenues. The organisation of the Comprehensive Privatisation Plan appears to be dispersed and not cohesive, with numerous agents on different levels. The execution of the programme is controlled at the top level by the State Commission on Economy Modernisation, led by the prime minister. The OECD consensus implies that the privatisation process be disclosed regularly to both the parliament and the general public (OECD, 2010). The Committee of State Property, the state assets registry and Samruk-Kazyna have provided appropriate and relevant information on the progress of the privatisation, supported with current data on their respective websites in several languages.

Past experience implies that any privatisation process should be controlled, *ex-post*, by an independent body reporting to the parliament (OECD, 2010). The supreme audit institution of Kazakhstan, the Accounts Committee, is subordinate to the president and reports to the parliament basically only on the execution of the budget. According to the recently adopted Law on State Audit and Financial Control the Accounts Committee reports quarterly to the parliament on the effectiveness of the management of state-owned assets, including the progress of the privatisation. The Accounts Committee should also have the tasks and powers required in the *ex post* control of the privatisation process and the responsibility to report appropriately to the parliament. The International Organisation of Supreme Audit Institutions' *Guidelines on Best Practice for the Audit of Privatisations* is a common set of good practices in this respect.

Preparing entities for privatisation

The implementation of the vast privatisation programme will be a huge challenge for the state administration, the holdings and the companies. It is a matter for debate to what extent the state owner should restructure the assets before privatisation.

Early planning and preparations are needed for the substantial adjustments of the functioning of a publicly owned entity to that of a listed company. A company planning to be listed must start preparations well in advance to fulfil the listing requirements set by the exchange. It must meet requirements concerning management, corporate governance and reporting. Its financial administration must be able to deliver financial reporting following international standards to the extent and comprehensiveness expected by the shareholders – and in three languages (Kazakh, Russian and English). Management must be able to organise annual and extraordinary general shareholder meetings for a large number of shareholders, including providing means for absentee voting. As an example of this process, KEGOC started preparations for listing in 2011, a year before the planned IPO. The preparations took a full year, and the company was ready in 2014 when the IPO became a reality after delays in the legislation process.

There are three aspects of an enterprise the owner might be willing to improve before sell-off to attract a better price: employment; management, board and governance; and capital structure (OECD, 2009). These aspects apply whether a company is to be privatised through listing or trade sale:

- Regarding **employment**, the labour and employment policies of Kazakhstan SOEs still follow those of the Soviet era. In many countries SOE employees enjoy better social benefits, such as housing or a larger pension, than their private-sector equivalents. Ironing out such differences post privatisation is challenging and sometimes results in the government assuming responsibility for certain benefits such as pensions for a long time afterwards. Such "grandfathering" of existing entitlements of civil servants and other public employees by the government is not regarded as good practice by the OECD (OECD, 2010). According to the Kazakhstani authorities such social privileges can be accessed only by civil servants and the employees of SOEs have similar conditions to their counterparts in the private sector.
- Also regarding **employment**, large SOEs employ large, often bloated workforces, a state of affairs maintained for political reasons. This over-employment has resulted in severe inefficiency, negatively affecting results. Such companies are not likely to interest private investors, particularly foreign investors. Layoffs are always unpleasant and politically challenging, but the government might be in a better position to mitigate the negative effects of personnel adjustments before the fact than private owners afterwards.

- Regarding **management and board composition**, a change in ownership should be reflected in the composition of the board and the management. Even if the state retains control, the number of government representatives should be reduced, the number of independent directors increased, and new owners of substantial stakes should have the opportunity to appoint their own candidates. New controlling owners, particularly in the case of a trade sale, will likely formulate the board, management and governance following their own preferences.[7]
- Lastly, it is advisable to adjust the **capital structure** of the entity being sold, ascertaining on one hand that the viability of the entity is not put at risk with change of ownership while on the other hand removing excess cash. A good price for cash is rarely obtained in connection with the sale of an enterprise.

Public service obligations of companies and the compensation for those obligations should be disclosed when the companies are being listed or sold. Among the companies identified for IPO, Kazakhstan Temir Zholy as the principal transportation enterprise of the country has public service obligations, and others may, as well. The fairness of the compensation should be evaluated by independent appraisers. Kazakhstan Temir Zholy has also been involved in the Samruk-Kazyna group's commitments, under the Law on Sovereign Wealth Fund, to finance and construct public facilities not directly connected with the business of the companies (Kazakhstan Temir Zholy, 2016). Continuing such practices after the listing would also severely conflict with the requirement for equal treatment of all shareholders.

Investors today are increasingly concerned about environmental risks. Remedying environmental damage is expensive and can be lengthy. Some of the SOEs to be offered for sale may be responsible for un-remedied environmental damages, and many more would bear the risk of such remediation costs. It will be challenging for the vendors to negotiate necessary remedial actions and any future responsibilities with potential purchasers, and this can substantially weigh on the final sale price.

The present owners of the SOEs to be privatised will need sufficient time to prepare the companies for sale and to ensure that they will remain viable under different ownership. The Comprehensive Privatisation Plan extends until 2020 but with annual targets. For example, in the opinion of KazAgro, which is required to dispose of several companies, only Food Contract Corporation JSC, the grain and cotton trader, has the resources, systems and operational methods required from a company with a mixed, possibly dispersed ownership.

Who will buy?

The primary challenge lies in finding buyers for the state-owned entities. The domestic demand for privatised state-owned assets is very limited, at least outside the big private conglomerates. The securities market is thin, illiquid and over-regulated, and the gross savings rate per capita is very low.

In OECD member countries, private pension funds are often important investors in local industries and thus active actors in securities markets. The National Pension Fund is not private and could rather be seen as a state agency. It invests in government securities, Kazakhstan corporate bonds and other credit instruments, not equity. The government's 2013 decision to consolidate all pension savings into a single, state-owned fund led to a sharp decrease in the liquidity of the market when the private pension funds, until then active institutional investors, disappeared (U.S. DoS, 2015). The absorptive capacity of the Kazakhstan market as a whole is, therefore, relatively small.

The success of the privatisation programmes depends to a large extent on foreign investors. Conditions in Kazakhstan's present economy will make it challenging to attract foreign money. Stability in the exchange rate is of great importance; large fluctuations can be very costly and make valuation of an asset difficult. (Desai and Wheeler, 2016)

Significant shares of the ownership of the privatised companies will need to be sold to attract strategic investors and to facilitate listing on international stock exchanges. Strategic investors are reluctant to invest where they are unable to influence the management of their investments. The government's belt-and-braces policy to dispose of only of 10% of the shares minus one share, effectively eliminates the possibility for minority shareholders to exercise their rights under the Law on JSCs and deters such strategic investors. The policy also sends a message to the market and to the companies that the government is likely to retain control of the company and will not allow a larger proportion of private ownership. This policy ultimately conflicts with the goal of reduced state ownership given the great weight in the Kazakhstan economy of Samruk-Kazyna and the companies proposed for listing. Moreover, the listing requirements of stock exchanges in OECD member countries do not usually allow such a high percentage of majority ownership. Companies' laws also normally include squeeze-out rules, whereby the owner of such a large majority has a pre-emptive right to purchase the shares of minority owners who themselves have the right to demand that the majority owner does so.

In direct trade sales, the strategic investor must agree to a number of undertakings and concessions regarding the investment and future management and operations of the company, which will reduce the attractiveness of the asset. This requirement is included in recent amendments to the Law on State Property. Such undertakings are very restrictive and will seriously hamper the investor's ability to improve the company's efficiency and productivity. In fact, the required undertakings appear contradictory: operational improvements should be made but nothing may be changed. The undertakings are to be specified in the sales contract between the vendor and the strategic investor. It is not stipulated how the fulfilment of the undertakings may be monitored and how the non-fulfilment or non-observance will be sanctioned. A clawback of the asset by the vendor is in practice most likely excluded.

Small companies to be auctioned through the electronic auction process will likely find any new owners in the domestic market. If domestic demand is limited, sales proceeds will be small. For larger and strategic entities, vendors have the option to use the structured two-stage auction. This allows vendors the possibility of negotiating with several buyers, imposing conditions and selecting the best new owner(s) for the future of the entity.

The possibility of management buy-outs (MBO), presently uncommon in Kazakhstan, should be reintroduced and encouraged where feasible. During the first privatisation programmes in the 1990s Kazakhstan experimented with management buy-outs but with discouraging results. However that was a quarter of a century ago and then many aspects of the Soviet legacy were still apparent in the entire economy. For SMEs, a MBO is favourable from the point of view of the entity itself, since competent management is aware of the existing problems and required remedies. Moreover, members of the management will be motivated as they will benefit from the gains in efficiency after privatisation. However, a successful MBO necessitates the ability of the purchasers to pay a fair price for the shares. If a company is sold at a heavily discounted price, there is no assurance that the management will be committed to running the entity well (OECD, 2003). An MBO is not to be confused with disposals, where the ownership of the entity is distributed to the entire personnel, for free or at a nominal price. Such operations in the past led often to the ownership of the entity falling into unwanted hands or to the demise of the entity because owners did not display interest.

Good things to follow

There is overwhelming support for the notion that privatisation brings about a significant increase in the profitability, real output and efficiency of privatised companies. Fully privatised companies perform better than partially privatised ones (OECD, 2003). Listed companies will enjoy the increase in efficiency through better governance and more professional leadership and management. Listed stock can be used to incentivise management. Daily stock prices provide a day-to-day performance indicator.

Shares to be listed will likely be offered, in large part, through foreign exchanges, and the KASE will also have an opportunity to increase its volumes substantially. When the listings are completed, the securities market of Kazakhstan will be much more active than today. Improving the local capital market is one of the stated priorities of the government and Samruk-Kazyna (Samruk-Kazyna, 2016).

A well-executed privatisation programme can improve government and national wealth, by providing finance for the general budget and for development programmes (OECD, 2016a). On the other hand, the government will forfeit the long-term dividend income that could be generated by the assets once they are privatised.

Conclusions and recommendations

The government has made several efforts since independence in 1991 to reduce the state's high share in Kazakhstan's economy, but the results have disappointing. Privatisation programmes have been incomplete and have been offset by the creation of new entities. The large number of fully state-owned registered legal entities is evidence of a certain over-organisation. Small functions, and similar operations in different locations have been incorporated into separate entities: for example, a large number of municipal sports clubs have been incorporated as LLPs. The number of all state-owned registered legal entities at the start of 2015 was 27 672. Consolidation into larger units would achieve substantial administrative savings. While bringing new owners into companies that will remain partly state-owned, ongoing privatisation programmes can also reduce the number of entities with state participation.

The organisation, administration and governance of state ownership in Kazakhstan do not yet meet internationally agreed good practices in many respects. A number of nations have used the OECD consensus as a benchmark for the reform of state ownership since the introduction of the OECD Guidelines in 2004. Their recent revisions were made in part to ensure their relevance to non-member countries and to provide guidance to countries in different economic circumstances, particularly those in transition to a market economy.

An important first step would be to develop an ownership policy – a step which is particularly important in view of the high state participation in the economy. The overall rationales of state ownership should be defined, written down and disclosed to the public.

The policy should be reviewed by the government at regular intervals. The government should also define the rationales of owning individual enterprises and review these regularly. Drafting, publishing and implementing such a policy would strongly enhance the government's future efforts to reduce state involvement in the economy. It would also create an opportunity to bring the government's ownership policies and practices more into line with the OECD consensus.

The ownership structure of SOEs in Kazakhstan should be clearly identified within the administration and preferably centralised in a single ownership entity. The Department of State Assets Management Policy at the Ministry of National Economy is the central policy-making authority. Although the Committee of State Property acts as authorised owner of state shares on behalf of the government, shareholders' rights of use and possession in numerous enterprises have been delegated to sector ministries, such as the Ministries of Agriculture, Health and Social Development, and Investment and Development. Meanwhile the largest weight of state ownership in Kazakhstan lies in the groups of companies owned and managed by Samruk-Kazyna and other national managing holding companies. This arrangement places a vast portion of the wealth and revenues of the nation outside the budgetary control of the parliament. A consolidated ownership entity should have the capacity and competencies to carry out its duties effectively. Currently it is not clear what degree of supervision the Ministry of Finance and the Ministry of National Economy can exercise over the boards of the national managing holding entities, where some of the government's most senior political office-holders sit. For example, the Committee of State Property may not be in a position to give directions to the board of directors of Samruk-Kazyna, which is chaired by the prime minister.

A centralised ownership entity could be established and located in the Office of the Prime Minister. This structure would reflect the importance of the state sector in the economy. During the first years of independence the ownership function of Kazakhstan was based on a single entity but this proved inefficient under those circumstances. Successful completion of the ongoing privatisation programme will give the opportunity to restructure the present ownership function into one more consistent with the OECD consensus. This would also ensure separation of the state's ownership from its regulatory functions, with the latter located in the Ministry of Finance and the Ministry of National Economy. The ownership entity would combine the policy-making tasks of the Department of State Assets Management Policy and the shareholder's powers and duties of the Committee of State Property, and take over the shareholding rights delegated to sector ministries. The ownership entity should be held accountable to the parliament. It should develop a consistent system of reporting on state ownership and publish an aggregate report at least annually.

The ownership entity should also have the shareholder's powers over the boards of the national managing holdings, and use this to appoint professional board members. These boards should be reorganised with professional corporate leaders taking over the responsibility from political office holders. The ownership entity should develop a consistent and transparent methodology to search, evaluate and choose talented and experienced candidates, both from home and from abroad, for membership on the boards of the important companies.

Box 4.5. **How could future scenarios affect implementation of privatisation strategies and the role of the state in the economy?**

Privatisation efforts have several motivations. They constitute a significant structural reform to move towards an economy where the private sector, sustained by improved competition law and practice, plays a more important role in the economy. This results in greater productivity in firms, possibly at the cost of net employment creation in the short run. Privatisation can also generate revenue for the public purse. Transforming the role of the state in the economy also relies on improvements in the ownership function of the state and the governance of state-owned enterprises (SOEs).

For details of the scenario storylines, please see section: *Anticipating trends and preparing for future challenges: scenarios for the future of Kazakhstan* in Chapter 1.

Scenario 1: "The New Commodity Super Cycle" would see a renewed natural resources bonanza that would reduce pressures to increase productivity in extractive sectors and test the government's resolve to reduce significantly the weight of the state in the economy. On the other hand, given their reduced price competitiveness, non-natural resource assets would most benefit from increased productivity. Moreover, liquidity in financial markets would allow for adequate revenue to be generated from privatisation efforts.

Conversely, in **Scenario 2: "The Great Dissipation"**, limited liquidity may reduce the efficiency of privatisation markets, while revenue would provide a strong motivation for continued privatisation efforts. In a depressed economy, the employment fallout of privatisation would need to be compensated for via active labour market policies or income support, to avoid further depressing internal demand. In this context, improvements in ownership and governance of SOEs would have great potential to increase productivity in a context of limited demand for privatisation, while allowing the state to cushion the employment fallout.

Scenario 3: "New Silk road and Central Asia Resurgence" would see greater trade integration with and through Central Asian economies which would shift the pattern of competitiveness of Kazakhstan, making productivity increases and complementary reforms – including in SOE governance – critical, to overcome higher labour costs in Kazakhstan. The opportunities offered by market-seeking foreign direct investment (FDI) could be capitalised and increase not only the quality of buyers, but also revenues raised from privatisation of manufacturing units and key export-driven state-owned companies.

Finding suitable buyers would be easier in **Scenario 1: "The New Super Cycle"** and especially in **Scenario 4: "New Technology Solution"**, when liquidity would be sufficient in the country and opportunities clear for private sector investors.

Notes

1. All direct references to laws of Kazakhstan are based on English translations provided by "Adilet", Legal information system of Regulatory Legal Acts of the Republic of Kazakhstan, Republican Center of Legal Information, *www.adilet.zan.kz*.
2. The President's State of the Nation address of 30 November 2015 called for pension fund management to move from the central bank to private entities. This policy had not been implemented at the end of 2016.
3. "Sales of republic ownership replenish budget", *Kazinform*, 8 January 2016.
4. "Government approves new privatization plan for 2016-2020", *The Astana Times*, 5 January 2016.
5. "About 60 major state-owned companies are going to be privatized in Kazakhstan", CIS Financial Markets, 23 September 2015.

6. The State Commission on Economy Modernisation is a special committee, headed by the prime minister, monitoring the progress of the development programmes Kazakhstan 2050 and 100 Concrete Steps.
7. Further guidance on boards of directors of state-owned enterprises can be found in OECD (2013a).

References

Baiterek National Managing Holding JSC (2014), *Annual Report 2014*, Baiterek National Managing Holding JSC, Astana, available at *www.baiterek.gov.kz/en/about/financial-reports/annual-reports/* (accessed 9 July 2016).

Christiansen, H. (2011), "The size and composition of the SOE sector in OECD countries", *OECD Corporate Governance Working Papers*, No. 5, OECD Publishing, Paris, *http://dx.doi. 10.1787/5kg54cwps0s3-en*.

Committee on Statistics of the Ministry of National Economy of the Republic of Kazakhstan (2015) *Statistical Yearbook "Kazakhstan 2014"*, Astana.

Desai, M. and E. Wheeler (2016), "Can Kazakhstan's privatization plan succeed?", *The Diplomat*, online, Tokyo, available at *http://thediplomat.com/2016/02/can-kazakhstans-privatization-plan-succeed/* (accessed 9 July 2016).

European Commission, International Monetary Fund, Organisation for Economic Co-operation and Development, United Nations, World Bank (2009), *System of National Accounts 2008*, New York.

Government of Kazakhstan (2015), Resolution of the Government of the Republic of Kazakhstan No. 1141 of 30 December 2015 "On Certain Issues of Privatization in 2016-2020" with Annexes.

Hess, K, A. Gunasekarage and M. Hovey (2008), *State Dominant and Non-state Dominant Ownership concentration and Firm Performance*, mimeo, Waikato Management School, University of Waikato, New Zealand, *http://dx.doi.org/10.2139/ssrn.1112383*.

KASE (2016), Kazakhstan Stock Exchange, website, *www.kase.kz*, accessed July 2016.

KazAgroFinance JSC (2015), 2014: *Annual Report*, KazAgroFinance JSC, Astana, available at *www.kazagro.kz/en/web/kaf/annual-reports* (accessed 9 July 2016).

Kazakhstan Temir Zholy (2016), *Annual Report* 2013, Kazakhstan Temir Zholy, Astana, available at *www.railways.kz/en/node/5362* (accessed 9 July 2016).

KEGOC (2014), *Annual Report* 2014, KECOC, Astana, available at *www.kegoc.kz/en/shareholders-and-investors/information-disclosure/annual-reports/2014* (accessed 9 July 2016).

Koske, I. et al. (2015), "The 2013 update of the OECD's database on product market regulation: Policy insights for OECD and non-OECD countries", *OECD Economics Department Working Papers*, No. 1200, OECD Publishing. *http://dx.doi.org/10.1787/5js3f5d3n2vl-en*

Lillis, J. (2015), "Kazakhstan: Central Bank steps in to prop up cash-strapped oil giant", Eurasianet.org, *www.eurasianet.org/node/74466* (accessed 9 July 2016).

Nazarbayev, N. (2015), "100 Concrete Steps: Modern state for all" established by President Nazarbayev, 20 May 2015.

Nazarbayev, N. (2012), "Strategy 'Kazakhstan 2050': New political course of the established state", speech delivered in Astana, 12 December 2012.

OECD (2016a), *Broadening the Ownership of State-Owned Enterprises: A Comparison of Governance Practices*, OECD Publishing, Paris, *http://dx.doi.org/10.1787/9789264244603-en*.

OECD (2016b), *Competition Law and Policy in Kazakhstan: A Peer Review*, OECD Publishing, Paris, available at *www.oecd.org/competition/competitionlawandpolicyinkazakhstan2016.htm*.

OECD (2015a), *OECD Guidelines on Corporate Governance of State-Owned Enterprises, 2015 Edition*, OECD Publishing, Paris, *http://dx.doi.10.1787/9789264244160-en*.

OECD (2015b), *G20/OECD Principles of Corporate Governance*, OECD Publishing, Paris, *http://dx.doi.org/10.1787/9789264236882-en*.

OECD (2014a), *Kazakhstan: Review of the Central Administration*, OECD Publishing, Paris, *http://dx.doi.org/10.1787/9789264224605-en*.

OECD (2014b), *The Size and Sectoral Distribution of SOEs in OECD and Partner Countries*, OECD Publishing, Paris, *http://dx.doi.org/10.1787/9789264215610-en*.

OECD (2013a), *Boards of Directors of State-Owned Enterprises: An Overview of National Practices*, OECD Publishing, Paris, *http://dx.doi.org/10.1787/9789264200425-en*.

OECD (2012a), *OECD Investment Policy Reviews: Kazakhstan 2012*, OECD Publishing, Paris, *http://dx.doi.10.1787/9789264121812-en*.

OECD (2012b), *Competitive Neutrality: Maintaining a Level Playing Field between Public and Private Business*, OECD Publishing, Paris, *http://dx.doi.org/10.1787/9789264178953-en*.

OECD (2010), *Privatisation in the 21st Century: Summary of Recent Experiences*, OECD Publishing, Paris, available at *www.oecd.org/daf/ca/corporategovernanceofstate-ownedenterprises/privatisationinthe21stcenturyinoecdcountries.htm*.

OECD (2009), *Privatisation in the 21st Century: Recent Experiences of OECD Countries*, OECD Publishing, Paris, available at *www.oecd.org/daf/ca/corporategovernanceofstate-ownedenterprises/privatisationinthe21stcenturyinoecdcountries.htm*.

OECD (2003), *Privatising State-owned Enterprises: An Overview of Policies and Practices in OECD Countries*, OECD Publishing, Paris, *http://dx.doi.org/10.1787/9789264104099-en*.

Samruk-Kazyna JSC (2016) Samruk Kazyna JSC website, *sk.kz/page/privatizatsija*, accessed December 2016.

Samruk-Kazyna JSC (2015), *Annual Report 2014*, Samruk-Kazyna JSC, Astana, available at *http://sk.kz/section/6928* (accessed 9 July 2016).

U.S. DoS (2015), *Kazakhstan Investment Climate Statement 2015*, U.S. Department of State, Washington, DC, available at *www.state.gov/e/eb/rls/othr/ics/2015/241613.htm* (accessed 9 July 2016).

Chapter 5

Towards better environmental regulations in Kazakhstan

Kazakhstan's impressive economic expansion since the late 1990s relied on high rates of energy use and generated significant pollution. These rates are not sustainable, putting at risk the country's development ambitions, while new international agreements add urgency to the need to reduce greenhouse gas emissions. This chapter shows how the current structure of Kazakhstan's system of environmental regulation, permitting and assessment impedes energy efficiency and pollution control. The emphasis on reforming the application of environmental permit fees and penalties as a means of raising revenue rather than on creating incentives to reduce efficiently environmental impact, adds to the cost of investing and doing businesses in Kazakhstan with limited environmental benefit. Better regulation also means designing policies and laws so that they achieve their objectives at minimum cost. These recommended reforms mostly involve bringing the policy into line with the benchmark OECD approach. Kazakhstan's emissions trading scheme presents a model of how the country can adopt effective mechanisms of environmental regulation to place the economy on a more sustainable development path, but it will be essential that this and other mechanisms are well implemented.

Kazakhstan's strategic framework for the environment and a green economy

Kazakhstan has been one of the most successful transition economies. Notwithstanding the recent global financial crisis, the country's gross domestic product (GDP) has doubled over the past decade. Export earnings have increased correspondingly over the same period. Yet much of this growth has depended on the extractive and heavy industries and on an intensive use of electricity produced from coal (Figure 5.1). Consequently, Kazakhstan is today one of the most energy-intensive countries in the world and the energy intensity has not improved during the last decade (Figure 5.2). The environmental damage inherited from the Soviet era has been exacerbated by the effects of energy production, accelerated extraction of oil, gas and other mineral resources, as well as pollution from heavy industry, from agriculture and from growing road traffic in urban areas.[1]

These imbalances pose serious risks to the country's future development path. The strong focus on primary commodities as principal export goods exposes Kazakhstan's export earnings to the high price volatility present in commodity markets. As these revenues mark a significant proportion of receipts of the state budget, that volatility introduces a high degree of uncertainty in medium and long-term budget planning. The recent external shocks of falling world oil and gas prices and shrinking export volumes have had an adverse impact on the economy of Kazakhstan. They add to significant internal vulnerabilities, including postponed investments, including those in large extractive projects. As a result average GDP growth in Kazakhstan has declined since 2014. The reliance on extractive industries also reduces the scope for innovative growth, as they offer limited scope for knowledge spill-overs to other sectors. Technology, human capital and knowledge from these industries tend to be highly sector-specific and may not be easily transferred to other productive uses. Adverse impacts of pollution from coal-based energy production and heavy industry have a cumulative long-term impact on the productivity of natural resources and result in significant negative impacts on the health of the population and excessive pressures on scarce water resources. For example, using monitoring station data from major cities in Almaty, Karaganda, Pavlodar and Ust-Kamenogorsk *oblasts* – on ambient air concentrations of total suspended solids – it was estimated that particulate matter pollution causes approximately 2 800 premature deaths and costs the economy over USD 1.3 billion annually (0.9% of GDP) in terms of increased health care costs (World Bank, 2013).

Given these challenges, Kazakhstan has undertaken steps to move towards a more sustainable model of development. These steps were outlined in two key strategic documents: the 2012 "Kazakhstan 2050 Strategy" and the 2013 "Green Economy Concept" (GEC). The 2050 strategy calls for widespread economic, social and political reforms to position Kazakhstan among the top 30 global economies by 2050. Among the important indicators of success were the acceleration of economic growth (GDP and per capita income); diversification of the economic structure, production and exports; increase in life expectancy; bolstering education parameters; as well as the adoption of an environmentally friendly and sustainable model of economic growth. The GEC outlined the path to ensure long-term growth based on climate-friendly technologies, energy efficiency measures, and the restoration and sustainable management of natural resources. The GEC also envisaged modernising deteriorating infrastructure, and set ambitious targets for the power sector, energy efficiency, water and agriculture. It stated that "...by successfully achieving these targets, the country will recover its water and land resources by 2030, and its resource productivity will largely be on par with the average indicators of the OECD members and other developed countries" (Box 5.1).

Figure 5.1. **Electricity mix in Kazakhstan**

Share of total electricity generation

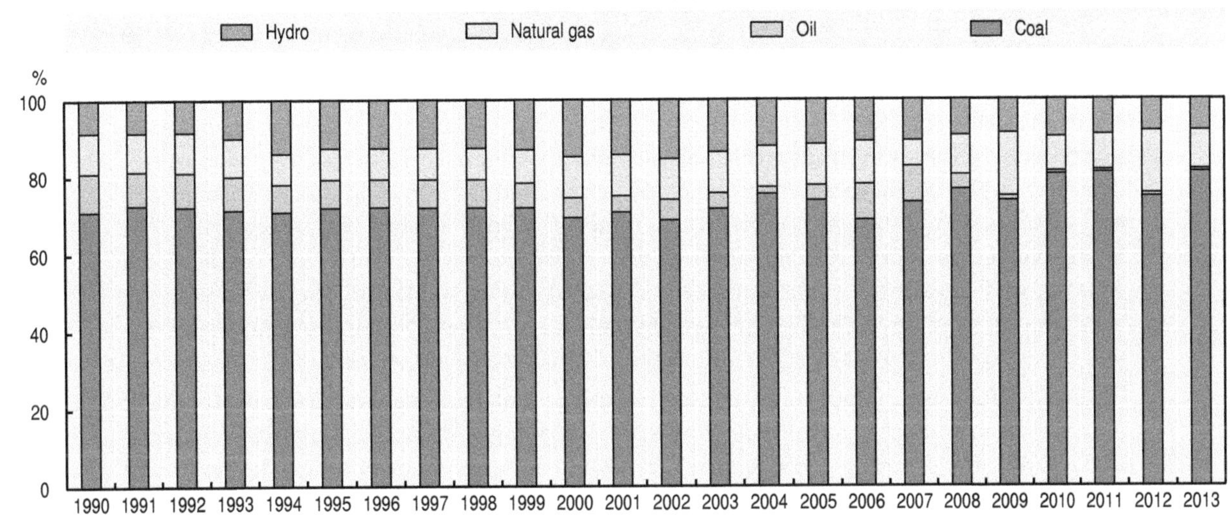

Source: IEA (2016).

StatLink http://dx.doi.org/10.1787/888933445644

Figure 5.2. **Energy intensity**

TPES/GDP, tonne of oil equivalent per thousand 2005 USD PPP

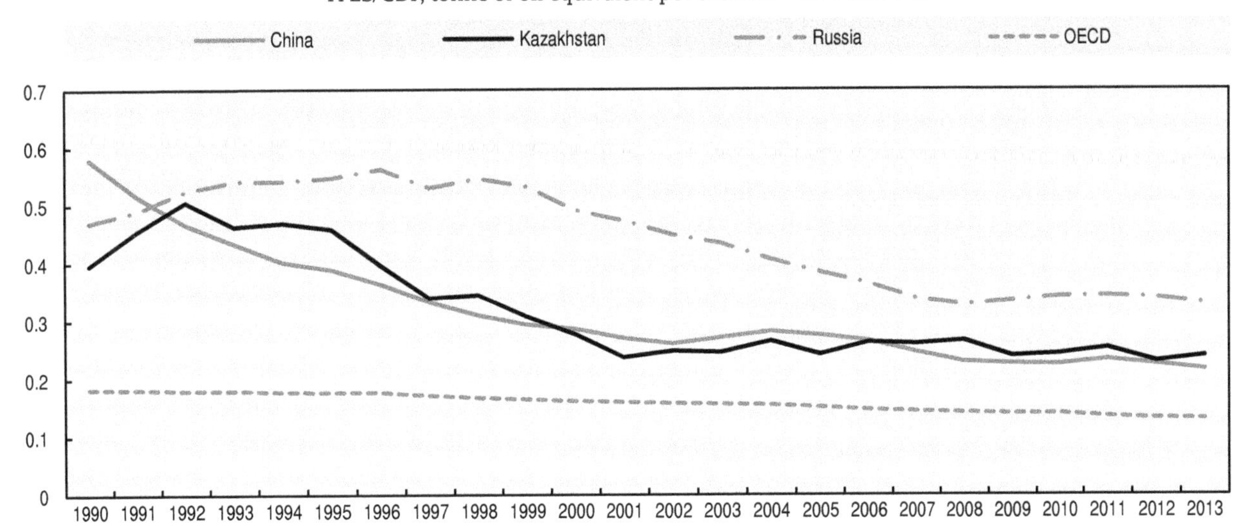

Source: IEA (2016).

StatLink http://dx.doi.org/10.1787/888933445659

The commitments to achieving the GEC targets were reinforced recently in Kazakhstan's Intended Nationally Determined Contributions (INDC) presented at the COP21 in December 2015 in Paris. The country intends to achieve an economy-wide target of a 15% reduction in greenhouse gas (GHG) emissions by 2030 compared to 1990, when emissions were at 389.5 million tonnes of CO_2 equivalent ($MtCO_2e$). Subject to international support, the government offered to raise this target to 25%. GHG emissions in 2012 stood at 303.6 $MtCO_2e$, 22% below 1990 levels (UNFCCC, 2016a).

Box 5.1. **Green Economy Concept**

The Green Economy Concept (GEC) was adopted in May 2013 in response to the United Nations Conference on Sustainable Development (Rio+20) the year before. The GEC is an aspirational, high-level document, prepared in co-operation with a number of stakeholders. It recognises the economic inefficiencies and environmental danger that exist in Kazakhstan, and describes the harmful impact that pollution has upon human health and the environment. The GEC implicitly identifies the nexus between modernised environmental stewardship and economic growth; green growth is synonymous with a more robust economy. The changes envisioned in the GEC involve realignment of economic priorities and mechanisms that not only protect the environment but constitute more viable and effective means for economic development. The GEC has set the goal that its transition into the green economy will increase GDP by 3%, and create more than 500 000 new jobs by 2050.

The GEC focuses on social and regional development and the need for investment. It emphasises in particular: sustainable water use; achieving sustainable and high-performing agriculture; energy saving and energy efficiency improvement; power sector development; better waste management; reducing air pollution; and the preservation and efficient management of ecosystems.

The GEC envisions job creation in five industrial clusters: "green construction", "agriculture", "new technologies in the energy sector", "waste management" and "closed-loop material handling", as well as "public water supply and water management".

The GEC set specific emission reduction and energy targets such as:

- reducing the economy-wide energy intensity of GDP by 50% in 2050 compared to 2013;
- ensuring that the share of alternative sources in electricity production is at least 50% by 2050;
- reducing the CO_2 emissions intensity of GDP in the production of electricity by 65% by 2050.

The GEC states that "...the total amount of investment required to implement the Green Economy Concept from now until 2050 will be on average USD 3-4 billion per annum." It further states that "the largest share of these investments (slightly more than USD 90 billion or three quarters of the total investment over the whole period until 2050) will be used for implementing energy-efficient measures and developing renewable energy as well as establishing gas infrastructure. Measures aimed at developing agriculture, water and waste management will be less demanding in terms of financing."

Source: Government of Kazakhstan (2013).

Implementation of the GEC has faced serious challenges, similar to those encountered in the previous attempts to mobilise support for greening economic growth. The previous attempts that have also faced challenges include the 2005 Concept on Kazakhstan's

Transition to Sustainable Development, the 2010-14 Zhasyl Damu (Green Development/ Growth) Programme, or the 2012 National Green Growth Plan. These challenges include:

- top-down and command-and-control approach based often on the Soviet standards of regulation, combined with frequent incidents of corruption to avoid heavy-handed non-compliance response;
- limited use of market-oriented, compliance promotion and information-based instruments to incentivise companies to invest in pollution reduction and technology modernisation;
- lack of willingness by local authorities to implement green reform because of fears of a decrease in the revenues from emissions payments or their reallocation away from local budgets; and
- strong vested interests in the energy-intensive sectors, such as domestic electric power, mining or chemical industries, in not allocating their own resources to the improvement of their environmental performance.

Regulatory framework for environmental management and green growth

Environmental and natural resource use management laws

Since Kazakhstan gained its independence in 1991, the legislative framework for environmental protection has been continuously, albeit slowly, strengthened. The 1997 Law on Environment Protection established the basic principles of environmental protection management, introduced the provisions for strengthening environmental monitoring, environmental information and its disclosure, environmental accident prevention and management, and control (inspections) of environmental protection. The law was amended in 2004 to include waste management and in 2005 to introduce mandatory and voluntary ecological audits.

A major change to the regulatory framework was brought by the Environmental Code, drafted and approved in a short period of less than a year in 2006/7. The code incorporated major elements of the existing national environmental legislation as well as requirements from many of the international environmental conventions.[2] It also outlined steps to move environmental management towards a more comprehensive and cross-sectoral regulatory framework based on a mix of regulatory, economic and information-based instruments (UNECE, 2008). Subsequently, Kazakhstan strengthened environmental protection in the energy sector with some new laws and amendments. The fundamental acts included the Law on Supporting the Use of Renewable Sources of Energy (2009), amendments to the Environmental Code to regulate greenhouse gas emissions (2011), and the Law on Energy Saving and Energy Efficiency (2012).

The adoption of the Green Economy Concept in 2013 stimulated yet another wave of regulatory reforms through the development of a Green Economy Law (GEL).[3] It was signed into law by the president of the Republic of Kazakhstan in April 2016. However, the GEL does not have major substantive provisions in and of itself. Rather, the GEL is an umbrella legislative enactment, which contains only limited amendments to other laws – including the Environmental Code – on issues pertaining to waste, water and protection of habitat. During the regulatory review and approval process in the Majilis's working groups provisions of the GEL were further weakened or eliminated. The draft of the GEL was left with very few concrete provisions and with an approach based on the principle of "no changes related to the economy, budget revenues and expenditure". For example:

- almost all provisions related to greenhouse gas regulatory reform and energy efficiency were removed from the GEL; these are, as noted above, areas which the GEC stated would require the greatest investment;[4]
- the provisions on air pollution, waste, and the use of payments collected from violations for the environment were also removed;[5] and
- renewable energy legislation remained partially intact, albeit still too weak for incentivising renewable energy projects.

Environmental standards

Despite the important reforms brought about by the Environmental Code, environmental pollution is still managed through regulations that include traditional post-Soviet mechanisms. Very few more modern systems derived from OECD countries' experiences are used in Kazakhstan. The basic instrument for pollution control is the system of environmental ambient quality standards (EQS), expressed through Maximum Allowable Concentrations (MACs).[6] These in turn provide a basis for setting emissions limits values (ELVs) for each individual facility or source of emissions ("resource users"[7]) which are developed as part of an environmental permit. The EQS and MACs were derived in the 1980s from the academically sound scientific theory of maximum absorptive capacity of the environment and atmospheric diffusion of pollution, and are based on the concept of zero risk to humans and the environment during the worst possible circumstances (e.g. worst-case meteorological conditions; most vulnerable part of population). Transposing these academic approaches to the legislative and regulatory framework resulted in very strict ambient quality standards and requires investments by industries to comply, which may not be feasible for most companies (OECD, 2010; World Bank, 2013). For example, unlike in the OECD countries, Kazakhstan's environmental standards for soil quality do not differentiate between different land uses and apply the same requirements for industrial use and the use of land for children's playgrounds.

In OECD countries, ambient quality standards are also based on sound scientific data, but are derived from a scientific assessment of acceptable risk levels under precautionary conditions. The desired level of "quality" is not only a scientific prescription, but also a political and social decision. In OECD countries, air or water "quality objectives" and "standards" have a different meaning, for example:

- water *quality objectives* are ambient thresholds to be maintained or achieved within a certain time period through phased pollution control requirements and water resources management measures. Objectives are set by a competent authority responsible for achieving them, in the context of territorial planning. It is, therefore, in the competent authority's interest to define the objectives that it has a reasonable expectation of achieving. Surface water quality objectives can be expressed in a variety of ways, for example: i) water quality should be suitable for a specific water use (e.g. abstraction of drinking water, recreation, etc.); ii) water quality should be suitable for the support and reproduction of certain fish species; or iii) a water body should attain a specified predefined condition (or class) by a certain date
- a surface water *quality standard* is a condition, expressed as a limit value for individual polluters, that a particular parameter is required to meet in order to achieve a surface water quality objective (OECD, 2010).

In Kazakhstan, as in many countries of the former Soviet Union, air or water "quality objectives" and "standards" (MACs) have been mistakenly interpreted to mean the same thing. In Kazakhstan, MACs are considered to be binding limits for all users of a given environmental medium. Individual limits of emissions (ELVs) to air, discharges to water and waste disposal are derived primarily from MACs. Any installation which emits, discharges or disposes of polluting substances is required by law to prove to environmental authorities that its incremental pollution will not lead to an infringement of the MAC.

The main purpose of ELVs is to ensure that the ambient EQS/MACs are not exceeded in the particular area as a result of emissions by individual sources. The calculation of ELVs for individual enterprises in a given region, or *oblast*, involves computer-based simulations of pollutants' dispersion in the space. Theoretically, ELVs are set at levels to ensure that the aggregate amount of emissions from all sources of pollution in a given location together with the existing level of pollution do not cause pollution levels in that location to exceed the EQS. However, most of the EQS were established before 1990 and the lists of ambient quality parameters have not been revised or harmonised with international standards since then. The lack of reform has resulted in a system that remains overly ambitious, covers hundreds of pollutants and mandates very low ambient concentrations of pollutants. Since environmental standards are the determinant factor in setting emission limit values in permits for individual installations, their excessive stringency imposes requirements that cannot be achieved even by applying best available techniques (BAT). This hinders the reform of the permitting systems and the introduction of integrated permitting based on BAT. For example, compared with equivalent EU regulations, Kazakhstan applies more stringent standards to surface water quality for water bodies to be used for abstraction of drinking water, for protection/breeding of freshwater fish, and for recreation. This is primarily because the standards are determined on the basis of zero impact on human health and ecosystems. In determining the standard, consideration was not given to the technical or economic feasibility of meeting it, which often becomes a problem when the standards are translated into effluent requirements for individual pollution sources.

There is also a mismatch between the scope of regulation and government regulatory monitoring. Kazakhstan's systems of surface water quality standards contain a substantially larger number of parameters regulated (over 1 000) than the equivalent EU directives but the number of parameters that is actually monitored is rather small. Notably, toxic pollutants are poorly covered in the current monitoring programmes. Moreover, laboratories are not always equipped to analyse monitored micro-pollutants at concentration levels corresponding to the MACs. At the same time, the EU Water Framework Directive Priority Substances are covered for about one-third of the parameters only.

There is now widespread recognition of the need to reform the EQS/MACs system in Kazakhstan. Some initial steps of the reform process have been taken, but new standards have not been introduced, so the old ones continue to be used for regulatory purposes such as setting effluent limits for individual polluters. The most serious obstacle to the reform comes from public authorities and stakeholders that benefit from the current system. For example, the general public is misled by the argument that more stringent standards lead to better health and environmental protection (health authorities insist that relaxation of some water quality standards would compromise public health), while environmental authorities are concerned about losing a part of revenues from pollution charges which are significant in case of non-compliance. The technical complexity of the subject matter and the lack of qualified specialists who would develop an alternative system are additional challenges.

Finally, inadequate financial resources are devoted to perform the analysis of air or water pollution sources and impacts on their quality which are the necessary first steps in the implementation of a new environmental standard system.

Environmental permits

In Kazakhstan, resource-users can legally emit pollutants into the environment as long as they hold an environmental permit that sets the Emission Limit Values (ELVs).[8] The permits are issued by competent environmental authorities at the national and regional level depending on the size of the operation. The objective of the permits, and the ELVs contained therein, is to ensure that the quality of the environment at the surrounding residential area or at the boundary of the so-called "sanitary zone"[9] meets the hygienic requirements for air or water quality, taking into account the background pollution level.

Since Soviet times the permitting procedures have been administratively complex and time-consuming, but have been streamlined on several occasions. For example, since 2002 the competent authorities has issued one multimedia permit instead of three single-medium permits (for air, water, waste separately). In 2005-06, the scope of documents to be reviewed for the purposes of issuing permits was broadened to include self-monitoring programmes and so-called "plans of environmental protection measures", which outline the measures that an enterprise would take to bring its production processes into line with environmental requirements.[10] In 2007, the country's permitting system underwent additional major changes, including the extension of the validity of permits from one to three years to decrease the administrative burden on the regulated community and the classification of enterprises into four classes of environmental exposure, with class I considered most hazardous and IV considered as least hazardous.[11] The Environmental Code also introduced integrated permitting on a pilot basis, following benchmarks established by the European Union's Integrated Pollution Prevention and Control (IPPC) Directive. However, as of early 2016 no applications had been submitted for an integrated permit.[12] Moreover, although the government approved a list of technologies eligible for complex permits in 2008 the list of industries which apply the relevant technologies for an integrated permit is limited and does not include the oil and gas sector.

In 2011 and 2014, the government and parliament adopted two additional sets of amendments to the Environmental Code intended to reduce the administrative burden on business. For example, deadlines for reviewing emission permit applications have been reduced from four months to two for class I facilities, one month for class II facilities and ten business days for category III and IV facilities; the issuing authority has been mandated to make a first check of the application within 15 days, instead of one month as previously; and the list of documents to attach to the application has been shortened by half.[13] Now, only the largest industrial facilities of class I apply for permits at the national level, while the rest of the industries can apply at the regional departments and a simplified procedure of permitting applies to class IV enterprises.[14] Finally, the permit validity period has been extended to ten years for class I, II and III facilities and is not restricted by any time limit for class IV facilities (compared to once every three years and even once a year before for class I facilities). Moreover, a gradual transition to electronic document flow (a system of submitting environmental permit applications electronically through a special web-portal) is also underway and most of the permits are issued electronically via the state database "E-licensing".

Despite improvements in the scope of permit conditions which brought the permitting system closer to the OECD standards, the permitting procedure is considered as administratively heavy and failing to guarantee a sufficient level of environmental protection (UNECE, 2008; World Bank, 2013). In practice:

- emission limits in the permitting process are based on the level of historic pollution and background concentrations rather than on the basis of emission limits that an industry could achieve when applying BAT. The approved BAT in place today in Kazakhstan provide only specific technical emission limits and reference methodologies for three industrial processes which should be the basis for approved ELVs in permits. This is insufficient compared to a variety of processes used by industrial facilities. The reference documents for BATs also do not clearly specify emission standards for all basic pollutants.
- although the ELVs should only be set for the pollutants for which the establishment of ELVs is mandatory, many of the environmental permit applications include ELVs for all identified emissions regardless of their quantities and potential hazard because of a lack of information about the mandatory list of pollutants for emission limits. This results in redundant paperwork both for responsible environmental specialists at industrial facilities and environmental regulators, without providing environmental/health benefits for industrial facilities and environmental regulators. It also leads to insufficient focus on the pollutants which cause most health impacts. In the European Union, ELVs are only set for the most hazardous emissions and based on emission limits that are possible to obtain when industries use BAT.
- Kazakhstan's industrial facilities typically obtain ELVs based on the highest level of emissions measured during the maximum production output. Although this offers a safety margin to ensure that the ELVs are not exceeded, it provides insufficient incentives to reduce the present level of emissions. Likewise, they can be based on the design capacity of process equipment, while in reality enterprises frequently do not work at full capacity which facilitates compliance without the improvement of technological processes, reduction of emissions and implementation of BAT. In addition, energy efficiency requirements have not been considered in permitting.
- although facilities which do not use the approved BAT and receive ordinary emissions permits are required to undergo environmental examinations every ten years they need to reapply for a new emission permit on an annual basis. This applies specifically to gas flaring since the amounts of pollution which the operators are authorised to emit are approved for a one-year term only. As a result, many of these facilities cannot forecast the required levels of emissions for an extended time period.

In 2014-15, the Ministry of Energy renewed efforts further to simplify the permit issuance process, to support investment planning and remove obstacles to project development. The procedures for issuing integrated permits were regulated by legislation in January 2015 and a list of best available techniques was prepared. Under the amendments submitted by the government to parliament in mid-2015, the authorisation to operate facilities and generate emissions would have been granted on the basis of the conclusions of the State Environmental Experts' Examination without requiring a separate emission permit. The proposed rules would have significantly reduced the time period required to obtain authorisation for emissions and perhaps made the established ELVs more justified. However, in June 2016 the Senate deleted the provisions regarding simplification of the emissions permits and shortening the procedures, thus undermining one of the main purposes of the legislation, and plans to launch a transition to integrated permitting have not been supported by the parliament.

There is an urgent need to optimise the present permitting and compliance control requirements. This should include shifting the focus of environmental requirements from "end-of-pipe" solutions to integrated pollution prevention and control. For the largest ("significant") polluters there should be a shift away from the command-and-control approach, which just penalises non-compliance, and re-incentivise it through integrated pollution prevention and control. Integrated environmental permits are one of the most effective ways of achieving better pollution control since the permit is linked to specific techniques (i.e. BATs) which are associated with lower emissions. In addition, firms can realise certain cost savings through a more simplified (integrated) permitting process where separate permits for each type of emission are not required. In instances where integrated permitting is relatively unknown or not well-understood pilots would be required to demonstrate the effectiveness of these new regulatory tools (World Bank, 2013).

Environmental Impact Assessment

Environmental Impact Assessment (EIA) is an important procedure that ensures that environmental implications are taken into account before investment decisions are made.[15] Consultation with the public is a key feature of these procedures to make them more effective and efficient. Facility-specific environmental permits are issued on the basis of a comprehensive EIA for both new and existing facilities. The EIA procedure is a two-phase process: the proper EIA, which is carried out by accredited private companies contracted by a developer, followed by the State Ecological Expertise Examination (SEEE) carried out by a competent government authority (Box 5.2).

Box 5.2. **Environmental Impact Assessment (EIA) and State Environmental Expert Examination (SEEE) in Kazakhstan**

New facilities are subject to an Environmental Impact Assessment (EIA) which is regulated by an Instruction for Conducting EIA Studies and a number of other regulatory documents establishing general requirements for this process. The Instruction lists the many documents that a resource-user must submit and establishes different requirements for EIA studies to be conducted in relation to facilities of each category of hazard. The environmental impact assessment must, among other things, include public hearings or discussions of the ecological aspects of the planned activities. The EIA procedure is performed before the permitting procedure and the developer has to attach the EIA report and the SEEE opinion together with the permit application.

There are different types of the EIA:

- A "preliminary" EIA is required at the investment feasibility study stage (except for class IV facilities). For a large-scale project, field prospecting should be conducted at this stage. Environmental impacts are estimated but precise emission limits are not calculated. An approved "preliminary" EIA is a prerequisite to receive a loan for implementing the project.
- A "fully-fledged" EIA, which is mandatory after the preliminary stage, requires very detailed information, including calculations of emission limit values (ELVs), emergency preparedness plans or monitoring programmes for all media.

Until 2011 a "post-construction" EIA was required for large projects with capital investments of over USD 50 million one year after the start of the operation. It aimed to confirm the environmental safety of the economic activity and to correct the plan of environmental protection measures.

Box 5.2. **Environmental Impact Assessment (EIA) and State Environmental Expert Examination (SEEE) in Kazakhstan** *(cont.)*

Once the EIA study is completed, its results, together with other documents relevant to the planned activity, must be provided for the State Environmental Experts' Examination (SEEE). The purpose of the SEEE is to assess project design, feasibility studies and other documents in relation to planned operations which may impact the environment (in the case of new facilities, the relevant documents must be filed together with the EIA). The SEEE also assesses the resource-user's preliminary Emissions Limit Values (ELVs). During the SEEE the competent authority checks the documents' quality, makes its own statement on them, and returns both to the developer. The statement takes into account the opinions and views expressed by the public and other authorities which have participated in the process. Currently, copies of minutes of public hearings and copies of the documents confirming the application in the media together with EIA materials have to be submitted for state environmental audit.

The whole procedure can take over two years (it should be noted that this does not include the permitting phase, which adds another one to two months). In practice, the timeframe for an SEEE has been reduced from three to two months for class I facilities, and up to one month for class II, III and IV facilities.* The number of required stages of EIA was reduced from five to three, through excluding an overview of the "status of environment" and "post-project analysis".

Resource-users operating facilities that already are in operation are required to apply periodically for a new permit, and hence they, too, must periodically revise their preliminary ELVs.

For any facility for which the SEEE is required, a public association can request a Public Environmental Experts' Examination prior to the completion of the SEEE. The state environmental experts must take the findings of the Public Environmental Experts' Examination (PEEE) into account during their review and provide a report as to what findings were addressed by them and what findings they dismissed. However, the PEEE has rarely any impact as it is usually completed after the SEEE.

Once a positive opinion of the state environmental experts is obtained, a resource-user can submit its application for an emissions permit to the competent authority. The environmental authorities review the application and the accompanying documents, and may request additional materials. The environmental authorities then decide whether they accept the application for final review, or decline it because of an insufficiency of data provided with the application or because the application does not meet the requirements of Kazakhstan law.

Note: * Timeframes have also been reduced for preliminary audits and repeated audits, respectively to five working days and one month for category I facilities.
Source: UNECE, 2008; World Bank, 2013.

Although the requirements for EIA were revised several times, procedures remain complicated and in need of further reform. Contrary to practice in the OECD or the European Union, an EIA in Kazakhstan is required, although to a different extent, for any project and facility, regardless of its size and the importance of its impact on the environment. The EIA has nonetheless been simplified for newly constructed industrial facilities. The stages of the procedures tend to repeat themselves and require provision of extensive volume of documentation to the authorities. Many of the documents tend to be voluminous, redundant and, in some parts, written in complex and overly technical language, impairing communication of the results of the EIA to the public and the responsible authority. Non-technical summaries of the results are not required. The EIA project developers typically outsource the preparation of EIA materials to specialised companies which must be licensed by the competent authority if they carry out the EIA for class I facilities. Licensing, however, is not a guarantee of quality: some 10% to 15% of EIA materials are declined because of poor quality (UNECE, 2008). There is anecdotal evidence that the EIA reports are falsified to fit the legislation requirements. Because of the increasing numbers of reviews, and therefore the increased administrative burden, most procedures are rather general, poorly enforceable and are made on the basis of theoretical estimates rather than in-depth analysis, particularly in the regions with the highest workload (e.g. Aktyubinsk, Karaganda, Pavlodar and North Kazakhstan *oblasts*).

According to the Environmental Code, all interested citizens and public associations are given the opportunity to express their opinion during the EIA procedures. The regulations approved in February 2016 require mandatory publication of the application for the EIA in the mass media by the project's proponents. The conclusion of the EIA has to be placed on the Internet site of the local executive body in charge of environmental protection within five working days after the receipt. Currently, the Public Council, which is the consultative advisory and monitoring body set up to develop proposals for improving interaction and co-operation between the administration and non-governmental organisations (NGOs) and citizens, have been co-operating with the Ministry of Energy to further improve the public participation procedures.

Despite progress, in the view of some NGOs public consultations on EIA are not systematic and public hearings are often seen as a procedural burden rather than a legitimate policy-decision mechanism. Some NGOs also consider that the EIA procedure is in many cases window-dressing and difficult to check by the public. Although several specialised NGOs, such as Kazakhstan's Green Salvation, are active in this area, further efforts by the public authorities are required to open the procedures to the public's active participation, especially at regional and local levels.

Effectiveness and efficiency of pollution payments linked to a system of permits

One of the key functions of the environmental permit has been to stipulate emissions limits for authorised emissions (ELVs). The permit limits also determine payments by the resource user for emissions below the relevant ELVs and those that apply to emission releases above the established limits. The system originated before 1991 and continues to exist, in various forms, in the environmental laws of many other post-Soviet states. In Kazakhstan the emissions below relevant ELVs have been subject to pollution charges (later on replaced by taxes) while emissions of pollutants above the ELVs have been subject to three distinct types of payments: i) pollution charges or taxes as indicated above, but multiplied tenfold; ii) administrative penalties; and iii) monetary damages. The combined amount of all three payments imposed for above-ELV emissions is substantial, with monetary damages constituting the largest of the three.

Pollution charges/taxes

The payments for authorised (below-limit) emissions (so called pollution charges) were based on each enterprise's ELVs for air and water pollutants and the volume of generated waste. There was also a large variation of base pollution charge rates (for emissions below the ELVs) among regions, reflecting the various patterns of economic activities and related differences in types and intensity of pollution. Air pollution charges per tonne of emissions from stationary sources varied by a factor of 20 between the *oblasts* with the highest (Atyrau) and the lowest (Karaganda) charge rates. Pollution charge rates were raised several times in line with the projected average annual inflation rate. The local authorities could further increase the rates discussed above.

In practice, the setting of pollution charges was for long guided by the desire to generate sufficient revenues for the support of regional or local budgets, and not to address environmental problems. A large number of air and water pollutants were subject to payment of emission charges which made the system quite complex and administratively onerous. The calculation of charges lacked transparency since there were no specific pollution charges for individual pollutants, only for aggregate emissions, measured in terms of so-called "notional tonnes".[16] The criteria for determining specific levels of pollution charges were obscure, and there appeared to be wide discretion in the application of the charges by the authorities (UNECE, 2008).

To address deficiencies in the system, the number of pollutants to be taken into account when determining emission limits for environmental permits and calculating emission charges was drastically reduced in 2008. The list distinguishes now only 16 types of air pollutants, including sulphur oxides (SO_x), nitrogen oxides (NO_x), volatile organic compounds (VOCs) and carbon monoxide (CO), and 13 water pollutants. The payment became subject to the provisions of the tax code as opposed to being regulated by administrative legislation in the past.[17] The collection of the payments is now no longer included in the competences of the administration in charge of environment protection.

As before, the tax payments for authorised emissions are based on each enterprise's ELVs. This leaves room for discretion in setting the ELVs, and is not in line with standard environmental tax principles which require a charge per unit of emissions, unless there is clear evidence of threshold effects. The tax code specifies the tax rates per kilogramme or per tonne (i.e. not notional tonne). Pollution tax rates are set as coefficients multiplied by the Kazakhstan monthly calculation index (MCI). The MCI is established by the government on an annual basis to take into account inflation and other factors and is then used to determine taxes, as well as penalties (as described below) and certain other payments.

Pollution tax rates for emissions within the ELVs in the permit are determined in a two-stage process. The tax code fixes the minimum or base tax rates which apply for each of the 16 regional entities (14 *oblasts* and two major cities, Almaty and Astana). Each *oblast* may then set a higher tax rate provided that such a rate does not exceed twice the base rate, with the exception of gas flaring by the oil and gas industry which may be subject to locally imposed tax rates 20 times the base rate. Most *oblasts* impose the highest possible rate of tax in each case. The proceeds of the emissions taxes are allocated to the budgets of the regions where the facilities are located.

For above-ELV emissions, the locally applicable rates are further multiplied by a factor of ten. For example, any gas flaring by the oil and gas industry in excess of ELVs in the *oblast* of Atyrau can be subject to tax at rate 200 times the base rate. Utilities and power plants are entitled to a reduction of emission tax rates by applying coefficients of 0.3 for air pollutants, 0.43 for waste water and 0.05 for ash.

With effect from January 2017, the tax code will be amended to remove the ten times multiplier applicable to emissions in excess of ELV. The base rates of tax for flaring by the oil and gas industry will be increased to and fixed at 20 times their current level; the *oblasts* will not have any discretion to change these tax rates. The base rates for other sources of emissions, the right of *oblasts* to increase the base rate twofold for other sources of emissions and the decreasing coefficients for utilities will remain in effect. As a consequence of these changes, the oil and gas industry will pay 67 times more per unit of emission than the heating and power plants.

Administrative penalties

While pollution charges/taxes are due for emissions or discharges both within and above the specified limits (ELVs), administrative penalties are imposed by authorities only for pollution exceeding the ELVs set in project documents and environmental permits (or in the absence of an environmental permit). Article 328 of the administrative code establishes that the penalty for emissions above the established ELVs for large businesses is in the amount of "1 000 % of the rate of the emissions payment (i.e. the tax code rates) for the excess amount of emissions." However, there are problems with the interpretation of the approach to the payment calculation. The authorities interpret this to mean that the penalty should be calculated not only by multiplying the rate times ten, but also then by multiplying the product by the amount of the relevant emissions, i.e. the same way that the tenfold tax is calculated (tax rate times ten times amount of excess emissions). The language of the administrative code's provision on administrative penalties does not clearly stipulate that the rate should also be multiplied by the amount of the relevant emissions, i.e. that the penalty is effectively equal to the tax amount for the excess emissions.

Monetary damages

In addition to taxes and administrative penalties, emissions of pollutants above the permitted ELVs are subject to monetary damages via a judicial system. Kazakhstan's environmental code defines the economic value of environmental damage as the cost of environmental remediation that can be assessed directly or indirectly. The direct method of assessment aims to determine the expenditure (in market prices) necessary to restore natural resources and living organisms through "most effective engineering, management and technological measures" in accordance with a time-specific project. The environmental code gives "priority" for the remediation to be undertaken by the party responsible for the damage. It also provides for the engagement of independent experts whose fee must be paid by the responsible party.

However, unlike the practice in OECD countries, the Kazakhstan environmental authorities mostly use the indirect method which is easier to apply and usually results in much higher monetary damages.[18] As in many Eastern Europe, Caucasus and Central Asia (EECCA) countries, this method determines the value of the "pollution damage" as a function of the current pollution tax rates and determines the "pollution damage" from each pollutant using a mathematical formula and then combines the resulting assessments of damage caused by each pollutant. The indirect method of calculating monetary damages relies on a pre-established formula and hence does not require measurements (or proof) of actual damage to the environment in determining the amount of compensation that must be paid.

A misconception of the Kazakhstan environmental code's damages regime is that it is only the indirect method for calculating damages that departs from OECD standards. However, both the direct and indirect methods, stipulated therein, contradict OECD legal principles because environmental liability for "damages" arises upon the exceeding of a predetermined limit in an emissions permit. "Direct" and "indirect" are mere calculation methodologies employed after the liability arising from exceeding ELVs in the permit has been established. In OECD countries the permit plays no role; liability for damages arises only upon a claimant bringing physical evidence of actual harm. The assessment of environmental damages in OECD countries is primarily based on resource equivalency analysis to estimate the needs and costs of restoring affected resources or environmental services.[19] The remediation scope may be mandated by law or left to the discretion of the competent authority, which determines specific measures using criteria such as technical feasibility, effectiveness and efficiency.

The OECD country experience shows that Kazakhstan should abandon fault-based concepts for damages that tie liability to exceeding a pre-determined limit in an emissions permit. It should instead adopt the strict liability/polluter-pays model based on evidence of actual harm to the environment. By contrast, environmental liability for pollution in Kazakhstan applies only if the emission permit limits have been breached (the fault standard), even in the absence of proof of environmental damage. Although some important legal changes are being introduced in other countries in the region, most notably in Russia, environmental liability in Kazakhstan remains focused on calculating and collecting monetary compensation for the state (essentially serving as a revenue-raising penalty) rather than on preventing and correcting the damage. There is very little regulatory guidance on how to assess the extent of the damage, needs and costs of remediation, and how to select clean-up measures.

Combined effect of the three pollution payments

The combined amount of all three payments (i.e. taxes, administrative penalties and damages) for the emissions above ELVs can be substantial, with monetary damages imposed by the courts constituting the largest of the three. For example, for 2013 payments for emissions within ELVs in the Atyrau region reached KZT 2 billion and KZT 34 billion in Kazakhstan overall. In the same year, the overall amount of charges for the emissions above ELVs including taxes, fines and damages was KZT 24.7 billion for Atyrau and KZT 31.4 billion for Kazakhstan (Kononenko et al, 2014).

The use of multiplied taxes and the indirect method for calculating monetary damages, with their focus on revenue raising, makes it impossible to gauge reliably the relation between pollution payments and marginal pollution reduction costs. A particularly acute illustration of the deficiency of Kazakhstan's pollution liability system relates to the formula that the government has adopted for calculating damages from gas flaring at upstream oil and gas facilities. The indirect damages formula until recently contained different (higher) coefficients for calculating damages for gas flaring than for the same amount of emissions/pollutants emitted from other stationary sources where there is less or no foreign investment. In June 2016 the government introduced amendments to the regulations which eliminated the discrimination between the calculation of damages resulting from gas flaring in oil and gas facilities and emissions by other industries (including mining and metallurgical). The government should be applauded for this change. The statutory discrimination in coefficients used in the indirect damages formula was analogous to the still existing tax and penalty discrimination by which, as noted above, the local authorities can multiply the taxes for excess emissions of pollutants from gas flaring by 20 times, as opposed to two times for excess emissions of the same pollutants from other stationary sources. As of 1 January 2017, instead of the 20 times tax multiplier for gas flaring emissions applied by the local authorities, the base tax rates on pollutants emitted from gas flaring will be 20 times the base rates for the same pollutants emitted from all other stationary sources. Similarly, since as noted above administrative penalties are established based on the tax rates, administrative penalties for gas flaring are higher than administrative penalties for emissions of the same pollutants from other stationary sources. The largest environmental lawsuits are brought by the environmental authorities against the major oil and gas projects and concern the gas flaring claims. The recently concluded court cases required major oil and gas companies to pay hundreds of millions of dollars in environmental payments based on the damage liability calculations described above (Box 5.3).[20]

Box 5.3. **Kazakhstan associated petroleum gas (APG) flaring reduction and damage payments**

Crude oil extraction from onshore or offshore oil wells in Kazakhstan is associated, as in many other oil-producing countries, with the release of raw natural gas which is brought to the surface together with the oil. Petroleum-producing plants typically process this gas for sale, for fuel, or to re-inject into the reservoir for pressure maintenance. The venting of raw gas is potentially very hazardous (especially when high levels of hydrogen sulphides are involved). In cases of non-routine events such as start-up, maintenance, technical breakdowns or operating condition deviations, modern processing facilities are designed to flare the extracted gas because it cannot be stored or further processed until plant conditions have been normalised.

Strengthening the requirements for gas flaring reduction, as well as collection and processing of associated gas, have become important for the Kazakhstan government not only to prevent environmental pollution, but also to incentivise the enterprises to use this valuable resource. To achieve these goals, gas flaring and venting were prohibited in Kazakhstan in 2004 ("Law on Introduction, Modifications and Amendments in some Legislative Acts of the Republic of Kazakhstan concerning subsoil use and carrying out petroleum operations in the Republic of Kazakhstan", No 2-III, 1 December 2004). Petroleum companies had received administrative notifications, issued by the central authorities requiring them immediately to start the full utilisation of the associated gas or otherwise face a reduction of production volumes, termination of previously concluded subsoil-use contracts or high penalties.

Abatement of gas flaring is a long-term process that requires proper investigation, comprehensive legislative insights and technological solutions, incurring major capital expenditure over many years. For many oil producers the ban created significant challenges and risks, including the inability to implement quickly gas transportation and processing programmes or obtain appropriate permits for treatment operations, attract sufficient financing and to adapt already approved permits and development plans.

Concerted appeals from the oil-producing companies resulted in the establishment of a new deadline of 2006 and the setting of the transition criteria to reduce gas flaring and venting by preparing a corresponding gas utilisation policy, analysing other countries' experience and enacting required amendments and modifications to the primary and secondary legislation. Since the operators required retaining the option to flare gas as the safest option for recovering from plant outages and equipment failures the 2010 Law on Subsoil and Subsoil Use allowed for technologically unpreventable flaring under specified conditions and authorised by the Ministry of Oil and Gas.

Since then several large operators in Kazakhstan have successfully reduced their emissions to a relatively modest level, after a period of more intensive gas flaring during start-up. Growing domestic demand for gas for power generation, clarification and strengthening of anti-flaring/associated petroleum gas (APG) use regulation, planned construction of national and regional pipelines now spur an increase in APG use projects. For example, the Tengiz oil field was flaring approximately 6.8% of inlet (impure) gas in the period 2005-06, but reduced that amount to 0.86% of inlet gas in 2010-11. As reported in 2014, the Tengiz operator managed to eliminate virtually all continuous flaring from gas processing, leaving only purge and pilot light flaring, together with some non–continuous flaring for maintenance repairs and process safety. Similarly, the Karachaganak oilfield has successfully reduced gas flaring to 0.19% of total volume of gas produced in 2014. Overall Kazakhstan has made substantial progress towards a 5% flare rate (gas utilisation rate 95%), indicative of elimination of routine flaring, which is commonly set as a policy target for flaring.

Box 5.3. Kazakhstan associated petroleum gas (APG) flaring reduction and damage payments *(cont.)*

Despite improvements, gas flaring continues to be the key target of the emission-focused liability system, and the associated fines and taxes are extremely large. In one of the biggest legal disputes the multinational consortium North Caspian Operating Company that developed the Kashagan oil field in the Caspian Sea was threatened with having to pay to pay KZT 152 billion (USD 845 million, using the prevailing exchange rate) in 2014 in taxes, fines and damages for alleged damage to the environment from flaring residual sour gas during start-up operations. In February 2016 Kazakhstan's Karachaganak Petroleum Operating Company, which operates one of the largest fields in the world* was ordered to pay a fine of KZT 526 million (over USD 1.5 million) for releasing pollutants into the atmosphere. In 2011, fines equal to USD 11.5 million were imposed on the Tengiz oil field operator for gas flaring.

Note: * The Karachaganak field located in the West Kazakhstan province accounts for 45% of the total volume of gas and 16% of liquid hydrocarbons produced in Kazakhstan.

Source: Carbon Limits, 2014, UNFCCC, 2016.

Oil and gas investors argue that the damages, taxes, and penalties result in assessments that significantly exceed gas flaring payments in OECD countries. They report that the largest environmental law suits concerning gas flaring claims are brought by the environmental authorities against the major oil and gas projects with foreign investment, adding discriminatory treatment of foreign investors by governmental conduct to statutory discrimination in the damages formula and tax multipliers. The operators also argue that the largest payments are imposed on emergency or technologically unavoidable gas flaring, while for Kazakhstan's power and other heavy industries the ELVs are set below the emissions levels that are achievable given the low efficiency of the ageing facilities: something that, as a whole, does not provide equal incentives to local and foreign operators to reduce emissions.[21]

Regulation of greenhouse gas emissions and the emissions trading system

Kazakhstan's obligations under international treaties to reduce its GHG emissions

Kazakhstan has been actively seeking ways to reduce emission of greenhouse gases (GHG), of which 83% come from the energy sector because of its heavy dependence on fossil fuel extraction and coal-based electricity generation (Figure 5.3). The country ratified the Kyoto Protocol in 2009 and submitted an economy-wide emissions reduction target of 15% compared with 1990 levels by 2020, under the United Nations Framework Convention on Climate Change (UNFCCC).[22] At the 2015 Paris Conference of the Parties to the UNFCCC Kazakhstan submitted its Intended Nationally Determined Contributions, committing to a further 15% reduction in emissions by 2030 from a 1990 baseline, and as much as a 25% reduction contingent on availability of international financing (Government of Kazakhstan, 2015).[23]

Emissions trading scheme in Kazakhstan (KazETS)

Kazakhstan's GHG reduction commitments have been reflected in the "Strategic Development Plan of the Republic of Kazakhstan to 2020". A general framework for regulating emissions of greenhouse gases was created by the 2011 amendments to the Environmental Code. Along with several regulatory instruments, the amendments included the provisions for the creation of an emissions trading system (KazETS) under which emissions from the highest-emitting sectors and activities are capped and allocated via tradeable emission allowances (quotas) to individual enterprises. This market-based mechanism provides for any excessive amount of GHG emissions to be offset (or compensated) with the relevant amount of quota units (either saved because of implementation of special GHG emission reduction measures or created by implementation of projects for the reduction or absorption of GHG) that can be purchased at the commodity exchange.[24] The quotas are allocated in the National Allocation Plan approved by the government and recorded in the quota certificates issued by the Kazakhstan competent authority.[25]

Figure 5.3. **Greenhouse gas emissions in Kazakhstan**

Million tonnes of CO_2 equivalent, 1990-2012

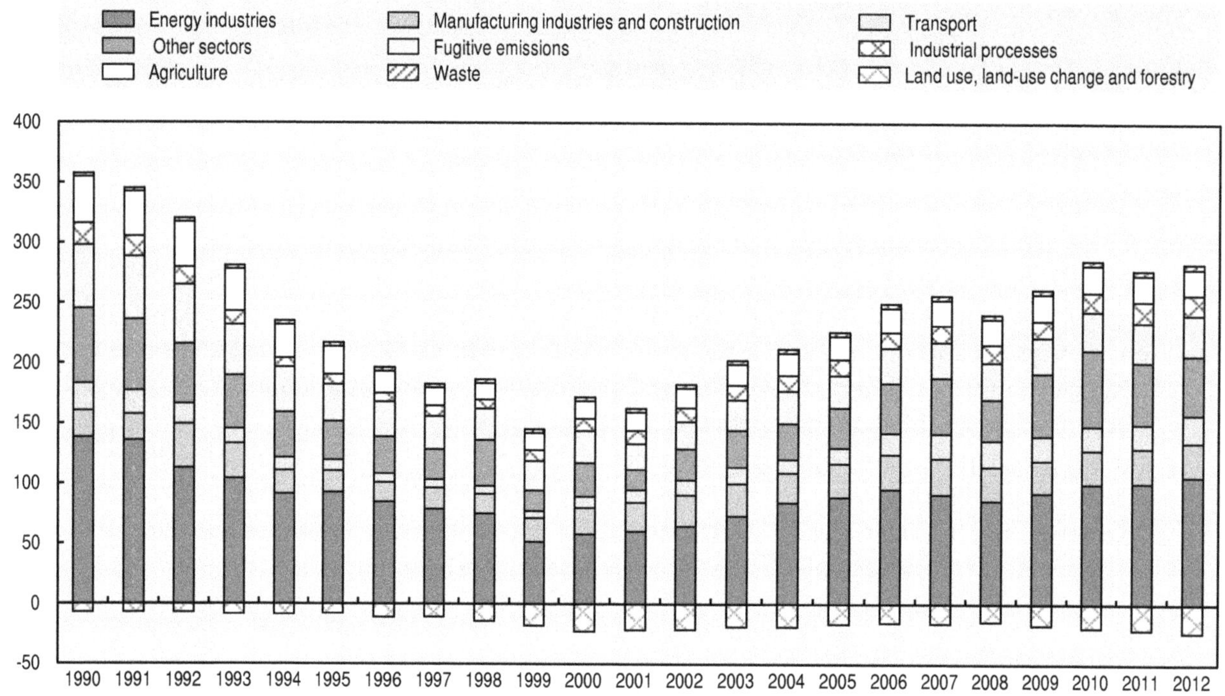

Note: Other sectors include Commercial/Institutional, Residential, and Agriculture/Forestry/Fisheries and other).

Source: UNFCCC (2016b).

StatLink http://dx.doi.org/10.1787/888933445661

Nearly half of Kazakhstan's GHG emissions are covered by the KazETS. The KazETS regulations cover companies in the oil and gas, power, mining and chemical sectors, which emit more than 20 000 tonnes of CO_2 per year (IETA, 2015).[26] Regulated entities must report and verify their annual emissions of CO_2 (carbon dioxide), CH_4 (methane), N_2O (nitrous oxide) and perfluorocarbons (PFCs). Only CO_2 emissions are currently capped under the KazETS, and discussions are on-going as to whether methane and other GHGs should also be capped by the scheme at a later date.

The KazETS was launched in 2013 with a pilot compliance period and was extended to the second phase (2014-15) in which 166 facilities participated. Allocations for phases I and II were provided for free, based on historic emissions (so-called "grandfathering"). For Phase III (2016-20), a National Allocation Plan was approved in December 2015 containing quotas for covered facilities, also based on grandfathering. The OECD country experience shows that a failure to move towards auctioning, or at least allocation less tied to historic emissions, usually weakens the environmental effectiveness of the system.

Even though the regulations and the rules for KazETS have been adopted, the KazETS has not yet been fully implemented. The government's rules do not contain clear provisions for how quotas are to be allocated. For instance, one regulation calls for allocations to be based on a facility-specific baseline (an average of each facility's actual emissions in the previous two years, as independently verified). Another regulation suggests that a baseline should be an average of similar facilities. Neither the Environmental Code nor the Rules for Allocation of GHG Quotas clearly provide how the obligations to reduce emissions for each year should be determined.

The Rules for Allocation of GHG Quotas provide that when the competent authority allocates quotas it should take into account voluntary measures to reduce greenhouse gases which were implemented in the three years preceding the quota year. However, the rules do not contain a specific mechanism or number of the additional quota units that the operator will receive. In addition, operators can keep or sell extra quotas only if they can demonstrate that GHG emissions have been reduced intentionally. If quotas were saved due to a decrease in production, even though the reductions would occur, they are expected to return unused quotas to the competent authority. This is an unusual practice for an emissions trading system.

The Administrative Code also provides that emissions of any amount of GHGs in excess of the quota (emissions not covered by allocated and purchased permits) shall result in a penalty. The penalty on the legal entities is the amount of five monthly calculation indices for each unit in excess of the quota which was not offset by purchased quota units.

The KazETS needs additional updates to bring it in line with international markets and prepare the system for future linking. In summary, the KazETS suffers from:

- a lack of clear and consistent implementation of regulations, and regulatory authorities have limited capacity and resources to facilitate its successful application;
- vaguely drafted, incomplete or inconsistent rules across regulatory documents, limited consistency or transparency regarding installation-level emissions, reduction activities, offset registration policies or procedures, which have led to an unclear carbon price;
- lack of co-ordination at a ministerial level on legal amendments and data-sharing, as well as inconsistent advice provided to enterprises on reporting accreditation and verification procedures, making it challenging or impossible for entities to comply fully;
- lack of verification regulations, standard and guidance to verifiers on how to conduct GHG verification activities, e.g. to apply risk-based approaches in the course of GHG verification;[27]
- errors in the existing emissions calculation rules that can overestimate emissions;
- lack of links with the Green Economy Concept and the renewable energy and energy efficiency laws, and only weak links to the "Kazakhstan-2050" Strategy in the form of a GHG emissions target for the power sector. For example, the INDC submitted to the UNFCCC is the sole national policy document that identifies these various activities as tools for achieving Kazakhstan's climate change goals.

Further reductions in emissions could be achieved if any KazETS revenues (e.g. from penalties or future auctioning) are reinvested in further GHG mitigation instead of being absorbed into the national budget.[28]

Ways forward

Observations and evaluations of errors and omissions in the many enactments regulating GHG emissions were aggregated in early 2014 from a variety of stakeholders. These included international donors, and were shared with the Ministry of Energy. The collective list contained approximately 200 comments (later consolidated into a sub-list of 70 comments), identifying incorrect definitions, missing provisions and inconsistencies in guidance between various sections of the Environmental Code. After numerous efforts to get these comments adopted as amendments to the Environmental Code, certain amendments were adopted by the parliament in March 2016 and signed by the president in April 2016.

Kazakhstan should be applauded for taking steps towards the implementation of a fully performant emissions trading system; and also commended for making commitments under international treaties to reduce its carbon footprint. Implementation will be critical in modernising the country's economy and integrating it into the international community of developed countries. Unfortunately, consistent with the trend across all environmental reform initiatives in Kazakhstan, the state has not matched its ambitious commitments with real legislative reforms. The KazETS has witnessed significant resistance to its implementation in the ministries, the parliament, regional governments, and the domestic business community. Despite some efforts, authorities have not succeeded in clarifying the regulations and the competent authority in charge of the KAzETS has been resource-constrained in its ability to provide adequate training, clarification and guidance to entities regulated under the KazETS. Also, the KazETS lacks access to more dynamic trading and offsets that could help to manage the costs of compliance.

In December 2015, in his letter to the parliament the prime minister emphasised the importance of the KazETS in fulfilling international commitments to reduce its GHG emissions. He also noted that failing to adopt the KazETS amendments would jeopardise support from international donors for climate change programmes. At the same time, the letter noted that a number of elements in the current legislation on the KazETS do not function correctly. He proposed suspending the applicability of a few sections of the Environmental Code relating to the ETS until 2018 and using the intervening period to improve the system's provisions, including the method of allocation of quotas; the creation and distribution of quotas from a reserve; certain definitions; and oversight of the carbon trading platform. This leaves uncertain what reductions will be required in 2018 by individual companies.[29] More generally, it is unclear what impact the suspension will have on Kazakhstan's ability to meet its national reduction commitments made at the various Conferences of the Parties (COPs) during the past few years. The suspension was signed by the president in April 2016 as part of an umbrella law on changing legislation on environmental issues.[30]

Companies lack the clear ability to comply with the KazETS requirements because of vague rules. Accordingly a risk exists that the KazETS could be reduced to another mechanism for penalising market participants for non-compliance rather than supporting the underlying environmental purposes of the programme.

The resistance in the governmental bodies and in parliament to make the necessary changes stems from domestic economic and social pressures. The implementation of the KazETS and other Green Economy programmes puts intense pressure on industries and the state to invest in modern infrastructure, thus reducing short-term profits and potentially disrupting economic and labour relations in communities that have for years relied upon Soviet-era factories. The KazETS already faced stiff resistance during the period of economic prosperity, but now with low commodity prices weakening the economy, local and national elites resist making the legislative and attitudinal changes needed to implement the KazETS as a tool that values environmental efficiency and sets Kazakhstan on a course to low emissions developments.

Conclusions and policy recommendations

Notwithstanding the recent global financial crisis, Kazakhstan's GDP doubled over the past decade while export earnings increased correspondingly over the same period. Yet, much of this growth was based on the extractive and heavy industries and on the use of electricity which is mostly produced from coal. Consequently, Kazakhstan today is one of the most energy-intensive countries in the world and the energy intensity has not improved during the last decade. The environmental damage inherited from the Soviet era was exacerbated by the impacts from energy production, pollution from heavy industry, accelerated extraction of oil, gas and other mineral resources, as well as from agriculture and from growing road traffic in urban areas.

Kazakhstan has undertaken steps to move towards a more sustainable mode of development which were outlined in two key strategic documents: the 2012 "Kazakhstan 2050 Strategy" and the 2013 "Green Economy Concept" (GEC) which outlined the path to long-term growth based on climate-friendly technologies, energy efficiency measures, and the restoration and sustainable management of natural resources. The GEC, in particular, envisaged modernising deteriorating environmental infrastructure, and set ambitious environment-related targets for the power generation, mining, industry and agriculture sectors and for the energy, soil and water use. It stated that "…by successfully achieving these targets, the country will recover its water and land resources by 2030, and its resource productivity will largely be on par with the average indicators of the OECD members and other developed countries".

However, the implementation of the GEC faces serious challenges, including:

- "top-down" and "command-and-control" approaches based often on the Soviet standards or regulation, combined with frequent incidents of corruption to avoid heavy-handed non-compliance response
- limited use of market-oriented, compliance-promotion and information-based instruments to incentivise companies to invest in pollution reduction and technology modernisation
- lack of willingness by local authorities to implement green reform because of fear of the reallocation of revenue from environmental payments away from local budgets; and
- strong vested interests in the energy-intensive sectors, such as the domestic electric power, mining or chemical industries seeking not to allocate their own resources in the improvement of their environmental performance.

In order to meet its ambitious targets, Kazakhstan urgently needs to develop and implement a set of measures and policies defined in the GEC and other key policy documents. Among many, one of the most important steps that could unlock vast green growth opportunities is the expeditious reform of a basic environmental regulatory framework. Despite recent progress, the uncoordinated implementation of environmental requirements together with the high volume of complex environmental regulations based on unrealistic assumptions has resulted in a regulatory environment that is complicated, burdensome and costly to both the administration and industry. What is more, the evidence suggests that it does not lead to actual environmental improvement. To address these fundamental flaws, further efforts to streamline and simplify these requirements are needed in a way that realistic objectives are set and environmental ambitions are not compromised. Better regulation also means designing policies and laws so that they achieve their objectives at minimum cost. Extensive preparations by the government of Kazakhstan for the upcoming EXPO 2017: Future Energy, the emphasis on green technologies and the overall business case for green economy are promisingly timed for new policy breakthroughs.

Box 5.4. **Main policy recommendations to promote better environmental regulations in Kazakhstan**

- Environmental quality standards need to be revised in the light of international best practices and domestic capabilities to technically feasible and enforceable levels, striking a balance between what is desirable from an environmental point of view and what is feasible from a technical and economic standpoint. The government should make the best use of limited technical capacity and prioritise the provision of the financial and human resources to regulate effectively those polluting substances that pose the greatest risk to human health and/or the environment.
- The present environmental permitting and compliance control requirements need to shift the focus of environmental requirements from "end-of-pipe" solutions to integrated pollution prevention and control. For the largest and "high impact" polluters there should be a shift away from the mentality of command-and-control regulation, which just penalises non-compliance, and re-incentivise it through integrated pollution prevention and control. Integrated environmental permits are one of the most effective ways in achieving better pollution control since the permit is linked to best available techniques (BATs) which are associated with lower emissions.
- Building on the reform and improvements of Environmental Impact Assessments (EIA) and State Environmental Experts' Examination (SEEE) there is a further need to simplify and shorten the procedures for medium and small-scale projects. Where possible the EIA/SEEE procedures should be combined with environmental integrated permitting. Further efforts are also needed by the public authorities to open the procedures to the public's active participation, especially at the regional and local levels. This should assist in building the procedures for more regular reporting on environmental pollution (and their impacts) in a consistent and standardised format.
- The OECD country experience shows that Kazakhstan should abandon fault-based concepts for damages that tie liability to exceeding a predetermined limit in an emissions permit and instead adopt the strict liability/polluter-pays model based on evidence of actual harm to the environment. By contrast, environmental liability for pollution in Kazakhstan applies only if the emission permit limits have been breached (the fault standard), even in the absence of proof of environmental damage.
- Although some important legal changes are being introduced, environmental liability in Kazakhstan remains focused on calculating and collecting monetary compensation for the state (essentially serving as a revenue-raising penalty) rather than on preventing and correcting the damage, reducing emissions over time and incentivising the use of BATs. Credibility in the regulatory system needs to be restored by reforming the laws governing environmental taxes, fines and damages so that they are aligned exclusively and transparently on environmental policy objectives and the international commitments Kazakhstan has made. The state should eliminate discrimination against specific industrial sectors, set rates for taxes and fines, which are uniform for all industry sectors and set rules for assessing damages, which are also non-discriminatory. The rates applicable to taxes and fines should be realistic, consistent with international practice, should not punish emissions associated with normal industrial practices using BATs and should not function as a form of taxation. Enforcement should also be transparent and even-handed. More regulatory guidance should be provided on how to assess the extent of the damage, needs and costs of remediation, and how to select clean-up measures

Box 5.4. **Main policy recommendations to promote better environmental regulations in Kazakhstan** *(cont.)*

- Kazakhstan should be applauded for taking steps towards the implementation of a fully performing emissions trading system for the reduction of greenhouse gases (KazETS) and making commitments under international treaties to reduce its carbon footprint. Implementation will be critical to modernise the country's economy and integrate it into the international community of developed countries. Consistent with the trend across all environmental reform initiatives in Kazakhstan, the state should match its ambitious commitments with real legislative reforms. Authorities should work jointly with relevant stakeholders to clarify the regulations. The competent authority in charge of the KazETS should be strengthened in order to provide adequate training, clarification and guidance to entities regulated under the KazETS.

Box 5.5. **How could the scenarios affect the context of implementation of smarter environmental strategies?**

For details of the scenario storylines, please see section: Anticipating trends and preparing for future challenges: scenarios for the future of Kazakhstan in Chapter 1.

The key recommendations in this report regarding environmental regulation relate to the alignment of environmental regulation with international best practice, including strengthening existing market-based mechanisms, the move from an environmental liability system focused on collecting monetary compensation towards one focused on preventing and correcting damage, and providing adequate incentives for the adoption of best available techniques.

Scenario 1: "The New Super Cycle", would see increased profitability of extractive industries, especially in fossil fuels which may increase and reinforce environmental risks linked to new operations. At the same time, more profitable operations would be better able to upgrade technology, making the transition towards environmental regulation that provides incentives for the adoption of best available techniques (BATs) most relevant. Increased international energy prices would be an opportunity to achieve structural change in energy production and usage in Kazakhstan with the aim of reducing carbon intensity, in particular through a change in fossil fuel usage for heating and electricity generation. Since diversification would be more difficult in scenario 1, dynamic manufacturing industries are likely to remain among the most carbon-intensive (metallurgy, petroleum refinery, chemistry), highlighting the need to lower emissions in other key activities.

In Scenario 2: "The Great Dissipation", proposed reforms would lower costs for compliant firms, by reducing the costs involved in the Environmental Impact Assessment procedures, in obtaining permits and by eliminating sector discrimination in the environmental regulation system. This would allow for an increase in competitiveness of firms in key sectors, including in green economy sectors, which would be potential new export sectors. On the other hand, in this scenario, choices to move away from revenue-generation views of environmental regulation may be more difficult in the light of tighter fiscal conditions.

Scenario 3: "New Silk road and Central Asia Resurgence" offers great opportunities for Kazakhstan which hinge on the development of transport corridors. These opportunities include greater trade integration with the Central Asia region and the world. Both large infrastructure projects and the ensuing higher transport activity are likely to impose environmental costs unless environmental regulation manages to limit risks and less polluting modes of transport, including rail, are further developed.

Scenario 4: "New Technology Solution" would offer great opportunity for advancing the regulatory agenda to accelerate the switch to low-carbon and low-emission solutions. Improved technologies would increase the value of integrating permitting approaches and incentivising the use of BATs. Importantly, this would necessitate that domestic price signals convey carbon costs, since otherwise, fossil fuel prices would fall in the medium term because of reduced global demand. Market-based mechanisms such as KazETS (the emissions trading scheme) would play an important role in ensuring that is the case.

Notes

1. For a detailed description of environmental challenges in Kazakhstan see OECD (2016), "Multi-dimensional Review of Kazakhstan - Vol. 1 - Initial Assessment".
2. Three main laws (Law on Environmental Protection, Law on Ecological Expertise and Law on Air Protection) were abrogated subsequent to their integration into the Environmental Code. Moreover, some 80 normative legal acts were abrogated after the adoption of the Environmental Code.
3. The full name of the GEL is the Law on Amendments to Legislative Acts of the Republic of Kazakhstan aimed at Transition of the Republic of Kazakhstan to Green Economy. The amendments in the GEL are made to the Water Code, Land Code, Environmental Code, Law on Local State Administration and Self-Administration in the Republic of Kazakhstan, and certain other laws.
4. Some provisions that were removed from the original drafts were reinserted under discussion in the Senate or introduced into the Environmental Code by another umbrella Law about changing of legislation on environmental issues. Among them were provisions for removing obstacles to invest to the extraction of coalbed methane, indexing feeding tariffs by pegging them to the exchange rate of foreign currencies, improvements of the connection of alternative energy sources to the national electrical grid, and the creation of a "reserve fund" to guarantee payments for alternative electricity.
5. Provisions related to public access to environmental information were removed from Green Economy Laws but some of them were introduced into the Environmental Code by another umbrella Law about changing of legislation on environmental issues.
6. They may also be expressed as Potentially Safe Concentrations (PSCs).
7. According to the Kazakh legislation resource-users are individuals and legal entities that emit pollution into the environment or otherwise use natural resources as part of their economic activities.
8. Some greenhouse gas emissions (GHG) are included into the list of pollutants for which a resource user must obtain an emissions permit regulation of general pollutants. Since 2013 emissions of GHG are permitted as long as they have been allocated a quota under the Emissions Trading System (Section 3).
9. The application has to be approved by the State Sanitary Inspectorate, which mainly looks at the proposed emission limit values and quantities.
10. Currently, this document is still required to be prepared by the companies but is not reviewed by the authorities for the purposes of issuing an emissions permit.
11. The classification depends upon: (i) human health risks; (ii) production capacity; (iii) type of production; (iv) emissions and exposure; and (v) operational mode. In practice, however, environmental authorities classify production facilities with the use of sanitary norms and rules adopted in 2013 which distinguish and define the size of sanitary zone (in meters) for more than 450 industrial activities.
12. The provisions for the integrated (complex) environmental permit envisaged issuing it for an indefinite term to environmental users who comply with the best available technologies (BAT) unless the technologies applied or environmental use conditions specified in the environmental permit change. The government approved a list of technologies eligible for integrated permits in 2008.
13. The application no longer includes a description of technologies at use, draft regulations on atmospheric emissions, a notarised copy of the agreement of environmental insurance, and the environmental audit report for the design of the intended activities with a section dedicated to environmental impact assessment.
14. Class IV facilities are no longer required to renew their permits on a regular basis.
15. The International Association for Impact Assessment (IAIA) defines an environmental impact assessment as "the process of identifying, predicting, evaluating and mitigating the biophysical, social, and other relevant effects of development proposals prior to major decisions being taken and commitments made." The EIAs are unique in that they do not require adherence to a predetermined environmental outcome, but rather they require decision makers to account for environmental values in their decisions and to justify those decisions in light of detailed environmental studies and public comments on the potential environmental impacts.

16. "Notional tonnes" were calculated by adjusting the volume of emissions for their maximum allowed (regional) concentrations.

17. Even though the list of pollutants subject to ELV was reduced there is a residual group of "other pollutants" that fall into specific hazard categories of MACs. Therefore, the enterprises are required to measure and keep records of a larger number of pollutants for statistical purposes.

18. Article 110 of the Environmental Code provides for the application of the indirect method for evaluation of economic damages in cases when "the direct method cannot be applied, namely for the discharges and emissions of pollutants into the atmosphere or excessive emissions when it is impossible to compensate the caused damage necessary for environmental rehabilitation, restoration of degraded natural resources and health improving of living organisms through the most efficient engineering, organisational, technical and technological measures".

19. In most OECD countries, liability for environmental damage is understood as an obligation for the responsible party to bear the costs of restoring the environment. This obligation, under the strict liability regime which is applied in OECD countries, does not require proof of negligence or regulatory non-compliance. The remediation is usually conducted by the party responsible for the damage under an administrative or court order, in accordance with a specific clean-up project. In a public health or environmental emergency, public authorities can directly proceed with remediation and then recover the remediation costs from the liable parties.

20. The claims of above-norm gas flaring often pertain to technologically unavoidable gas flaring resulting from statistically predictable malfunctions of equipment. Sometimes they also pertain to maintenance flaring which the authorities had approved, but which was carried out in a different period from that indicated in the resource user's pre-approved maintenance plan.

21. According to the information provided by the government in its submission to the Paris COP, fugitive emissions of CO2 emitted by the oil and gas industry fallen from 5.8 million tonnes in 1992 to 2.4 million tonnes in 2011. By contrast, the same source indicates that the energy industry in Kazakhstan reduced its emissions from 113 million tonnes of CO_2 in 1992 to 93 million tonnes in 2011 Kazakhstan (UNFCCC, 2016).

22. Kazakhstan indicated that according to the updated "with measures" scenario total national GHG emissions in 2020 are projected to be 15.6% below the 1990 level. The projections show that Kazakhstan could reach its 15% emission reduction target by 2020 but these are not consistent with the GHG emission projections as reported in Kazakhstan's sixth national communication (NC6), which indicate that Kazakhstan's 2020 target under the Convention could not be achieved under the "with measures" scenario. The expert review teams recommends that Kazakhstan enhance the transparency of its reporting by providing the information on mitigation actions and their effects included in the updated "with measures" scenario in the subsequent biennial report.

23. But the goal to reduce emissions until 2030 does not mean further reduction of emissions before 2020.

24. The 2011 Environmental Code amendments contain a principle that only GHG emission reductions *not* due to a reduction in production can be sold on the market. In practice, procedures to ensure/verify the origins of such reductions were not clear. As of March 2016, this principle is expected to be removed as part of a pending package of amendments to the Environmental Code.

25. Kazakhstan aims periodically to determine the amount of "carbon units" based on the amount of units allocated under international treaties, the amount of units absorbed by Kazakhstan facilities or acquired in the international market. The Kyoto Protocol and the Environmental Code define this aggregate amount as the Established Quantity. Under Kazakhstan law, the Established Quantity is divided between the Established Quantity Reserve and the National Allocation Plan for Emissions of Greenhouse Gases (NAP).

26. Technically, the KazETS also cover GHG emissions from the agricultural and transport sectors, although in practice these sectors do not receive allocations and thus are not presently regulated. The inclusion of the agricultural and transport sectors is still being debated.

27. To date 15 companies have been accredited by the Ministry of Energy to perform these accreditations, and this list is published online. Companies are accredited by submitting an application and identifying personnel with experience in key industrial sectors or accreditation under an existing international carbon market. The threshold for being accredited is low by international standards, and there are no minimum requirements for training, testing, or conflict of interest. It should be noted that in April 2016 the competence for validation and verification of accreditations was transmitted from the Ministry of Energy to the Committee on Technical Regulation and Metrology under the Ministry of Investment and Development.

28. To date, revenue from the ETS has been relatively small, coming only from small penalties collected in 2015.

29. It should be noted however that despite the suspension of the KazETS until 2018, users of natural resources must submit reports on the greenhouse gas inventory to the authorised body.

30. The Law of the Republic of Kazakhstan of 8 April 2016, No.491-V, "On the Introduction of Changes and Additions to Several Legal Acts of the Republic of Kazakhstan on Environmental Issues".

References

Carbon Limits (2014), *Associated Petroleum Gas Flaring Study for Russia, Kazakhstan, Turkmenistan and Azerbaijan*, Final Report for the EBRD and the Global Gas Flaring Reduction Partnership, Oslo, *http://www.ebrd.com/downloads/sector/sei/ap-gas-flaring-study-final-report.pdf*.

Government of Kazakhstan (2015), *Intended Nationally Determined Contribution - Submission of the Republic of Kazakhstan*, *http://www4.unfccc.int/submissions/INDC/Published%20Documents/Kazakhstan/1/INDC%20Kz_eng.pdf*.

Government of Kazakhstan (2013), *Concept for Transition of the Republic of Kazakhstan to Green Economy*, approved by the Decree #557 of the President of the Republic of Kazakhstan on 30 May 2013, *https://www.awex.be/fr-BE/Infos%20march%C3%A9s%20et%20secteurs/Infossecteurs/Documents/PECO/Green%20Economy%20Concept_En.pdf*.

International Energy Agency (2016) *World Energy Balances*, IEA World Energy Statistics and Balances (database). DOI: *http://dx.doi.org/10.1787/data-00512-en* (accessed on 15 March 2016).

International Emissions Trading Association (2015), *Kazakhstan: An Emissions Trading Case Study*, International Emissions Trading Association (IETA), CDC Climate Research, Environmental Defence Fund, Brussels/Paris/Boston, *http://www.ieta.org/resources/Resources/Case_Studies_Worlds_Carbon_Markets/kazakhstan_case_study_may2015.pdf*.

Kononenko, V. et al. (2014), *Urgent Issues When Applying Tax and Environmental Legislation to Subsoil Use*, Deloitte *https://www2.deloitte.com/content/dam/Deloitte/kz/Documents/media/KZ_Urgent_issues_when_applying_tax_and_enviromental_legislation_to_subsoil_use_Kononenko.pdf*.

OECD (2016), *Multi-dimensional Review of Kazakhstan, Volume 1: Initial Assessment*, OECD Development Pathways, OECD Publishing, Paris, *http://dx.doi.org/10.1787/9789264246768-en*.

OECD (2014), *Kazakhstan: Review of Central Administration*, OECD Public Governance Reviews, OECD Publishing, Paris, *http://dx.doi.org/10.1787/9789264224605-en*.

OECD/EAP Task Force (2012), *Liability for Environmental Damage in Eastern Europe, Caucasus and Central Asia (EECCA): Implementation of Good International Practices* , Task Force for the Implementation of the Environmental Action Programme for Central and Eastern Europe (EAP Task Force), Paris, *http://www.oecd.org/env/outreach/50244626.pdf*.

OECD/EAP Task Force (2010), *Surface Water Quality Regulation in EECCA Countries: Directions for Reform*, Task Force for the Implementation of the Environmental Action Programme for Central and Eastern Europe (EAP Task Force), Paris, *http://www.oecd.org/env/outreach/41832129.pdf*.

OECD/EAP Task Force (2009), *Determination and Application of Administrative Fines for Environmental Offences: Guidance for Environmental Enforcement Authorities in EECCA Countries*, Task Force for the Implementation of the Environmental Action Programme for Central and Eastern Europe (EAP Task Force), Paris, *http://www.oecd.org/env/outreach/42356640.pdf*.

UNECE (2008), *Environmental Performance Reviews: Kazakhstan, Second Review*, Environmental Performance Reviews Series No 27, UNECE Environmental Policy Committee, United Nations, New York/Geneva, *http://www.unece.org/fileadmin/DAM/env/epr/epr_studies/kazakhstan%20II.pdf*.

UNFCCC (2016a), *Summary of GHG Emissions for Kazakhstan*, GHG Emission Profiles for Non-Annex I Parties, UN Framework Convention on Climate Change, *http://unfccc.int/files/ghg_data/ghg_data_unfccc/ghg_profiles/application/pdf/kaz_ghg_profile.pdf*.

UNFCCC (2016b), *GHG emission profiles for non-Annex I Parties*, *http://unfccc.int/ghg_data/ghg_data_unfccc/ghg_profiles/items/4626.php*.

UNFCCC (2015) *Report of the Technical Review of the First Biennial Report of Kazakhstan*, UN Framework Convention on Climate Change, FCCC/TRR.I/KAZ, *http://unfccc.int/resource/docs/2015/trr/kaz01.pdf*.

World Bank (2013), *Towards Cleaner Industry and Improved Air Quality Monitoring in Kazakhstan*, Joint Economic Research Program (JERP), World Bank and Ministry of Environment and Water Resources of the Republic of Kazakhstan, *http://www-wds.worldbank.org/external/default/WDSContentServer/WDSP/IB/2014/01/10/000461832_20140110182738/Rendered/PDF/839150WP0P133300Box0382116B000UO090.pdf*

ORGANISATION FOR ECONOMIC CO-OPERATION AND DEVELOPMENT

The OECD is a unique forum where governments work together to address the economic, social and environmental challenges of globalisation. The OECD is also at the forefront of efforts to understand and to help governments respond to new developments and concerns, such as corporate governance, the information economy and the challenges of an ageing population. The Organisation provides a setting where governments can compare policy experiences, seek answers to common problems, identify good practice and work to co-ordinate domestic and international policies.

The OECD member countries are: Australia, Austria, Belgium, Canada, Chile, the Czech Republic, Denmark, Estonia, Finland, France, Germany, Greece, Hungary, Iceland, Ireland, Israel, Italy, Japan, Korea, Latvia, Luxembourg, Mexico, the Netherlands, New Zealand, Norway, Poland, Portugal, the Slovak Republic, Slovenia, Spain, Sweden, Switzerland, Turkey, the United Kingdom and the United States. The European Union takes part in the work of the OECD.

OECD Publishing disseminates widely the results of the Organisation's statistics gathering and research on economic, social and environmental issues, as well as the conventions, guidelines and standards agreed by its members.

OECD DEVELOPMENT CENTRE

The OECD Development Centre was established in 1962 as an independent platform for knowledge sharing and policy dialogue between OECD member countries and developing economies, allowing these countries to interact on an equal footing. Today, 27 OECD countries and 25 non-OECD countries are members of the Centre. The Centre draws attention to emerging systemic issues likely to have an impact on global development and more specific development challenges faced by today's developing and emerging economies. It uses evidence-based analysis and strategic partnerships to help countries formulate innovative policy solutions to the global challenges of development.

For more information on the Centre and its members, please see *www.oecd.org/dev*.

OECD PUBLISHING, 2, rue André-Pascal, 75775 PARIS CEDEX 16
(41 2017 01 1P1) ISBN 978-92-64-26919-4 – 2017

www.ingramcontent.com/pod-product-compliance
Ingram Content Group UK Ltd.
Pitfield, Milton Keynes, MK11 3LW, UK
UKHW051501290926
15471UKWH00008B/1352

9 789264 26919